D0952642

CONSCIOUS BUSINESS

HOW TO BUILD VALUE
THROUGH VALUES

FRED KOFMAN

Forewords by Peter Senge and Ken Wilber

SOUNDS TRUE

Sounds True, Boulder CO 80306

Printed in Canada

10 9 8

Grateful acknowledgement is made to the following for permission to reprint previously published material:

From *The Kabir Book* by Robert Bly. © 1971, 1977 by Robert Bly, © 1977 by the Seventies Press. Reprinted by permission of Beacon Press, Boston.

From *Good Business* by Mihaly Csikszentmihalyi. © 2003 by Mihaly Csikszentmihalyi. Used by permission of Viking Penguin, a division of Penguin Group (USA) Inc.

Excerpt from "Little Gidding" in *Four Quartets*. © 1942 by T.S. Eliot and renewed 1970 by Esme Valerie Eliot. Reprinted by permission of Harcourt, Inc.

"The Gift Outright" from *The Poetry of Robert Frost*, edited by Edward Connery Lathem. © 1923, 1969 by Henry Holt and Company. © 1951 by Robert Frost. Reprinted by permission of Henry Holt and Company, LLC.

478 words from *All You Need Is Love and Other Lies About Marriage* by John W. Jacobs, M.D. © 2004 by John William Jacobs, M.D. Reprinted by permission of HarperCollins Publishers.

Li Po, "Zazen on Ching-t'ing Mountain," translated by Sam Hamill, from *Crossing the Yellow River: Three Hundred Poems from the Chinese*. © 2000 by Sam Hamill. Reprinted with permission of BOA Editions, Ltd.

Excerpt from "Last Night as I Slept" from *Lands of Castile* by Antonio Machado, introduced and translated by Paul Burns and Salvador Ortiz-Carboneres. Published by Aris & Phillips, 2002. Reprinted by permission of Aris & Phillips, an imprint of Oxbow Books Ltd.

By Thomas Merton, from *The Way of Chuang Tzu*. © 1965 by The Abbey of Gethsemani. Reprinted by permission of New Directions Publishing Corp.

"My Daily Affairs Are Quite Ordinary" [p. 35] from *The Enlightened Heart: An Anthology of Sacred Poetry*, edited by Stephen Mitchell. © 1989 by Stephen Mitchell. Reprinted by permission of HarperCollins Publishers.

"These Days" from *The Collected Poems of Charles Olson*, by Charles Olson. © 1987 Estate of Charles Olson. Published by the University of California Press.

"The Rabbi's Gift," as it appears in M. Scott Peck's Prologue from *The Different Drum* by M. Scott Peck. Reprinted with the permission of Simon & Schuster, 1987.

Excerpt from "The Man Watching" [p. 105]: "When we win . . . constantly greater beings" from *Selected Poems of Rainer Maria Rilke, a Translation from the German and Commentary* by Robert Bly. © 1981 by Robert Bly. Reprinted by permission of HarperCollins Publishers.

"In the Driest, Whitest Stretch" by Jalal al-Din Rumi, translated by Andrew Harvey. Published in *The Way of Passion: A Celebration of Rumi* (Berkeley: Frog Ltd./North Atlantic Books, 1994: J.P. Tarcher, 2001). Reprinted by permission of Andrew Harvey.

Excerpt from "Checkmate" and "Guest House" and "The Worm's Waking" in their entirety by Jalal al-Din Rumi, translated by Coleman Barks, published in *The Essential Rumi* (San Francisco: HarperSanFrancisco, 1997). Reprinted by permission of Coleman Barks.

"A Ritual to Read to Each Other." © 1960, 1998 by the estate of William Stafford. Reprinted from *The Way It Is: New & Selected Poems* with the permission of Graywolf Press, Saint Paul, Minnesota.

Kofman, Fred.
  Conscious business: how to build value through values
  ISBN-10: 1-59179-517-6
  ISBN-13: 978-1-59179-517-9
  Library of Congress Control Number: 2006928854

Table of Contents

Foreword

◆

by Ken Wilber

The dictionary definition of *business*, dry and prosaic, is "occupation, work, trade, commerce; serious, rightful, proper endeavor." *Conscious* means "having an awareness of one's inner and outer worlds; mentally perceptive, awake, mindful." So "conscious business" might mean engaging in an occupation, work, or trade in a mindful, awake fashion. This implies, of course, that many people do not do so. In my experience, this is often the case. So I would definitely be in favor of conscious business—or conscious anything, for that matter.

That starts to sound interesting. Still, I wonder exactly what "conscious" or "mindful" might mean, especially since under "conscious" we find the provocative phrase, "aware of inner and outer worlds." Just how many worlds are there, and do I have to be conscious of all of them in order to be really conscious?

Here, I think, is where the entire idea of conscious business starts to become truly intriguing. Worlds, terrains, landscapes, environments: it's a big world, and the better we understand that world—both inner and outer—the better our navigation of it will be.

A map of the outer world would help; so would a map of the inner world. Together they would provide a tool that would dramatically improve my navigation through any environment, any world, including the world of business. A comprehensive map that combines the latest knowledge of both inner and outer worlds would provide an extraordinary means for fulfilling any goals that I might have. It would also provide the key to being conscious of both inner and outer worlds. Conscious business—in fact, conscious living—would start to become a very real possibility.

BIG WORLD, BIG MAP

A map, of course, is not the territory, and we definitely do not want to confuse any map, no matter how comprehensive, with the territory itself. At the same time, we don't want to have an inadequate, partial, broken map either. The fact is, most human endeavors, including most business practices, operate with incomplete and often misleading maps of human potentials. These partial and fractured maps of inner and outer realities consistently lead to failures in both personal and professional endeavors.

In the past few decades there has been, for the first time in history, a concerted effort to take all of the known maps of human potentials, both inner and outer, and combine them into a more comprehensive, inclusive, and accurate map of reality. This "Big Map"—sometimes called an Integral Map—represents the most comprehensive and balanced overview to date, and as such offers an unparalleled navigational aid in defining and fulfilling virtually any goals, personal or professional.

How comprehensive is this Big Map? It started with an exhaustive cross-cultural comparison of all the known interior maps offered by the world's major cultures, including psychological maps from Freud to Jung to Piaget; Eastern maps, including those offered by yoga, Buddhism, and Taoism; the extensive results of cognitive science, neurobiology, and evolutionary psychology; typologies from the Enneagram to Myers-Briggs; transformation tools from ancient shamans to postmodern sages. The idea was simple: what psychological map or model could account for, and include, all of those possibilities? Because human beings have in fact proposed all of those various schools and systems, there must be a model comprehensive enough to account for all of them, and the Integral Model, as far as we can tell, does exactly that.

The result in the interior domains is that there appears to be a spectrum of consciousness available to men and women. This spectrum ranges from body to mind to spirit; from prerational to rational to transrational; from sub-conscious to self-conscious to superconscious; from emotional to ethical to spiritual. The point is that all of those potentials—body to mind to spirit—are important for a comprehensive approach to any situation, personal or professional, because those realities are in fact operating in all humans in any event, and you either take them into conscious account or they will subconsciously sabotage your efforts at every turn. This is true in any human endeavor, from marriage to business to education to recreation.

In addition to these interior or psychological realities, the Integral Model also includes the most recent maps of the outer world, maps offered by widely respected empirical sciences, from dynamic systems theory to complexity and chaos theories. Combined with interior maps, the result is indeed an Integral Map of inner and outer worlds—a map that therefore is the measure of what it means to be really conscious.

Complex as this Integral Map sounds (and is), it actually shakes down into a handful of fairly simple factors that can be quickly mastered. The easiest way to summarize the Integral Map is that it covers a spectrum of consciousness operating in both inner and outer worlds: the Integral Approach includes body, mind, and spirit in self, culture, and nature.

We have already briefly examined the first part of that equation—namely, "body, mind, and spirit"—which we saw as the spectrum of consciousness that constitutes the interior realities or worlds. The second half of the integral equation—"in self, culture, and nature"—represents the three most important worlds themselves; that is, the three most fundamental environments, realities, or landscapes through which the spectrum of consciousness operates.

"Self" simply refers to my own interior world or subjective realities, which can be accessed by introspection, meditation, and self-reflection. "Culture" refers to the world of shared values, mutual understanding, and common meanings that you and I might exchange, such as a common language, an interest in business, a love of classical music, or any shared meaning or value.

This is not subjective but intersubjective, a world accessed by interpretation and mutual understanding. And "nature" refers to the exterior world of objective facts, environments, and events, including exterior human nature with its products and artifacts. Because the human organism is a part of nature, the products of human organisms, such as automobiles, are products of nature and can be approached with natural sciences such as systems theory and complexity theory.

These three major landscapes—self, culture, and world—are often called the Beautiful, the Good, and the True. Or Art, Morals, and Science. Or simply I, We, and It. They are also sometimes called "the Big Three," so fundamental and important are these three worlds in which human beings are always operating. Conscious living—and certainly conscious business— would therefore necessarily take these three worlds into account when planning any activity, because, again, these worlds exist in any event, and you will either take them into conscious account or they will subconsciously sabotage your every move.

INTEGRAL BUSINESS

Conscious business—business that is conscious of inner and outer worlds— would therefore be business that takes into account body, mind, and spirit in self, culture, and nature. Put differently, conscious business would be mindful of the way that the spectrum of consciousness operates in the Big Three worlds of self, culture, and nature. This means very specifically that integral business leadership would use the tools that have been developed to best navigate and master self, culture, and world.

It's not surprising, then, that business management theories break down into three large categories covering the Big Three landscapes: approaches that focus on individual motivation; those that emphasize corporate culture and values; and those that focus on exterior objective systems, flow patterns, and quality control. The whole point is that integral business leadership would use the tools of all of them in a coordinated and integrated fashion for maximum results, or else settle for less than optimal results.

For example, integral business leadership would use systems theory to understand the dynamic patterns of the exterior world. The systems approach to business has been made popular by writers such as Peter Senge, Meg Wheatley, and Michael C. Jackson, among literally hundreds of others. The systems approach is also widely used to track business cycles, as in the groundbreaking work of Clayton Christensen on disruptive technologies.

But integral business leadership would also use the tools of the interior spectrum of consciousness in individuals—tools such as emotional intelligence, made popular by Daniel Goleman; Myers-Briggs, already widely used as a management aid; and personal motivational tools, from Tony Robbins to Franklin Covey.

But integral business leadership would not stop with self and world. It would also draw on our extensive knowledge of corporate culture, shared values, and company motivation. Every company has a culture, and specific business cycles seem to be most effectively navigated by different types of corporate cultures, as suggested by the important research of Geoffrey Moore or the empirical research of Jim Collins. Both point to the overriding importance of corporate values and intersubjective factors in long-term success, which any integral leadership would take into account if it wanted to be mindful and awake in the world of corporate values and maximum effectiveness.

In other words, all of those major theories of business management and leadership—from systems theory to emotional intelligence to corporate-culture management, covering the Big Three landscapes faced by all humans—have an important place in a true Integral Model of conscious business. Although this might at first seem too complicated, the undeniable fact is that any less than integral approach is doomed to failure. In today's world, nobody can afford to be less than integral, because the guaranteed costs are otherwise much too high. Body, mind, and spirit—and self, culture, nature—are all there, all exerting an influence, all actively shaping events, and you either consciously take them into account in any human endeavor or stand back and watch the roadkill.

BIG MAP, BIG MIND

I have attempted to give a simple summary of this overall approach to business in *A Theory of Everything: An Integral Vision for Business, Politics, Science, and Spirituality*. But perhaps the best place to begin an integral approach to business is with oneself. In the Big Three of self, culture, and world, integral mastery starts with self. How do body, mind, and spirit operate in me? How does that necessarily impact my role in the world of business? And how can I become more conscious of these already operating realities in myself and in others?

This is the great value of Fred Kofman's *Conscious Business: How to Build Value Through Values*. Integral mastery begins with mastery of self, at an emotional level, a mental-ethical level, and a spiritual level. Anything more than that is not needed; anything less than that, disastrous.

Fred Kofman is a living example of what he preaches, a man of sensitivity, impeccability, and keen consciousness. It's not just that this makes him a better, more effective, more successful businessperson, but that it makes him a more admirable human being, whom I am proud to call a friend. I highly recommend that you take the following journey with Fred, learning to transform body, mind, and spirit as a prelude to transforming self, culture, and world. And in that integral embrace, neither you nor the world will ever be the same.

Foreword

◆

by Peter Senge

The past ten years have seen an explosion of how-to management books. The only problem is that most how-to books aren't very practical. Life is much too contingent, complex, and emergent ever to conform to a formula. Knowing what should be done and being able to do it are two different things. Consequently, it often seems that the more we learn about great companies, winning competitive strategies, or visionary-change leaders, the less we are actually able to build such organizations, effect such strategies, or be such leaders. Management "know-about" has vastly outpaced management "know-how."

What is missing? Ironically, I believe that it is exactly what bestselling management books say makes the difference: the human dimensions of the enterprise. Yet such books rarely discuss how to cultivate and activate those human capabilities, which, after all, determine whether any significant change ever gets implemented. There is wide agreement on what needs to happen, but very little help for those who seek to make it happen.

I believe that what is missing, most fundamentally, is a deep understanding of what it means to develop an organization as a conscious human community. Fred Kofman argues that a conscious organization starts with what matters most to us: a commitment to achieving a vision that exceeds any individual capacities, a vision that connects people in a common effort with genuine meaning. Such commitment is grounded in people taking unconditional responsibility for their situation and for their ways of responding to it.

We then must choose what matters more to each of us—knowing or learning. Real learning opens us to the fear of uncertainty and the embarrassment of incompetence, as well as the vulnerability of needing one another. We begin to see day-to-day work as a continual dance of learning with and from one another, where what we achieve rests on the quality of our conversations—because our working together centers on how we talk, relate, and commit to one another and to our aims. Ultimately, Fred argues, an enterprise flourishes or fails based on its technical *and* its emotional intelligence, integrity, and capacity to nurture "success beyond success." More importantly, Fred shows in-depth what is needed to work together in building such capabilities. In effect, he offers a detailed map and an instruction manual for developing collective consciousness.

When I first met Fred, he was a young professor of accounting at MIT, a rather unusual professor of accounting. For example, he often started his classes by having his students listen to Beethoven, taking the same piece of music and playing it a half dozen times so that people could see that *each time* they heard something different. How could they keep hearing something new when the same music was played again and again? Because, they gradually came to realize, the music was not in the CD but in *their listening*.

This, Fred pointed out, was the first principle of accounting: the information's only value is in how it is interpreted through the mental models of the "listener." Fred argued that the only justification for performance measurement was to enhance people's capacities to produce outcomes they truly desired. If this was taken seriously, it followed logically that the truth was not in the numbers but in the meaning we made from them. Moreover, the distinction between accounting that led to learning and accounting that did not lay in the cultivation of the accountants and the managers they served. Was their real aim learning and improvement? Did they treat the data they collected as the truth, or were they open to continually challenging and improving the assumptions upon which such data was collected? Were they part of a larger human community learning how to shape its future, or were they merely keeping score of a game whose players they neither identified with nor cared about? Did the business have a larger purpose, and how could accounting contribute to this purpose?

Then, as now, Fred argued that the key to organizational excellence lay in transforming our practices of unilateral control into cultures of mutual learning. When people continually challenge and improve the data and assumptions upon which their map of reality is grounded, as opposed to treating their perspectives as *the* truth, tremendous productive energy is unleashed.

Needless to say, Fred's course was not for everyone. Most students regarded it as a life-changing experience; that's probably why they selected him Sloan School Teacher of the Year. But every semester there would be at least one or two who would urge the deans to fire the lunatic who was teaching managerial cost accounting as a spiritual practice.

Nor is this book for everyone. If you are looking for a book to fix others, you are in the wrong place.

The inventor Buckminster Fuller used to be fond of saying, "If you want to change how a person thinks, give up. You cannot change how another person thinks. Give them a tool the use of which will gradually lead them to think differently." Fred Kofman provides some of those tools. Now it is up to serious practitioners to use them.

Prologue

◆

Everything said, is said by someone.
HUMBERTO MATURANA

Whatever you have to say, leave
the roots on, let them
dangle
And the dirt,
Just to make clear
where they come from
CHARLES OLSON, "THESE DAYS"

◆

I grew up under a military dictatorship in Argentina. Everything seemed under control—I went to school every day, the economy was stable, and the terrorist attacks that had plagued the country in previous years had stopped. I played soccer, went to the movies, and had fun with my friends. Life was good. Or better said, it *appeared* good to me.

In the late '70s rumors began to circulate: kidnappings, concentration camps, tortures, murders, and thirty thousand *desaparecidos* ("missing"). Mostly, the information came from foreign sources—the national media was under government censorship. I felt enraged. I was told, and believed, that this was an anti-Argentinean campaign. The country was plastered with bumper stickers that read, "Argentineans are human and righteous" (a word play on the "human rights" that foreigners alleged were being violated).

Obviously, we thought, *if we are human and righteous this cannot be true*. I guess we didn't *want* it to be true. If the grim reports were accurate, we would face an impossible dilemma: Inaction would turn us into accomplices to mass murder; action would turn us into victims of mass murder. In Argentina we have a saying: "Nobody's more blind that the one who doesn't want to see." There were plenty of signs for us to see, but we were afraid to look and to assume responsibility for what we found. It was much easier to remain unconscious.

Unfortunately, it all turned out to be true. This period was later known as the Dirty War. In order to protect the "Western and Christian Values of the Homeland" (as the slogan said), the military followed a policy of systematic extermination. Anybody who didn't adhere to its nationalist right-wing doctrine was an enemy. Even volunteering for soup kitchens or teaching illiterate adults how to read indicated dangerous left-wing tendencies. In order to protect against an amorphous terrorist threat, the military arrested and killed anybody who looked suspicious to them. "If out of ten people killed, one is a terrorist, the other nine are worth the price," said one general.

I lived in a nice neighborhood and went to a private school. I was a good student and didn't get in trouble. I did not feel the evil around me. I was completely oblivious. The bus I took to school stopped daily at the Navy School of Engineering, a beautiful building with a manicured lawn. Its basement held hundreds of prisoners, most of whom never made it out alive. People were tortured and killed there regularly. This ostensibly respectable institution hid a death camp beneath its polished floors.

I am Jewish, so waking up to the horrible circumstances that had surrounded my life had a tremendous impact on me. In school and at home I repeatedly heard how the Germans had stood idle while six million Jews were exterminated. Self-righteous judgment came easily to me. "How awful! How evil! How could anybody do something like this?" Well, I now occupied the place of the "awful" and the "evil." Thousands of people had been carried to concentration camps under my own nose, and I didn't see it.

For many years I felt deep shame. I had been so unconscious. *How could I not know? How could I have been so blind! Was I evil?* After years of wrestling with these questions, I accepted that I had done the best I could in the moment. To redeem myself, I committed to learn from the experience and work so that it would not happen again. I wanted to stop the violence at its roots, teaching people to be more conscious and more respectful of diversity. I finally mustered enough compassion to forgive myself and the Germans of World War II. Nobody is immune from unconsciousness. The best way to deal with it is not to judge it, but to touch it with compassion and awareness.

Looking back years later, I have learned that unconsciousness is not the exclusive property of Argentineans. I've been in many business meetings, where the sole purpose hasd been to obscure the truth. Worse yet, I suspect that everyone in those rooms knew what was going on, but nobody dared to speak up and deal honestly with the situation. There are great rewards for those who go along, and equally great threats for those who rock the boat. There are no death camps in corporations, but many apparently successful companies hide great suffering in their basements.

I have seen professional identities destroyed in meeting rooms through innuendo, rumors, and negative opinions. Although sometimes an ill-intentioned act, this is more generally an unconscious expression. The problem is not that people think differently, the problem is that somebody thinks that he is right, and anybody who does not think like him must be wrong. Thus, the "different ones" become an enemy to eliminate. Instead of seeing the alternative view as a valuable perspective that can be integrated, power-hungry individuals take it to be a stumbling block. Not surprisingly, they don't want to waste their time engaging with it in dialogue. They simply want to get rid of it by any means and move on. The seeds that sowed the Dirty War lie within everyone's heart.

As Aleksandr Solzhenitsyn, the Russian Nobel laureate, wrote in *The Gulag Archipelago,* "If only it were all so simple! If only there were evil people somewhere, insidiously committing evil deeds, and it were necessary only to separate them from the rest of us and destroy them; but the line dividing good and evil cuts through the heart of every human being. And who is willing to destroy a piece of his own heart?"

I vowed as a child that when I grew up I would never fall for easy lies again, but growing up is not simply a matter of time. When I was in college, the military government started a war with Great Britain by occupying the Falkland Islands. The espoused goal was to redeem Argentina's sovereignty over its territory; the real goal was to divert attention from its domestic situation. Throughout the short war, the state-controlled media constantly reported that Argentinean forces had the upper hand. Every morning's paper repeated the same optimistic news, "We're winning, we're winning, we're winning!" until one afternoon when the commander of the armed forces appeared on TV to report starkly, "We lost." I had known that the daily reports were propaganda, but I was still shocked. I realized then that awareness is not a one-time decision. Staying conscious is an ongoing process that demands constant attention and commitment. I vowed to keep my eyes open and look beyond appearances.

Years later, working as a consultant, I discovered that without a commitment to the truth, individuals and groups are prone to degenerating into manic delusions. Everyone receives tranquilizing information while leaders trumpet the importance of "positive thinking" and "being a team player." This makes it seem as if "we are winning" until the last possible moment, when it is announced that the project failed, the division will be sold off, the company is going under. "We lost."

I always dreamed of being a professor, so when I finished college I left Argentina to pursue a doctorate in economics at the University of California at Berkeley. I chose game theory as my specialization. I wanted to get away from all the human craziness I'd experienced in Argentina. I wanted to deal with rational agents and understand how they make rational decisions. I was doing very well with my studies until I made a decision that ruined my career. I got married.

The problem was not that I got married, but how I decided to get married. I still remember the phone conversation in which I told my father, "Dad, I'm getting married." "Are you crazy?" he challenged me. "Absolutely,"

I answered, "You've got to be crazy to get married." If you do the math, the risk/benefit ratio is a total turn-off. Marriage is not about cold calculation; it is about love.

I found that I could not continue to embrace the theories I was studying. The assumption of perfect rationality no longer made sense to me. I now understood that human beings are not just rational beings that calculate; we are emotional-spiritual beings that seek meaning. I had spent seven years working on decision theory, but I threw them out the window when I fell in love. If I did not use rationality to make the most important decision of my life, how could I assume that others would?

While I continued to study economics, I began to explore philosophy. Berkeley had a top-notch department. I met great teachers who opened my mind to the philosophy of language, philosophy of mind, metaphysics, ethics, existentialism, and hermeneutics. Paradoxically, I found these disciplines much more practical than my mathematical models. I finally began to understand how human beings really make decisions. I learned how we organize our perceptions, build an image of the world, and act accordingly. I studied language. I saw how communication enables an "I" to join a "Thou" and form a "We." Most important, I learned that happiness and fulfillment do not come from pleasure but from meaning, from the pursuit of a noble purpose.

A deep thirst for transcendence brought me to spirituality. My traditionalist Jewish upbringing had led me to believe that religion was a matter of faith and folklore, not of meaning. But as I read the great philosophers I discovered that spirituality was much more than belief in a supernatural being and ritual. I became fascinated by the Eastern traditions, particularly by Zen Buddhism and Advaita Vedanta. I started to meditate and developed an invaluable practice that I still maintain today. Meditation has kept me sane through my most difficult times. It has also driven me insane, challenging my most cherished beliefs about myself and life in general. I worked with many wonderful teachers who helped me discover "the pathless path to the gateless gate."

I also discovered the personal transformation movement. California was still teeming with workshops promising enlightenment in a week. I couldn't pass up the offer, so I took most of them. Among the New Age psychobabble, I found valuable nuggets of truth. I like to think that I kept these babies when I threw out the bath water.

When I graduated, I took a job teaching management accounting at the Massachusetts Institute of Technology. I was in heaven, until I wasn't. All my life I'd been climbing the proverbial ladder, but when I reached the zenith of my academic career, I realized that I had placed it against the proverbial wrong wall. I was interested in teaching people how to make things happen, not how to account for the things that others made happen. Leadership development became my passion, one unsuitable for a university professor. Leadership is about being more than knowing; about emotion more than cognition; about spirit more than matter. I couldn't teach greatness in a traditional classroom style.

I couldn't stay, and I couldn't leave. Losing my affiliation with MIT scared me to death. Losing my job was like losing my identity. *What would be left of me if I didn't have my teaching position? Would there be anything left of Fred Kofman if you took away the MIT professorship?* This feeling was reflected in the difference between my objective business card and my subjective experience of it.

Here's what my business card looked like:

Fred Kofman, Ph.D.

Professor of Management Accounting
and Information Systems

MIT

Here's what my experience of the card was like:

I discovered how much of my identity was based on my job. I saw how little I knew about myself and how much effort I'd put into proving my self-worth through achievements. I realized also that I wasn't the only one. When I shared this story in my seminars, most managers confessed to having the same fear. Losing a job is not just an economic blow; it is a blow to your identity.

With great trepidation, I left MIT. I lost my professorship and found myself. I refocused on my psycho-spiritual explorations. For the following ten years, I took to the path of self-discovery and self-improvement. But at some point even this pursuit fell away. I realized that my true identity transcended my professional circumstances, my successes, and my failures—even the spiritual success of enlightenment. I am who I am, and perfectly so. I am not perfect; I am perfectly imperfect in my own unique way. And so is every-thing. So what is there to do? Let the dream become lucid. See every fake identity for what it really is, a phenomenal disguise of The One.

I started what later became Axialent, a consulting company devoted to helping leaders realize their true greatness and express it at work. I worked with leaders throughout the world to achieve extraordinary success through the development of cooperative relationships and dignified human behaviors. It's been a great journey.

Conscious Business is the result of fifteen years of work with leaders of major corporations in the United States, Europe, and South America. My associates at Axialent and I have worked with all levels of management, from first-line supervisors to senior executives, in a wide range of industries. The material has been refined and tested in the real world by thousands of leaders from companies such as Microsoft, Yahoo!, EDS, Cisco, Google, General Motors, Chrysler, Shell, Citibank, Unilever, and many others.

These leaders realized that to be successful they needed more than technical competence; they needed to grow as people. As they learned the skillful means necessary to run a business with wisdom and compassion, they helped all of us at Axialent make the material that we present in our seminars—and that I present in this book—user-friendly and practical.

What did these leaders learn? First, they learned that freedom, responsibility, and integrity are the keys to success, but that these qualities demand the courage to face existential anxiety. They learned that speaking the truth is essential, but that the truth that needs to be said and heard is not the one most people call "truth." They learned that "win-win" is a powerful concept for negotiations, but only mature human beings can implement it. They learned that impeccable commitments are essential for cooperative relationships, but that they require a strong foundation of personal values. They learned that they needed to manage their emotions, but not in the stoic way they had adopted. They learned that who they are is the main determinant of what they can and cannot do. And they learned that when all is said and done, service to others is the highest spiritual and business imperative.

They also learned how to embody their freedom with confidence and inner peace. They learned to find the essential truth in themselves and others. They learned to express it and receive it with dignity and respect. They learned to tap their imagination to create options when at an impasse. They learned to establish, maintain, and repair networks of trust and coordinated actions. They learned to maintain equanimity in the face of the most difficult circumstances, simultaneously keeping their hearts open and their minds sharp. They learned that who they are is the most amazing space of possibilities in which Life manifests its creative potential. And they learned how to serve others without betraying their highest goals and values. They learned, in short, to succeed beyond success.

They learned all this. And if you read this book, I hope that you will too.

◆

I've presented some of my background to show you where this book is coming from. Now, I invite you to think where you want this book to take you. What made you pick it up? What do you want from it? Why is this search important to you? What can you accomplish if you find what you're looking for? How can you use this knowledge for your own benefit and that of those around you? It is important to ponder these questions. As the Cheshire Cat told Alice, if you don't much care where you want to get to, then it doesn't matter which way you go. On the other hand, if you know what you want, you will be able to use almost anything to go in that direction. Like a skillful sailor who can use any wind to navigate toward his destination, you will be able to use any concept to pursue your goals.

The main difference between a workout tape and real exercise is participation. When you go to a gym, you have to expend effort to get any benefit. Just so, with a book you have to get involved in the text in order to take full advantage of it. I invite you to read with a pencil in hand, agreeing, discussing, analyzing, challenging, and linking ideas with real situations in your life. The ideas are incredibly simple, but they are not easy. They sound like common sense, but they are not common practice. If you want to learn to put them into practice, you'll need to participate. You'll have to get up close and personal to get the most benefit. Learning is a contact sport.

You shall no longer take things at second or third hand, nor
   look through the eyes of the dead, nor feed on the spectres
   in books,
You shall not look through my eyes either, nor take things from me,
You shall listen to all sides and filter them from your self.

WALT WHITMAN, FROM "SONG OF MYSELF"

Acknowledgments

◆

First of all, I'd like to thank the president of the social club who organized the dance where my mother met my father in Argentina almost fifty years ago. Thanks to him and other innumerable factors, I was born, have lived, and have written this book. No, I'm not kidding. In thanking this man, I'd like to honor the unimaginable convergence of forces that created this present. If we look at anything closely, we discover that it doesn't exist as a separate or independent thing, that everything that seems isolated is nothing other than a node in an infinite network of crisscrossing energies. There's no such thing as a book independent of all the things that influenced the life of its author.

Tom, Dick and Harry think they have written the books that they sign ... But they exaggerate. It was a pen that did it, or some other implement. They held the pen? Yes, but the hand that held the pen was an implement too, and the brain that controlled the hand. They were intermediaries, instruments, just apparatus. Even the best apparatus does not need a personal name like Tom, Dick, or Harry.

If the nameless builders of the Taj Mahal, of Chartres, of Rheims, of a hundred cathedral symphonies, knew that—and

avoided the solecism of attributing to their own egos the works
that were created through their instrumentality—may not even a
jotter-down of passing [management] notions know it also?

WEI WU WEI[1]

I'd like to thank the people who have had a positive influence on my profes-
sional life and made this book possible. Many of them I don't even know.
Some of those I remember are Guido Di Tella, Albert Fishlow, Drew
Fudenberg, Fernando Flores, Pat Sculley, Greig Trosper, Marcia Clark,
Dave Meador, Dave Prett, Jerry Golden, John Sequeira, Frank Trogus, Dale
Holecek, Wendy Coles, Dave Sharpe, Fred Schaafsma, Fernando Esquivel,
Eugenio Beaufrand, Therese Lenk, Cheryl Van, Sheryl Sandberg, and David
Neenan. I also want to thank my partners in Axialent for their support and
friendship: Andy Freire, Ana Diniz, Ricardo Gil, Patrick Campiani, Cristina
Nogueira, and Carolyn Taylor.

I'd also like to thank everyone who has participated or will participate
in my programs. Your questions, challenges, input, and energy are constant
sources of enthusiasm and motivation for me. In the crucible of learning,
we all melt, mix, and are separated again. In the end, everyone takes away a
piece of everyone else. I feel that my life has become immensely richer every
time I've poured myself into that process.

I am indebted to two teachers, two intellectual and spiritual giants on
whose shoulders I stand: Peter Senge and Ken Wilber. Peter Senge men-
tored me with overwhelming generosity. From the start, he pushed me and
nurtured me; he challenged me to grow and try new things. A number of
times, he vouched for my work when companies doubted putting their
senior executives in the hands of an unconventional thirty-year-old professor. I hope that someday I can return such kindness by encouraging other
people's growth as Peter did with me. Ken Wilber is a phenomenon. If he
weren't so human, I'd think he was an extraterrestrial. I believe he's one of
the most important philosophers of all time. To read his books, get to know
him, and finally work by his side has been a privilege.

Ted Rose spent hundreds of hours trying to make my thoughts understandable: a grueling task if there ever was one. His editing skill, effort, and commitment to this project have gone well beyond the call of duty. Of course, any remaining mistakes are a consequence of my stubbornness.

Tami Simon, my publisher, dear friend, and Dharma sister, has always encouraged me to speak the truth. I hope I can honor the name of her company with an offering that really Sounds True.

Finally, I'd like to thank my wife Kathy and our children Michelle, Paloma, Tomás, Rebecca, Sophie, and Janette for their love and support.

Boulder, Colorado, 2006

CHAPTER 1

Conscious Business

◆

Cogito ergo sum. (I am conscious, therefore I am.)
RENÉ DESCARTES

Greatness is not a function of circumstance.
Greatness ... is a matter of conscious choice.
JIM COLLINS[1]

◆

I love molecules," explains Marcus. "You apply a certain amount of heat and a certain amount of pressure, and you know exactly what's going to happen. At the start of my career I did great working with molecules, but now I work with people. People are unpredictable. You apply a certain amount of heat and a certain amount of pressure, and you never know what's going to happen."

Marcus, a research manager at an oil company, has two doctorates. He is an intellectual wonder and a management disaster. Technical excellence propelled him into management, exposing his social incompetence. Marcus deals with people in the same way he dealt with molecules. This doesn't work. In contrast to molecules, people have minds of their own.

As they climb the corporate ladder, managers like Marcus stumble and fall. They fail to make the transition from the operational requirements of the lower rungs to the leadership requirements of the higher ones. Ironically, some of the traits that drove their success as individual contributors derail their success as leaders.[2] Success in business requires dealing with human beings, which is to say *conscious* beings. This book presents the basic principles and skills needed to deal with people while honoring their conscious nature. Although this is helpful for anybody who works, it is fundamental for those who manage and lead others. Great leadership is conscious leadership.

In his book *Good to Great*, Jim Collins studies what drives average companies to take a quantum leap and become extraordinary. He concludes that a crucial component of greatness is a group of leaders with a paradoxical blend of personal humility and professional will. These leaders, whom Collins calls "Level 5," channel their ego ambition away from themselves into the larger goal of building a great company. "All of the companies in the study that went from good to great," says Collins, "had Level 5 leadership in key positions, including the CEO, at the pivotal time of transition." However, Collins couldn't answer a central question: how to develop Level 5 leadership. "I would love to be able to give you a list of steps for becoming Level 5, but we have no solid research data that would support a credible list." The inner development of a person remains a "black box."[3] This book is my effort to unlock the black box of great leadership. My key is the set of attitudes and skills that I call "Conscious Business."

Living consciously is a state of being mentally active rather than passive. It is the ability to look at the world through fresh eyes. It is intelligence taking joy in its own function. Living consciously is seeking to be aware of everything that bears on our interests, actions, values, purposes, and goals. It is the willingness to confront facts, pleasant or unpleasant. It is the desire to discover our mistakes and correct them … it is the quest to keep expanding our awareness and understanding, both of the world external to self and of the world within.

NATHANIEL BRANDEN[4]

CONSCIOUSNESS

Consciousness is the ability to experience reality, to be aware of our inner and outer worlds. It allows us to adapt to our environment and act to promote our lives. All living beings possess consciousness, but human beings have a unique kind. Unlike plants and other animals, we can think and act beyond instinctual drives and conditioning. We can be autonomous (from the Greek, "self-governing"). While this autonomy is a possibility, it is not a given. We must develop it through conscious choices.

To be conscious means to be awake, mindful. To live consciously means to be open to perceiving the world around and within us, to understand our circumstances, and to decide how to respond to them in ways that honor our needs, values, and goals. To be unconscious is to be asleep, mindless. To live unconsciously means to be driven by instincts and habitual patterns.

Have you ever driven down the highway on cruise control, engaged in a conversation or daydreaming, only to realize that you missed your exit? You didn't literally lose consciousness, but you dimmed your awareness. Relevant details, such as your location and the actions needed to reach your goal, receded from the forefront of your mind. Your eyes were open, but you didn't see. This is a poor way to drive—and an even poorer way to live.

When we are more conscious, we can better perceive our surroundings, understand our situation, remember what's important to us, and envision more possibilities for action to attain it. Consciousness enables us to face our circumstances and pursue our goals in alignment with our values. When we lose consciousness, we are swept away by instincts and habits that may not serve us. We pursue goals that are not conducive to our health and happiness, we act in ways that we later regret, and we produce results that hurt us and those we care about.

A unique characteristic of human consciousness is self-awareness. We not only perceive the external world, we can also bear witness to our internal world. We can pose questions like, "Why am I thinking what I am thinking?" "Do I have sound reasons for my conclusions?" "Am I letting my desires cloud my judgment?" Self-awareness allows us to consider the deepest aspects of our existence. We can ask ourselves, "Who am I?" "What is my mission in life?" "What values should guide me?" "How should I live?" "Is my behavior aligned with my values and purpose?" "Am I happy?"

Not only do we experience self-awareness, we also recognize "other-awareness." I'm talking about something more subtle than perceiving other people from an external perspective. We know that beyond people's observable behavior, they are conscious, choosing their actions based on their reasoning. We can ask, "What leads you to think what you are thinking?" "Do you have evidence for your conclusions?" "Why is this issue important to you?" "What do you really want?" Other-awareness enables us to inquire into others' deeper motivations, posing such questions as, "What is most meaningful in your life?" "What are your hopes and dreams?" "What values guide your behavior?" "What makes you happy?"

Another unique characteristic of human consciousness is its capacity for abstraction. We can transcend our concrete experiences through our intellectual ability to understand, judge, and reason. Intellect allows us to organize information in order to understand and manage complex situations. We may not be able to look at every tree, but we can consider the whole forest. As our cognitive capacity develops, we operate at higher and higher levels of abstraction, from immediate experience to symbols to concepts. At the highest level, we wonder, "What is true?" "What is beautiful?" "What is good?" Abstract reason enables us to transcend our immediate circumstances and consider human existence: "What is human nature?" "Are there moral imperatives derived from such nature?" "What is a good life?" "What brings authentic happiness?" A conscious life is concerned with such questions.

And so is a conscious business. Business is an essential part of our lives, so doing business consciously is an essential aspect of living consciously. In order to do business consciously, we need to ponder the most fundamental questions pertaining to reality and human existence and let these insights guide our business choices.

A conscious business promotes mindfulness for all of its stakeholders. Employees are encouraged to investigate the world with rigorous scientific reasoning, and to reflect on their role in it with equally rigorous moral reasoning. They are invited to contemplate their own selves, finding what it means to live with virtue, meaning, and happiness. They are also asked to think of their colleagues as human beings, rather than as "human resources." Finally, they are required to understand their customers, offering them products and services that support their growth and well-being. A conscious business fosters peace and happiness in individuals, respect and solidarity in the community, and mission accomplishment in the organization.

Most of us recognize that companies need employees with a high level of technical knowledge if they are to succeed in the information economy. I believe it is more important, and far less recognized, that companies also need employees with a high level of consciousness. Without conscious employees, companies cannot achieve greatness—let alone survive. How many companies have gone out of business because of the arrogance of their executives? How many have imploded because of the disengagement of their employees? How many millions of dollars have been wasted by managers who are in denial? How many corporate leaders have chosen the immediate gratification of quarterly earnings at the expense of long-term profitability? Conscious employees are an organization's most important asset; unconscious employees are its most dangerous liability.

CONSCIOUS EMPLOYEES

I use seven qualities to distinguish conscious from unconscious employees. The first three are character attributes: unconditional responsibility, essential integrity, and ontological humility. The next three are interpersonal skills: authentic communication, constructive negotiation, and impeccable coordination. The seventh quality is an enabling condition for the previous six: emotional mastery. These qualities are easy to understand, but hard to implement. They seem natural, but they challenge deep-seated assumptions we hold about ourselves, other people, and the world. This is why although most of us know *about* them, we don't know *how* to enact them. They are common sense, but not common practice.

Conscious employees take responsibility for their lives. They don't compromise human values for material success. They speak their truth and listen to others' truths with honesty and respect. They look for creative solutions to disagreements and honor their commitments impeccably. They are in touch with their emotions and express them productively.

Unconscious employees do the opposite. They blame others for problems, seek immediate gratification regardless of ethics, and claim to always be right. They hide significant information, sweep conflicts under the table, and negotiate to beat their opponents. They expect to get what they need without asking, make irresponsible promises, and don't honor their commitments. They repress their emotions or explode irrationally.

Of course, productive employees must have the necessary cognitive power, knowledge, and technical skills to do their jobs. If you don't know engineering, you're the wrong person to build a bridge. But productive employees must also have conscious business skills. If you know engineering but can't communicate, negotiate, and coordinate, you are the wrong person to work on the construction team.

Conscious employees require conscious managers if they are to fully commit their energy to organizational goals. Unless they feel acknowledged, supported, and challenged by their managers, conscious employees will withdraw. Conscious managers create the right environment for employees to blossom as professionals and as human beings. They enable employees to contribute their best. Nothing is more vital for exceptional performance than conscious management.

No matter what type of business, the *only* way to generate a competitive advantage and long-term profitability is to attract, develop, and retain talented employees. The top management of the company can provide an inspiring vision and a solid strategy, but these aren't enough. Managers at all levels determine the everyday world of employees. Only conscious managers can elicit employee engagement. Unfortunately, managerial consciousness is in short supply. Warren Bennis and Burt Nanus report that less than one out of every four employees works at full potential. Half said they only do what's necessary to keep their jobs, and three out of four say they could be more effective than they are.[5] The good news is that there's lots of room for improvement. If companies could harness the lost energy, organizational performance would surge.

... if management views workers not as valuable, unique individuals but as tools to be discarded when no longer needed, then employees will also regard the firm as nothing more than a machine for issuing paychecks, with no other value or meaning. Under such conditions it is difficult to do a good job, let alone to enjoy one's work.

MIHALY CSIKSZENTMIHALYI[6]

CONSCIOUS MANAGERS

In *First, Break All the Rules,* Marcus Buckingham and Curt Coffman report the results of a twenty-year research project on organizational effectiveness undertaken by The Gallup Organization. The study focused on a single question: "What do the most talented employees need from their workplace?"

After surveying over a million individuals from a broad range of companies, industries, and countries, the study concluded: "Talented employees need great managers. The talented employee may join a company because of its charismatic leaders, its generous benefits, and its world-class training programs, but how long that employee stays and how productive he is while he is there is determined by his relationship with his immediate supervisor."[7]

This led to the researchers' next question: "How do the world's greatest managers find, focus, and keep talented employees?" Gallup surveyed four hundred organizations, interviewing a cross section of eighty thousand great and average managers. To determine who was great and who was average, they used objective performance measures such as sales, profit, customer satisfaction, and employee turnover. The combination of both these studies resulted in the most extensive empirical research ever carried out on this subject.

The researchers found that exceptional managers created a workplace in which employees emphatically answered "yes" when asked the following questions:

1 Do I know what is expected of me at work?
2 Do I have the materials and equipment I need to do my work right?
3 At work, do I have the opportunity to do what I do best every day?
4 In the last seven days, have I received recognition or praise for doing good work?
5 Does my supervisor, or someone at work, seem to care about me as a person?
6 Is there someone at work who encourages my development?
7 At work, do my opinions seem to count?
8 Does the mission/purpose of my company make me feel my job is important?
9 Are my co-workers committed to doing quality work?
10 Do I have a best friend at work?
11 In the last six months, has someone at work talked to me about my progress?
12 This last year, have I had opportunities at work to learn and grow?[8]

These results are not just true for individual performers and their immediate supervisors; they hold at all levels of the organizational hierarchy. Top management's primary responsibility is to populate the company with what I've called "conscious employees." Senior managers do not just set the corporate mission and policy; they also create an environment that attracts, retains, and develops their junior managers. To attract conscious employees, managers need to exercise conscious leadership.

The worst leader is he who people despise. A good leader is he who people worship. A great leader is he who makes people say: "We ourselves did it."

LAO TZU, *TAO TE CHING*

CONSCIOUS LEADERSHIP

Leadership is the process by which a person sets a purpose for other persons and motivates them to pursue it with effectiveness and full commitment. Leadership transforms individual potential into collective performance. The leader's job is to develop and maintain a high-performing team. Her effectiveness is demonstrated by the performance of the team.*

Anyone who manages people has a leadership responsibility. Formal authority is never sufficient to gain enthusiasm from those to be managed. An essential part of the manager's job is to enlist the full cooperation of those she leads, shifting their motivation from external compliance to internal commitment. Thus, great leadership is a necessary condition for great management. A team that is well managed, and thus well led, operates in alignment, because each of the team members takes the team goal as his own. Great managers (i.e., great leaders) earn the trust and respect of their subordinates. Without trust and respect, followers will rarely exert more than a minimal effort in the pursuit of the goals set by a leader.

Asking whether someone is a manager or a leader is like asking whether someone is a soccer player or a ball-kicker. Kicking the ball is the way in which a soccer player plays soccer. It is ridiculous to say that Joe is a good soccer player but a bad kicker, or that we have too many soccer players but not enough kickers. By the same token, leadership is a necessary skill for anyone who manages. Leadership is the way in which a manager manages.

How does a great manager earn the trust and respect of her subordinates? First, she needs to demonstrate the cognitive and technical competence to do her job. Note the word "demonstrate" here. Not only does a leader need to have the competence, she needs to convince her followers that she is management-worthy. The manager does not need to show that she can do the subordinates' jobs; she must show that she can do *her* job. In other words, she needs to prove

---

*Everything in this book applies to all people, regardless of their gender. When I speak about individuals, I could use "him or her" every time, but I find this cumbersome and distracting. Instead, I will alternate between "him" and "her." Either way, I refer to both genders.

that she can perform managerial functions, such as selecting the right people to join the team, assigning tasks appropriately, providing context for how all the tasks fit together in the pursuit of the team goal, and so on.

Second, she needs to exercise conscious leadership. That is to say, she needs to lead with the seven qualities of conscious business I described earlier in this chapter. A great manager leads through unconditional responsibility, essential integrity, ontological humility, authentic communication, constructive negotiation, impeccable coordination, and emotional mastery. In addition, she fosters—and demands—the enactment of these qualities in her subordinates. A great manager holds not only herself accountable for conscious behavior, but everybody else as well; and she holds everybody else accountable for holding everybody else—including the manager herself—accountable. This creates a culture in which everybody supports and calls for everybody else's consciousness.

… Leadership begins with what the leader must Be, the values and attributes that shape the leader's character … *Leadership is a matter of how to be, not how to do.*

BE-KNOW-DO: *LEADERSHIP THE ARMY WAY*[9]

THE THREE DIMENSIONS OF BUSINESS

Every organization has three dimensions: the impersonal, task, or "It"; the interpersonal, relationship, or "We"; and the personal, self, or "I." The impersonal realm comprises technical aspects. It considers the effectiveness, efficiency, and reliability of the organization. The interpersonal realm comprises relational aspects. It considers the solidarity, trust, and respect of the relationships between organizational stakeholders. The personal realm comprises psychological and behavioral aspects. It considers the health, happiness, and need for meaning of each stakeholder. Just as material objects exist in three-dimensional physical space, businesses exist in three-dimensional organizational space. Every object has length, width, and depth; every business has It, We, and I.

When we look at an organization from the impersonal It perspective, we consider its ability to achieve its goals, pursue its vision, and fulfill its mission in a way that enhances its capacity to continue to do so in the future. In the impersonal realm, the goals of a business include making money today and in the future, increasing shareholder value, and gaining market share. (The goal of a nonprofit could be to care for the sick, feed the hungry, or educate children.) In this dimension, the concern is for efficiency, attaining the maximum output with the minimum consumption of resources.

Impersonal success is essential. Without it, the survival of the organization is at risk. If it does not fulfill its reason for being, it will be unable to draw energy and resources, and it will collapse. For a business to get raw materials it needs to pay its suppliers; to get the contribution of employees it needs to offer them an attractive compensation package; to get revenue from its customers it needs to offer them attractive products or services; to get funding from its investors it needs to offer them attractive expected returns. If the business cannot appear attractive to its stakeholders, it will fail.

Instead of looking at the business world as a three-dimensional space, most managers—and investors—focus only on the It. It is as though they wear polarized lenses that filter out the We and the I. Stripped of the human dimensions, business appears to be an unconscious activity in which success and failure depend exclusively on the management of mindless things. However, business success essentially depends on the leadership of conscious beings.

When we look at an organization from the interpersonal We perspective, we examine its ability to create a community that works with solidarity, trust, and respect. In the interpersonal realm, the goal is to build a network of collaborative relationships—a community in which people feel included, respected, and enabled to contribute their best.

Interpersonal success is also indispensable to survival. Human beings are social beings. In order to offer their full engagement to the organization, people demand to feel accepted, respected, supported, acknowledged, and challenged. Monetary compensation alone cannot accomplish this. This is why solidarity is so fundamental to long-term business success. If people do not cooperate and respect each other, the organization will fail.

When we look at an organization from the personal I perspective, we focus on its ability to foster well-being, meaning, and happiness in each one of its stakeholders. In the personal realm, the goal is to cultivate psychophysical health and a high quality of life. Every person wants to feel whole in body and mind, to know that her life is meaningful, to be happy. A conscious organization's goal in the personal realm is to promote the self-actualization and self-transcendence of everyone it touches.

Finally, personal success is critical. Without it, no organization can last. Happy people are much more productive and able to cooperate with others.[10] They are resilient when suffering setbacks and enthusiastic when facing opportunities. They trust themselves to respond appropriately to life's circumstances, to connect with others, and to deliver exceptional results. If people are not happy in their jobs, they will not remain engaged; they will not last as productive employees. They may not quit formally, but they will quit emotionally. In order to obtain energy from its employees, the organization needs to provide them with opportunities for physical, emotional, mental, and spiritual well-being. If an organization's people do not experience this well-being, it will fail.

Over the long term, the It, We, and I aspects of this system must operate in concert. Although it is possible to achieve good financial results in the short term with unhappy people, cold relationships, or wasteful processes, the gains will not endure. Strong profits will not be sustainable without equally strong interpersonal solidarity and personal well-being.

BEING, DOING, HAVING, AND BECOMING

"The best way to do is to be," said Lao Tzu nearly 2,500 years ago. The recommendation is still valid, even though it goes against our instincts. Our attention is normally drawn to that which we can see (the effect), which obscures the importance of what remains hidden (the cause). We focus on results (the having) and forget the process (the doing) necessary to achieve those results. We are even less aware of the infrastructure (the being) that underlies processes and provides the necessary capabilities for their functioning. Achieving specific results requires behaving in a way that produces such results, and behaving in such a way requires *being* the type of person or organization capable of such behavior. Thus, the highest leverage comes from *becoming* the person or organization capable of behaving in the way that produces the desired results.

Consider a computer. At the level of *being* (platform or infrastructure) it relies on an operating system. For example, my computer uses Microsoft Windows. This master program enables the operation of the application programs, which appear at the level of *doing* (processes or behaviors). I wrote this text using Microsoft Word. At the level of *having* (products or results) we find the output of the application program. I produced a text file that has been published as the book you are now reading. If the operating system couldn't support the application programs, they would not run properly. In order to yield the correct output, the operating system must provide the process capabilities required by the applications.

FIGURE 1 An Integral Perspective of Organization

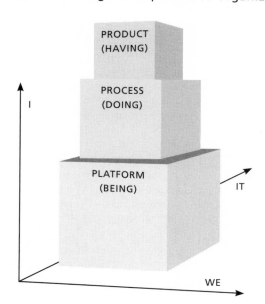

This sequence of platform, process, and product occurs in the three dimensions I described earlier: It, We, and I. Imagine three cubes stacked on top of one another (see figure 1). The bottom cube represents the platform, the middle cube the process, and the top cube the product. In each cube, the height represents the I or personal dimension, the width represents the We or interpersonal dimension, and the depth represents the It or impersonal dimension.

The impersonal aspect of the platform (the bottom cube) is the business infrastructure: the material, technological, economic, and administrative base comprising of property, plant, equipment, financial structure, information systems, organizational design, etc. The interpersonal aspect is the organization's culture: the shared beliefs, values, and norms that let people know how to behave and what they can expect from others. The personal aspect is the individual's mental model: her beliefs, values, and psychological structures.

The impersonal aspect of the process (the middle cube) is the functional tasks: procurement, sales, marketing, operations, etc. The interpersonal aspect is the interaction of the organization's stakeholders: communication, negotiation, and coordination. The personal aspect is the behavior of these individuals: their thinking, feeling, and acting.

TABLE 1 Organizational Map			
	(I) Individual Personal Self	(We) Relationship Interpersonal Community	(It) Task Impersonal Organization
Product Result (Have)	Well-being Meaning Happiness	Solidarity Connectedness Belonging	Mission Accomplishment Profitability Growth
Process Behavior (Do)	Thinking Feeling Acting	Communicating Negotiating Coordinating	Selling Delivering Planning, etc.
Platform Structure (Be)	Mental Model: Personal Values, Beliefs, and Practices	Culture: Shared Values, Beliefs, and Practices	Capital: Administrative, Technical, and Economic Infrastructure

The impersonal aspect of the product (the top cube) is the business results: mission accomplishment, profitability, and growth. The interpersonal aspect is the experience of community: the group's sense of solidarity, connectedness, and belonging. The personal aspect is the quality of life of each of the individual stakeholders: her wellness, happiness, and sense of meaning.

Table 1 is a convenient summary, but it obscures an important fact. These are neither three independent columns put side by side, nor three independent rows stacked on top of each other; they are a system. Each element relates to every other element; each one influences and is influenced by the others. It is possible to influence the system starting from any element, so the critical question is, "Where is the best place to focus improvement efforts?"

I believe that the highest leverage can be gained by focusing on culture. I also believe that the strongest determinant of an effective, healthy culture is conscious leadership. Developing consciousness in its top managers is the most efficient way for an organization to improve.

CONSCIOUS CULTURE

No man is an island. Human beings are social animals who band together in families, clans, tribes, and organizations. Our biological and psychological survival requires relationships with other people. Thus, we look for signals about how to fit within a certain community, and we adapt our behavior accordingly. If we cannot adapt, we leave or are ejected. Every group exerts pressure on its members to conform to its cultural norms. Those who fail in their acculturation suffer ostracism.

Culture is best described as the standard beliefs and expectations of "how we do things around here." Culture develops from the messages that group members receive about how they are expected to behave. It comprises shared goals, beliefs, routines, needs, or values. Cultures exist in all groups, from corporations to sport clubs, from schools to families.

Developing a conscious culture is a business imperative. Culture undergirds an organization. It enables the execution of the organization's strategy, the achievement of its goals, and the fulfillment of its mission.

Culture is as essential a part of the organization's infrastructure as its technology; perhaps it is even more essential. Collins found: "Technology and technology-driven change has virtually nothing to do with igniting a transformation from good to great."[11] Yet typical companies channel the bulk of their investment toward the purchase of unconscious capital while spending relatively little on the development of conscious (human) capital.

The key infrastructure question is, "What culture do we need in order to execute our strategy and fulfill our mission?" Although specific missions entail specific cultural attributes, at the core of every productive culture are the seven qualities of conscious business. These qualities are rare in people, but they are even rarer in organizations. Establishing them as the organizational way of doing things requires a cultural change.

To change a culture, the leaders have to change the messages people receive about what they must do to fit in. When people understand that there are new requirements for belonging, they adjust their behavior accordingly. Cultural change starts with a new set of messages. Culture-changing communication is nonverbal—the "doing" rather than the "saying"—and comes most vividly from leadership behaviors. The behavior of leaders exemplifies what people with power—and those who aspire to have it—are supposed to do. A small change in a senior manager's behavior can send a big message. For example, a CEO who begins to hold his reports accountable for treating others with respect—perhaps demoting a notoriously disrespectful high performer—would show that respect is now a cultural norm.

The good news is that a cultural change inevitably leads to an organizational change. If the leadership can change people's beliefs about "the way things are done in this organization," things will definitely be done differently. Those who adjust and fit into the new culture will thrive; those who don't will leave. As the culture changes, its thoughts, behaviors, interactions, systems, processes, and results will change.

The bad news is that changing a culture is exceedingly difficult. Culture is not something that leaders can change by decree. They can only reshape it through new behaviors. The chicken-and-egg problem is that leadership behaviors are strongly determined by the existing culture. Furthermore, those who have reached leadership positions are the ones who thrived in the old culture. How can they lead the organization away from the patterns that helped them succeed? Only through a change in consciousness. The spark that ignites a process of cultural change is a change in the attitudes, beliefs, and behaviors of top management: in other words, a shift from unconscious to conscious leadership.

> In the hands of a mature, healthy human being—one who has achieved full humanness—power … is a great blessing. But in the hands of the immature, vicious, or emotionally sick, power is a horrible danger.
>
> ABRAHAM MASLOW[12]

TABLE 2 Unconscious versus Conscious Business	
Unconscious Attitudes	**Conscious Attitudes**
Unconditional Blame Essential Selfishness Ontological Arrogance	Unconditional Responsibility Essential Integrity Ontological Humility
Unconscious Behaviors	**Conscious Behaviors**
Manipulative Communication Narcissistic Negotiation Negligent Coordination	Authentic Communication Constructive Negotiation Impeccable Coordination
Unconscious Reactions	**Conscious Responses**
Emotional Incompetence	Emotional Mastery

UNCONSCIOUS ATTITUDES

Three attitudes lie at the source of unconscious organizations. They establish a toxic infrastructure that leads to disastrous results in the impersonal, interpersonal, and personal dimensions.

Unconditional blame is the tendency to explain all difficulties *exclusively* as the consequence of forces beyond your influence, to see yourself as an absolute victim of external circumstances.

Every person suffers the impact of factors beyond his control, so we are all, in a sense, victims. We are not, however, *absolute* victims. We have the ability to respond to our circumstances and influence how they affect us. In contrast, the unconditional blamer defines his victim-identity by his helplessness, disowning any power to manage his life, and assigning causality *only* to that which is beyond his control.

Unconditional blamers believe that their problems are always someone else's fault, and that there's nothing they could have done to prevent them. Consequently, they believe that there's nothing they should do to address them. Unconditional blamers feel innocent, unfairly burdened by others who do things they "shouldn't" do because of maliciousness or stupidity. According to the unconditional blamer, these others "ought" to fix the problems they created. Blamers live in a state of self-righteous indignation, trying to control people around them with their accusations and angry demands.

What the unconditional blamer does not see is that in order to claim innocence, he has to relinquish his power. If he is not part of the problem, he cannot be part of the solution. In fact, rather than being the main character of his life, the blamer is a spectator. Watching his own suffering from the sidelines, he feels "safe" because his misery is always somebody else's fault. Blame is a tranquilizer. It soothes the blamer, sheltering him from accountability for his life. But like any drug, its soothing effect quickly turns sour, miring him in resignation and resentment. In order to avoid anxiety and guilt, the blamer must disown his freedom and power and see himself as a plaything of others.

The blamer feels victimized at work. His job is fraught with letdowns, betrayals, disappointments, and resentments. He feels that he is expected to fix problems he didn't create, yet his efforts are never recognized. So he shields himself with justifications. Breakdowns are never his fault, nor are solutions his responsibility. He is not accountable because it is always other people who failed to do what they should have done. Managers don't give him direction as they should, employees don't support him as they should, colleagues don't cooperate with him as they should, customers demand much more than they should, suppliers don't respond as they should, senior executives don't lead the organization as they should, administration systems don't work as they should—the whole company is a mess. In addition, the economy is weak, the job market tough, the taxes confiscatory, the regulations crippling, the interest rates exorbitant, and the competition fierce (especially because of those evil foreigners who pay unfairly low wages). And if it weren't difficult enough to survive in this environment, everybody demands extraordinary results. The blamer never tires of reciting his tune, "Life is not fair!"

Essential selfishness is the exclusive focus on ego gratification, without concern for the well-being of others. It is the drive toward immediate satisfaction, without considering the long-term consequences of your actions on others—or even on yourself.

The selfish individual is single-mindedly focused on her desires. She seeks pleasure, assuming that getting what she wants is both necessary and sufficient for a good life. Winning is everything for her; all her attention is on "taking care of number one," coming out on top, being first at any cost. She is ready to do anything to achieve her goals: bend some rules, break others, use people if convenient, disregard them if not, sack them if necessary. The selfish individual respects no moral or legal boundaries in her pursuit of ego gratification. She may obey the law, but only out of fear of punishment—not because of any sense of morality. She is ruthless and relentless in her pursuit of pleasure. She sees other people as a means whose only role is to serve her purposes. She is guided by greed, envy, and jealousy, consumed by possessiveness. Her desire is never satisfied; she always wants more, more, and more.

The blindness of the selfish individual is that her attachment to success is the ultimate source of her suffering. Her endless cravings lead her to a hellish realm of anxiety, fear, frustration, and depression. In the Buddhist tradition these individuals are called "hungry ghosts" and are depicted as having huge mouths and long thin necks, which make them unable to swallow what they bite off. Their bodies are emaciated since they cannot get any nourishment. Spiritual traditions of East and West teach that attachment to egoic desire always leads to suffering. The selfish individual disregards this wisdom, trusting that the satisfaction of her endless appetite is the key to happiness.

For the selfish individual, work is just another place in which to get as much as possible while giving back the least possible. Her contributions are to be minimized and her compensations are to be maximized. She always seeks to take advantage of situations and people, regardless of whether this may hurt others. Cutting corners is all right if it allows her to succeed now—even if it is harmful in the long term.

Unflattering portrayals of selfish business people often appear in the news. Their greed and unscrupulousness give business a bad name. They see their companies exclusively as means for their own gratification. They exploit employees, lie to investors, squeeze suppliers, and take advantage of customers, all for their own personal gain.

Ontological arrogance is the claim that things are the way you see them, that your truth is the *only* truth. It is the belief that the only valid perspective is the one you hold, and that anybody who sees things differently is mistaken.

The ontological arrogant (ontology is the branch of philosophy that asks what actually exists) does not distinguish his personal opinions from objective truth; for him, his opinions *are* the truth. Neither does he distinguish his subjective experience from objective reality; for him, his experience *defines* reality. He lives in a dream world, and takes it to be the real world. He acts as though his views are absolutely right and whoever disagrees with him must be wrong. For the ontological arrogant there is only one way of thinking: his. Diversity of thought is anathema to him; his goal is to get everybody to surrender to his ideas. He is intent on showing that he is right, and will argue passionately to prove his point—even if he is not sure about it. He is the classic know-it-all, always pontificating about how things are, how they ought to be, and what everybody else should do.

The ontological arrogant "loves his face more than he loves the truth." He refuses to question his views, even against overwhelming contradictory evidence. His self-esteem depends on being right—or at least looking like he is. His self-image is brittle and would be shattered if he were forced to acknowledge a mistake. This makes it impossible to have a productive conversation with him. His self-righteous assertions antagonize those who hold different perspectives. His behavior polarizes people and touches off quasi-religious wars in which each camp tries to prove that it owns the truth. This prevents groups from integrating the information of all their members into a more inclusive perspective.

The current work environment means trouble for the ontological arrogant. The information economy requires humility and a willingness to learn from others. In the old days, a manager was able to do most jobs under his supervision better than his employees. Nowadays, employees know better than managers what is happening in their areas and what to do about it. The manager has a role in aligning individual efforts as parts of a team strategy, but the most effective tactical responses come from the employees with local knowledge. The arrogant manager, however, cannot listen to his employees. He uses his formal authority to impose his perspective. This demotivates his subordinates into compliance or even malicious obedience. Nobody feels like offering his best to someone who does not listen to him.

When unconditional blame, essential selfishness, and ontological arrogance become the toxic infrastructure of an organization, they lead to three types of perverse interactions: manipulative communication, narcissistic negotiation, and negligent coordination.

UNCONSCIOUS INTERACTIONS

At work, we interact in three basic ways. We communicate to understand each other, we negotiate our differences to make decisions, and we coordinate our actions through mutual commitments. Each type of interaction poses a challenge in the It, We, and I dimensions.

The challenge of communication is to share difficult information with honesty and respect in a way that honors your values, deepens your relationships, and improves your (and the organization's) performance. To understand this challenge, consider how you would tell a colleague, in a way that helps both of you work better together, that you think his proposal is a terrible idea.

The challenge of decision making is to turn disagreement into consensus, taking care of each party's concerns. To understand this challenge, consider how you would go from your wanting to do "A" and your colleague wanting to do "B" to the two of you freely deciding (and committing) to doing "X" in a way that builds self-esteem, connection, and excellence.

The challenge of coordination is to make and fulfill commitments in the face of uncertainty and change. To understand this challenge, consider how you would honor your word, enhance trust in your relationships, and accomplish your (and the organization's) goals when you make promises that are subject to risk.

There are conscious and unconscious ways to address these challenges. Unfortunately, most people tend to act unconsciously.

Manipulative communication is the choice to withhold relevant information in order to get what you want. Those who communicate manipulatively seek to pursue their personal agenda above all else. They hide data that does not support their arguments and fabricate information to buttress their positions. If necessary, they are willing to deceive others to reach their goals. They have no desire to present a full picture of the situation and enable others to make free, informed choices. They only convey information that supports their arguments. Simultaneously, they have no curiosity about what others really think. They only care about getting others to think what they think. Thus, their questions attempt to undermine others' positions and advocate their own. Genuine inquiry is anathema to them, since it may allow others to present information that contradicts their view.

When people communicate manipulatively, there is a wide gap between public speech and private thoughts. On the outside, it may seem as though a polite conversation is taking place. But significant facts and opinions remain hidden in each person's mind. This leads to serious problems. From a task perspective, miscommunication destroys effectiveness and creates escalating errors. It is impossible to operate successfully if people don't share relevant information. It is equally impossible to cooperate without a frank discussion in which people understand each other's views and needs. From a relationship perspective, it is impossible to experience mutual respect and connection when relating dishonestly. In order to develop a sense of community it is necessary to view the other person as a legitimate partner, one who deserves to be heard and make her own decisions freely and with full information. From a personal perspective, the gap between your real thoughts and your messages sets off a feeling of hypocrisy. Hiding relevant parts of your truth produces stress because it violates your sense of honesty.

Narcissistic negotiation is the attempt to prove your worth by beating up your opponent. The narcissist's primary goal is not to achieve what he wants, but to show the other "who's the boss." The narcissist puts others down as a way of pulling himself up in comparison. In a negotiation, the narcissist seeks to *win over* the other, as opposed to *win with* the other. Instead of trying to satisfy every party's needs, narcissistic negotiators focus only on having their demands met. This prevents them from exploring options that could address their underlying interests without clashing with the other person's needs. Narcissistic negotiation prevents shared problem solving and escalates conflict.

When people use disagreement as an arena in which to prove that they are more valuable than their opponents, performance suffers. For starters, the expectation that differences of opinion will degenerate into fights encourages people to avoid necessary discussions and sweep disagreements under the table. I explained earlier how these manipulative conversations seriously hurt personal, team, and organizational performance. Beyond that, in a narcissistic negotiation, even when people share their information and engage in discussion, the decision-making process is politicized and fraught with personal attacks. Narcissists become identified with their opinions and consider any disagreement a personal affront. They are unable to distinguish a challenge to their ideas from a challenge to their identity. So the discussion is never really about the relative merits of the contending points of view—although it may look like it on the surface. The discussion is all about who wins and who loses, who gets the right to trounce the other. A resource allocation process based on such contentiousness cannot yield a good outcome. On the contrary, decisions tend to be erratic and based on power rather than logic.

Narcissistic negotiations destroy relationships. People see each other as enemies competing for scarce resources. There is overt competition for material things but, more damaging, there is covert competition for what appears to the opponents as a fixed and limited amount of self-esteem. This sets up a zero-sum game in which one player wins only what the other loses. There is no room for cooperation, creativity, synergy, or solidarity. It's a dog-eat-dog world in which one person ends up on top and all the others on the bottom. The rivalry usually goes beyond the individuals directly involved in the conflict. As representatives of different organizational factions, participants engage their "allies" in the fight. Additionally, it is typical for the contenders to stab each other in the back by going to a senior person to advocate their case against the other. This is seriously detrimental because it engages the managers in the subordinates' turf wars.

Negligent coordination is a careless way to collaborate, making promises without a serious commitment to honor them. Collective action requires counting on each other's word: a word kept by making and fulfilling commitments. If people let each other down, performance suffers, trust disappears, and anxiety reigns. The situation is even worse when the would-be collaborators don't know how to make clear requests and hold others accountable for their promises. There is a perfect convergence of careless requests, groundless promises, fulfillment breakdowns, and ineffective complaints that destroys coordination, reliance, and integrity.

Some typical examples of negligence in *making a request* include not asking for what you want; expecting the other to read your mind and fulfill your unstated wishes; failing to address your request to a specific person; not defining the concrete deliverables that you are asking for; leaving undetermined the time by which you want the request to be fulfilled; and assuming that because the other didn't explicitly decline your request, he promised to fulfill it. Some typical examples of negligence in *responding to a request* include accepting a request without understanding it; promising to deliver something that you have no skills or resources to produce; committing to do something without really intending to do it; and leading the requester to believe that you are committed when you are truly not, with a weak response such as "I'll do my best" or "I'll see what I can do." Some typical examples of negligence in *honoring a commitment* include failing to plan for risk mitigation and being blindsided by predictable events; not alerting the requester when you realize that you may not be able to fulfill your promise; letting the requester know of the risk but not taking responsibility (using "victim" justifications that blame external events); not working with the requester to minimize disruptions; and failing to contact the requester to apologize and repair the damage even after the deadline, or worse yet, reacting with anger to the requester's legitimate complaint.

As if these perverse attitudes and interactions were not enough to overwhelm individuals and organizations, their effects are compounded by a seventh factor that undermines people's attempts to remain conscious: emotional incompetence.

UNCONSCIOUS REACTIONS

Emotional incompetence manifests in two ways: explosion and repression. The first is acting out your feelings, indulging in counterproductive behaviors that only serve to discharge your emotional impulses. The second is hiding your feelings behind a facade of stoicism, pretending that nothing is going on while you are seething inside. We tend to display both behaviors in cycles. Repression builds up a charge to the point where we cannot contain it and we explode—with disastrous consequences for ourselves and others. The pain and guilt we feel after such an episode triggers a new cycle of repression, which is surely followed by another explosion, and so on.

Emotions can take over your mind and trigger actions that you later regret. As you reflect, it is shocking to realize that you lost your cool and behaved irrationally. Even if, under normal conditions, you can fight off the pressure to think and behave perversely, your psychological defenses are inclined to collapse under emotional stress. Grief, fear, anger, and guilt are typical emotions that can debilitate your mind to the point where you revert to automatic patterns of fight or flight. Such biological programming is entrenched in the most primitive part of your nervous system, known as the reptilian brain. When intense emotional energy overcharges your system, you blow the proverbial fuse. The ensuing short circuit puts the rational part of your mind off-line and allows atavistic impulses to take over.

While in the throes of passion, most of us have caused harm. Some of us have concluded that it is better to suppress our emotions. Pushing them into a dark corner of our minds, however, defeats our purpose. In the shadows, beyond the reach of awareness, they grow until they become strong enough to mount an assault and take control. If we manage to repel them, they revert to covert tactics, creating stress, anxiety, depression, and other psychosomatic diseases.

If we get overwhelmed by our emotions, we revert to active and passive aggression. Even though they always end up backfiring, these tactics are deeply ingrained. They seem to protect us in the short term, but they harm us (and those around us) in due course. They promise relief, but they deliver only suffering.

Over the course of this book, I will explore the transition from these unconscious attitudes, interactions, and reactions to a more conscious way of doing business. I will present concepts, tools, and practices to foster a more vibrant, more rewarding, and more productive (business) life.

AN INVITATION TO CONSCIOUS BUSINESS

You know that there is more to work than making money. You know that it is possible to experience great joy as you engage in meaningful work of which you are proud; soulful work that confronts you with challenges and develops your skills; work that is aligned with your mission in life. This is work you enjoy doing for its own sake, work that provides you with significant material and spiritual rewards.

While you do this work, you feel fully absorbed. Time seems to stop and you enter into an extraordinary reality. Difficulties become creative challenges. You feel in control—not because you can guarantee the result, but because you trust yourself and know that you can respond skillfully. This is an ecstatic world that "stands outside" everyday dullness, a world that captures you so thoroughly that you forget yourself. There's a sense of flow, an experience of hard work performed with ease. Life seems to be living itself effortlessly, and everything that needs to get done gets done.

You may be alone, but you don't feel lonely. You feel connected to something larger than yourself. Whether people are physically present or not, you feel a bond with a community of purpose. You feel an exquisite intimacy, a sense of belonging to something larger than yourself, and yet completely at one with your true self.

Some people say that work is hell. I claim that work can be heaven. Heaven and hell are not realms of the afterlife; they are states of mind. When you live and work unconsciously, situations seem hellish, but when you intensify the light of awareness, the same situations seem heavenly. I hope this book helps you brighten the light of consciousness for yourself, your organization, and the world.

A big, tough samurai once went to see a little monk. "Monk," he barked, in a voice accustomed to instant obedience, "teach me about heaven and hell!"

The monk looked up at the mighty warrior and replied with utter disdain, "Teach you about heaven and hell? I couldn't teach you about anything. You're dumb. You're dirty. You're a disgrace, an embarrassment to the samurai class. Get out of my sight. I can't stand you."

The samurai got furious. He shook, red in the face, speechless with rage. He pulled out his sword, and prepared to slay the monk.

Looking straight into the samurai's eyes, the monk said softly, "That's hell."

The samurai froze, realizing the compassion of the monk who had risked his life to show him hell! He put down his sword and fell to his knees, filled with gratitude.

The monk said softly, "And that's heaven."

ZEN PARABLE

CHAPTER 2

Unconditional Responsibility

◆

The basic difference between an ordinary man and a warrior
is that a warrior takes everything as a challenge,
while an ordinary man takes everything as a blessing or a curse.
DON JUAN, YAQUI SHAMAN[1]

We who lived in the concentration camps can remember
the men who walked through the huts comforting others,
giving away their last piece of bread. They may have been
few in number, but they offer sufficient proof that
everything can be taken from a man but one thing:
the last of human freedoms—to choose one's attitude
in any given set of circumstances—to choose one's own way. ...
It is this spiritual freedom—which cannot be taken away—
that makes life meaningful and purposeful.
VIKTOR FRANKL[2]

◆

Y ou're late, Al," says John with a grimace. "Again."
John is the procurement vice president for Al's largest client and he is clearly not a happy customer.

"I'm sorry, John, my previous meeting ran over. The client was late and everything got delayed."

Al's explanation doesn't appease John. "It's not the meeting, Al, it's the delivery. We are still waiting for your shipment, the one that was supposed to arrive last week!"

"Well, that's not my fault," says Al. "The freight company dropped the ball. They screwed up the paperwork and delayed the whole thing."

"I don't give a damn whose fault is it. We can't afford delays. Our plant is starved for parts: *your* parts."

Al leaves John's office muttering under his breath, "I'm not responsible for my previous meeting running over or for the shipping company's mistake. He's blaming *me* for problems *I* didn't create. People are so unfair …"

Next time a colleague is late for an appointment, listen to his explanation. Maybe, like Al, your tardy associate will blame another meeting "running over"; maybe he will complain about traffic. If the previous meeting had finished on time or the freeway had been clear, he would have been on time. His explanations may be accurate, but they are ineffective. To understand why, let's take a closer look at the consequences of this conversation between Al and John.

For starters, they failed to resolve the shipping problem. Furthermore, there's little reason to believe that similar problems won't arise in the future. When confronted with John's demands, Al offered explanations that didn't solve anything. According to his logic, as long as other people make him late, Al will continue to be late. As long as Al's business associates make mistakes, his clients will suffer delays. There's more. On the interpersonal level, the conversation hurt the relationship. John was left distrusting Al while Al was resentful toward John. It's hard to imagine an effective supplier-customer relationship based on mutual exasperation. Finally, it is safe to assume that both John and Al finished the conversation feeling worse than when they started. Each probably felt some combination of stress, grief, anger, and fear. It's not a stretch to imagine each of them complaining about the other to anyone who will listen.

Unfortunately, this conversation is typical of many that I've witnessed in corporations, nonprofit organizations, families, and friendships. When blame meets avoidance, conflicts escalate and people feel alienated. How can you avert these disasters?

You must take unconditional responsibility; you need to see yourself as a "player," as a central character who has contributed to shape the current situation—and who can thus affect its future. This is the opposite of seeing yourself as a "victim," subject to forces beyond your control. The player is *in* the game and can affect the result. The victim is *out of* the game and can only suffer the consequences of others' actions.

While Al's explanations were true, they weren't the whole truth. In fact, they were the weakest and most unproductive part of the truth. His explanations disempowered him and his partner. They made it more difficult for them to resolve the problem, heal the relationship, and be at peace.

There are many ways to look at any problem. Some promote power and achievement; others promote weakness and failure. In order to pursue personal and organization greatness, you need to adopt the former and eschew the latter. You need to address every situation from a player's stance. You need to claim your unconditional *response-ability*. In this chapter, I will define unconditional responsibility and explore why it is so critical to the health of individuals, teams, and organizations. I will also show why, in spite of its obvious benefits, it is so rare. Let's start with a distinction between two typical characters: the victim and the player.

RESPONSE-ABILITY

Response-ability is your ability to respond to a situation. You can respond to an offer by choosing to buy or not buy. You can respond to a complaint by choosing to listen or argue. I call response-ability "unconditional" because your responses are not determined by external circumstances or instinct. They may depend on external factors and inner drives, but you always have a choice. As a human being, you are an autonomous (from the Greek, "self-ruling") being. And the more conscious you are of your autonomy, the more unconditioned your responses will be.

Ability to respond does not mean ability to succeed. There is no guarantee that what you do will yield what you want. The guarantee is that as long as you are alive and conscious, you can respond to your circumstances in pursuit of your happiness. This power to respond is a defining feature of humanity. Our response-ability is a direct expression of our rationality, our will, and our freedom. Being human is being response-able.

Unconditional response-ability is self-empowering. It lets you focus on those aspects of the situation that you can influence. When you play cards, you have no control over the hand you are dealt. If you spend all your time complaining and making excuses for your cards, you will feel disempowered and will most likely lose the game. But if you see yourself as having a choice in how to play those cards, your feelings will change. You will have a sense of possibility. Even if you don't win, you can always do your best with the cards you've got.

When you live in this world, you have no control over the hand you are dealt. You will live a sorry life if you keep blaming fate for the unfairness of your lot. Response-ability is looking at your cards and making the best of them. Response-ability is knowing that no matter how bad things appear, there is always a possibility to express your truth in the face of a challenge.

Response-ability is not guilt. You are not responsible *for* your circumstances; you are response-able *in the face of* your circumstances. Let's take an extreme example: You are not responsible for world hunger. You didn't start it and you didn't worsen it. It exists independently of you. You are, however, able to respond *to* world hunger. In fact, world hunger is such a pervasive problem that you cannot not respond to it. You can ignore it, you can read about it, you can donate money, you can work in a soup kitchen, you can volunteer for the Peace Corps, or you can devote your life to feeding the hungry. Whatever you do, that is your choice, your expression of your response-ability in the face of world hunger.

Response-ability is the source of power and integrity, the power to influence your situation and the integrity to do so in alignment with your values.

WHY DOES THE PEN FALL?

In my seminars I conduct a simple experiment. I pick up a pen and let it fall to the ground. Then I ask the group, "Why did the pen fall?" "Gravity" is usually the first answer. Sometimes people point out that I dropped it. Both answers are correct. Both gravity and my releasing of the pen caused it to fall. Most problems involve multiple factors as well, yet when we analyze them we don't look at all the causes. Normally we focus on a single reason. We look for a simple explanation. The question is, which reason is the most useful? In order to assess usefulness, we need to examine our goals. What are we trying to accomplish through our explanation?

If you want to prevent the pen from falling again, pointing out that the pen falls "because of gravity" will not help you. As long as there is gravity, the pen will fall and, according to your explanation, there is nothing you can do about it. On the other hand, if you want to argue that the fall of the pen "is not your fault," gravity is the perfect explanation. (Perhaps that's why my kids, who've seen me do the pen experiment, argue that the food that falls on the floor does so "because of gravity.")

If you say that you dropped the pen, however, there is something you can do about it. Now you have a role in the drama and you can pursue your goal actively. If you do not want the pen to fall, hold on to it. "Gravity" places causality in the realm of the uncontrollable; "I dropped it" puts me in control. Of course, most situations are more complex, but the example demonstrates an important distinction between self-disempowering explanations and self-empowering ones. It distinguishes between the explanatory styles of the *victim* and the *player*.

THE VICTIM AND THE PLAYER

The victim pays attention only to those factors he cannot influence. He sees himself as somebody who suffers the consequences of external circumstances. The victim keeps his self-esteem by claiming innocence. His explanations never include him, since he has nothing to do with the problem. He never acknowledges any contribution to the current situation. When things go wrong, the victim seeks to place blame. He points his finger at other people's mistakes. For him, problems always come from other people's actions. Self-soothing explanations placate him. They allow him to maintain the illusion of blamelessness when confronted with the reality of failure.

When an information systems manager-as-victim receives a customer complaint, for example, his automatic response is to blame the problem on his programmers. The programmers may indeed have made mistakes, but his explanation conveniently avoids the fact that he is supposed to supervise their work. When an account executive-as-victim loses a client, he immediately claims that the shipping department did not deliver on time. This may also be true, but overlooks the fact that he may have failed to ask the shipping department if it could meet the deadline.

The player pays attention to those factors she can influence. She sees herself as somebody who can respond to external circumstances. She bases her self-esteem on doing her best. Her explanations focus on her, since she realizes that she is an important contributor to the problem. When things go wrong, the player seeks to understand what she can do to correct them. She chooses *self-empowering explanations*, explanations that put her in control.

If the information systems manager were a player, he would recognize his contribution to the undesirable outcome; that is, the role his supervision played in producing the customer's complaint. If the account executive were a player, he would choose to focus on his contribution to the problem; that is, on the ungrounded commitment that led to the late shipment and consequent loss of the customer.

The victim knows the way to innocence. "If you want to look good," he thinks, "you can't be seen as part of the problem. You have to blame external circumstances over which you had no control." The player knows the way to power. "If you want to be part of the solution," she thinks, "you have to see yourself as part of the problem. Unless you recognize your contribution to a bad situation, you won't be able to change it."

For a player, the world is full of challenges that she feels empowered to face as a "warrior"—as don Juan says in this chapter's epigraph. The player does not feel omnipotent. She understands that there are external factors beyond her control. She takes these factors neither as a blessing nor a curse, but simply as challenges.

Several years ago, as I presented the victim-player dichotomy in one of my seminars, an irate black man stood up and announced that my argument was worthless, that people of his race had been abused for generations, and that I was a typical clueless white guy. I was touched by his grief, and a little scared by his anger. I listened to him without interruption. When he finished, he headed for the exit. I asked him to stay and consider listening to my response. To my great relief, he agreed.

I told him that I had no intention of denying that there are people — black people among them — who have suffered great injustices. I explained that I had grown up a Jew under an anti-Semitic military dictatorship and felt the same fear that many minorities experience daily throughout the world. I hadn't been physically harmed, but several people I knew had "disappeared." Most likely they were kidnapped, tortured, and killed by military death squads. I told the man that I considered his outrage perfectly valid and assured him that I wanted to correct and repair these injustices as much as he did.

I then shared an insight that I had gleaned during those dark years in Argentina. I realized that the people oppressing me had absolutely no concern whatsoever for my well-being. I realized that the only way I could improve my situation was to take responsibility to protect myself. I stopped expecting the rulers, who only had ill will toward me, to change. I decided to do what I could, given that *they* wouldn't.

I noticed that the man was nodding slightly. I told him that perhaps I was a bit paranoid, but after my experience in Argentina I didn't trust government officials — or anyone who feels antagonistic toward me — to place my interests above theirs. So I have gone to great lengths to minimize my dependency on others. "Although I may have done it in an incompetent way," I explained, "my only goal was to invite you to realize that you are much better suited to take care of yourself than those who are intent on discriminating against you."

He smiled and nodded. As he returned to his seat I added, "Taking care of ourselves does not preclude educating abusers or removing them from our organizations."

Reverend Andre Scheffer was a minister of the Dutch Reformed Mission Church in Africa. He had a dry sense of humor and liked to poke fun at us. "You know," he would say, "the white man has a more difficult task than the black man in this country. Whenever there is a problem, we (white men) have to find a solution. But whenever you blacks have a problem, you have an excuse. You can simply say, *'Ingabilungu'* ... a Xhosa expression that means, 'It is the whites.'"

He was saying that we could always blame all of our troubles on the white man. His message was that we must also look within ourselves and become responsible for our actions—sentiments with which I wholeheartedly agreed.

NELSON MANDELA[3]

No one is simply a victim or a player. The victim and the player are archetypes that capture two basic tendencies in human beings: openness and defensiveness. Each represents a different lens through which we provide explanations for the many occurrences in our lives. We may take on each of these roles at different times. My acting like a victim in one particular instance doesn't preclude my acting like a player under different circumstances, and vice versa. Some people, for example, operate in full player mode when they are at work and return home to become perfect victims.

Regardless of which role you adopt, there are always factors that will be beyond your control. You must choose whether to focus on the ones within your control and be a player, or on those beyond your control and be a victim. Choosing the stance of the player is clearly more effective. Yet there are powerful reasons why so many of us choose to act like victims. Let's take a look at the "benefits" of victimhood.

　　　　　　　　　　　　　　　　　　　　CONSCIOUS BUSINESS

IT'S GOOD TO BE A VICTIM

We take the victim stance to protect ourselves from blame. We want to look good and project an image of success—or at least to avoid the tarnish that comes with failure. Victimhood is an attempt to cover up our incompetence so that we look more capable than we really are. Whether we like to admit it or not, many of us depend on other people's approval for our sense of achievement and happiness. Thus, we expend a great deal of energy building an "unblamable" public image.

Many executives explain poor results by fixing blame on economic factors such as inflation, deflation, or taxes or competitive factors such as low Asian wages, currency valuations, or trade barriers. Other common explanations focus on technological change, shifting consumer tastes, or an insufficient pool of competent job applicants. All those factors may be real but, like gravity, they are out of any executive's control. They are not determinants of poor results but environmental conditions that call for responses. It is much more comfortable, however, to shift responsibility to external factors than to take it for oneself.

For many of us, responsibility is synonymous with guilt and therefore to be avoided. It is a connection we made in early childhood. One of our first lessons in "self-defense" was to argue that we were always innocent. Some time ago, my three-year-old son, Tomás, walked into my office in a forlorn mood. With his best puppy-dog look, he said, "Daddy, I did it by accident." Naturally, I was concerned. "What did you do?" I asked. Tomás quickly changed his statement. "Daddy, *it* was an accident," he said and then grabbed my hand and led me to the dining room. I noticed the lamp was on. "Tomás, you plugged in the lamp. You know I don't want you to mess with electricity!" "But Daddy," he pleaded, "*it* was an accident."

Children believe that finding external causes for problems, or reporting that they did things unintentionally, erases their responsibility. That is why they often say such things as, "The juice spilled," implying that they had nothing to do with the cup tipping over; "The toy broke," as though the toy committed suicide right before their eyes; or the lamp turned itself on by accident. Another favorite phrase is "I didn't mean to ... ," which assumes that good intentions make up for bad behavior and poor results.

A third popular strategy is, "You made me do it." If, after interrupting one of their fights, I ask one of my kids, "Why are you hitting your sister?" his self-righteous answer will be something like, "Because she teased me." This answer implies, "She is responsible for my hitting her; I'm just a mechanism that reacts automatically to her teasing. Actually, it's not me who hit her; she hit herself through me." Of course, when I ask my daughter why she was teasing her brother, her self-righteous answer will be something like, "Because he stuck his tongue out at me first."

Many adults act in this same fashion. In coaching a client who had called me because he felt disconnected from his team, I asked him why he had answered the phone during a staff meeting. He told me, "Because it rang." This was true. The phone did ring, but his explanation didn't account for his choice to take the call while his staff waited. Taking the call hurt his relationship with the team, yet he couldn't see that he had exercised a choice. Similarly, a manager from a hospital told me how she heard a nurse yell at a patient's family member. When the manager informed the nurse that her outburst was unacceptable, the nurse offered a startlingly childish response: "He yelled at me first." As I was helping two executives repair their relationship, I heard the first say, "You ignored my request." To which the other responded, "That was not my intention, I was too busy." (That's the grownup way of saying, "I didn't mean to do it" or "I did it by accident.")

You are not a robot. You make choices. You choose to act as you do because you think it is the best way to pursue your interests in a given situation. External facts are *information*, not stimuli. You don't answer the phone *because* it rings. You *choose* to answer the phone *when* it rings, *because* you *want* to. You assess—perhaps automatically—that you are better off taking the call. External circumstances and internal impulses *influence* your behavior but they don't *determine* it. You are a conscious human being; you *always* have a choice.

Acknowledging that you have a choice is uncomfortable. "Choicelessness" is a great place to hide. When a phone rings in the middle of a meeting and you say, "Excuse me, I *have* to take this call," you are really deceiving yourself and others. You do not *have* to take the call. You are *choosing* to take it, because you find it preferable to continuing the conversation. It is awkward admitting that the phone call is more important to you than the conversation—so you mask the thorny truth. It is much easier to blame the phone than to take responsibility for the interruption. It is much safer to hide behind the ringing phone and relinquish accountability for your choice. It is also much weaker.

I am not suggesting that you dispense entirely with social graces. They are an effective lubricant for normal conversations. Neither am I proposing that you explicitly evaluate every choice you make. Habitual responses are extremely useful in normal circumstances. But in difficult situations, unconscious routines can be dangerous. When operational, interpersonal, or personal problems arise, you need to disconnect the automatic pilot and fly the plane consciously. You need to understand how your past choices contributed to the problem, and take accountability. You need to fully own the response-ability and the power that you have in the present. If you pick up the phone because it rings, the phone is in control. If you pick up the phone because you choose to, you are in charge.

Take the case of Esteban, a South American sales executive. He had learned that the human resources department had scheduled his staff's vacations without checking with him. Now his department would be under-staffed at a critical time. He was furious. "This is unbelievable!" he told me. "How dare they let people take vacations in February? Are they out of their minds? Those jerks don't know that our biggest clients are in the Northern Hemisphere. February is our busiest month!"

I asked him, "Esteban, whose problem is this?"

"Theirs, of course," he answered angrily. "They should have checked with me before scheduling *my* staff's vacations."

I insisted, "Who's suffering because of their decision?"

"I am, of course!" he said.

"So," I repeated, "whose problem is it?"

There was a long silence, and in that moment I saw a spark of under-standing in his eyes. "I didn't avoid talking to HR; *they* avoided talking to me. They screwed up; how can it be *my* problem?" he asked in disbelief.

"You didn't make the decision," I acknowledged, "but you are suffering the consequences. *If you are the one suffering, you are the one who has the problem*. And that means that you are the one who had better take corrective action. If you expect the ones who made the decision that suited *their* needs to solve *your* problem, I wish you luck."

Esteban followed my train of thought, but he wasn't ready to give up his victim story. "Why do I have to solve a problem that I am not responsible for?" he asked. "They broke it; they ought to fix it."

"Because you are the one who is being hurt by it," I told him. "You may not have caused the problem, but if *you* are hurt, you had better make it *your* problem. If you want things to change, you've got to deal with the problem yourself. You may not be responsible *for* the problem, but you can respond *to* it. *You* can make it better *for yourself.* Either that or you can continue to blame others. That may soothe you, but I think you'd be better off trying to change the situation. Feeling sorry for yourself in self-righteous indignation won't solve anything."

"But that's not fair," he argued. "This is not my fault!"

"Esteban," I said somewhat sadly, "life is not fair. If you wait for things to be fair you will spend a lot of your time stuck in resentment and resignation. Give up the illusion that other people will take care of your problems just because you think they caused them. You'll feel much better if you deal with the situation yourself. It does not matter if you are the one who broke it; you are the one who needs to fix it. Even if you don't succeed, just taking charge and doing your best—doing something that makes you proud of yourself—will reestablish your sense of power and integrity."

Why do we take the victim stance? Because we choose to. Why do we make this choice? Because, perhaps without giving the matter much thought, we feel that we will be better off as victims than as players. Yet as Esteban's story suggests, there is a huge cost to clinging to victimhood. Since the victim does not see himself as part of the problem, he cannot imagine himself as part of the solution.

For the victim, life is a spectator sport. His favorite place is on the sidelines, not on the field. His only option is to criticize those who play the game. This makes him feel safe because, although he can do nothing to help his team, he cannot be blamed when it loses. His routine is to blame the players, the coach, the referees, the opponents, the weather, bad luck, and everything else. Although his explanations are technically correct (just as it is correct that the pen falls because of gravity), they are also disempowering. This is the sharp hook behind the bait of innocence. The price of innocence is powerlessness.

Forsaking responsibility in the face of problems that are not of your making may seem justifiable, but if your ship encounters a storm you couldn't very well say, "This isn't my mess; I don't have to deal with it." A captain accepts that everything that happens during his watch is his responsibility. You are the captain of your life. You must sail as best you can no matter how "unfair" the weather is.

This may seem overly demanding, but when you think about it, victimhood is a terrible alternative. Consider the situation of psychiatrist Viktor Frankl, who was imprisoned at Auschwitz during World War II. It is hard to imagine a situation more unfair and tragic than his. Yet even amidst the horrific conditions, he woke up each morning and found a reason to survive. To paraphrase Nietzsche, Frankl realized that whoever has a "why" can withstand almost any "how." Even though all of the prisoners suffered extraordinarily, Frankl later noticed an important trait shared by many of the camp's survivors. Despite their lack of control over their exterior circumstances, they never relinquished control over their inner experience. Certainly, many prisoners who maintained this discipline also perished, but they never lost their integrity, gave up, or took their own lives. Frankl discovered that a human being's fundamental dignity lies in his capacity to choose his response to any situation—his *response-ability*.

Any situation—from the horrific to the mundane—can be explained from the point of view of determinism or of free will. Freedom distinguishes a human being from every other type of being; *being human means being able to choose*. Perhaps the most important exercise of this freedom is the decision about whether to live as a victim or a player.

To cover all the earth with sheets of hide—
Where could such amounts of skin be found?

But simply wrap some leather round your feet,
And it's as if the whole earth had been covered!

Likewise, we can never take
And turn aside the outer course of things.
But only seize and discipline the mind itself,
And what is there remaining to be curbed?

SHANTIDEVA, *THE WAY OF THE BODHISATTVA*[4]

THE PLAYER: UNCONDITIONAL FREEDOM

The traditional definition of freedom describes it as our capacity to do what we want. We want to be "free from" constraints. This freedom is "relative" or "conditional" because it depends on factors beyond our control. Life is full of constraints. We can't stop our bodies from aging or following the laws of physics. We can't make others think and feel as we wish. We can't start a company (at least not legally) without the necessary government licenses. We have different degrees of relative freedom, but nobody is "totally free."

The essential or unconditional definition of freedom is our capacity to respond to a situation by exercising our free will. According to this definition, every person is free. Essential freedom is a basic condition of human existence. We *always* respond to situations the way we choose. If we face an armed robber threatening to take our money or our life, we have plenty of options: hand him the money, attack him, try to escape, shout, seek help, etc. What we *cannot* choose is the criminal not being there to attack us. Another thing we cannot choose is whether our strategy will be successful. Essential human freedom is unconditional because, *as we face* our situation, we can choose to do what we deem best.

We are always free to choose our behavior; we are even free to choose to deny ourselves this freedom and feel as though we were not free. Take Nancy, for example, an engineering manager. She felt victimized by her boss who "forced" her to attend a meeting I was facilitating between the engineering and sales departments. When I asked her why she attended the meeting, she replied,

"Because my boss sent me." It was true that her boss had asked her to come to the meeting, but not the whole truth. It was also true that she *chose* to accept her boss's request. Nancy's interpretation led her to feel resentment and resignation. She was physically present at the meeting, but her heart and mind were somewhere else. I challenged her gently, asking her if *she* hadn't *agreed* to attend the meeting when her boss had requested it. The obvious implication was that she could have chosen not to come to the meeting in spite of her boss's request.

"No, I couldn't disagree with my boss and miss this meeting. My job is on the line," Nancy argued. I pointed out that she could have missed the meeting but instead chose to attend because the consequences of declining her boss's request were worse than the consequences of accepting it. "Well, it's the same thing," she said. "The difference is purely semantic."

The difference is not just semantic. To own her power, Nancy must stop denying her freedom. Once she realizes that she is free to respond to her boss (even though she is not free *from* her boss's authority), Nancy could try to negotiate not attending the meeting, or if the meeting was that distasteful for her, to risk declining her boss's request anyway. This could result in unwanted consequences: Nancy cannot choose to keep her job if her boss fires her, but quitting her job in protest for being sent to the meeting is an option (although probably not the most desirable one). Freedom does not mean doing what you want without consequences; it means having the capacity to choose, in the face of a situation, the response that is most consistent with your values.

Unconditional freedom is the player's secret weapon. The player understands that all results are a consequence of the interplay between a certain challenge and her ability to respond to it—what we've been calling *response-ability*. If the challenge is greater than her capacity to respond, the result will be negative, a failure. If her capacity to respond is greater than the challenge, the result will be positive, a success. Thus, she can increase her chances of success by either increasing her response capabilities or by reducing the challenge she is facing. In situations where the challenge is beyond her control, trusting success to luck is a risky proposition—a chance that a player is not willing to take. (The victim, on the other hand, assumes that other people and the forces of the universe should go her way.)

The player always describes herself as a significant part of her problems. She is willing to take the hit of accountability because it puts her in the driver's seat. Self-empowering explanations let her understand how she contributed to the situation, and find ways to improve it. When she understands what she did or didn't do that contributed to the problem, she understands what she can do or not do to prevent the problem from recurring.

Let's go back to Esteban and his scheduling problem. "Fine," he granted begrudgingly. "Let's say that this is my problem. What am I supposed to do now?"

"First, you need to understand how you contributed to it," I answered.

"What?" he burst out. "This is too much! *I didn't do anything* wrong. They made the mistake. Why do you want me to take the blame?"

"I don't want you to take the blame, Esteban. I want to find your part in the problem."

"And why is that?" he asked.

I said, "I have three reasons: First, it will help you think of ways in which you can be a part of the solution; second, it will allow you to have a conversation with the HR guys that starts non-confrontationally; and third, it will let you avoid falling into the same trap in the future."

"Okay," Esteban accepted, "let's try it."

After some inquiry we established that Esteban's contribution to the problem was that, as he had said, *he hadn't done anything*. Specifically, he hadn't told the HR department that February was his busiest month, and that he needed all his staff. This was not *wrong*; it was subject to improvement. We agreed that the best way to proceed would be for him to have a conversation with the HR department to try to change the current schedule. I will describe in detail how to tackle this type of conversation in chapter 5, but let me give you a preview here. I asked Esteban to do a reverse role play. "You play the HR guy and I'll play you," I instructed. "Improvise using your best judgment. Don't make him easier than you think he would be, but don't make him a monster either. I'll use my judgment to play you. If you feel I say something that you wouldn't honestly say, interrupt me and let me know, okay? So what's your nemesis's name?" Esteban sneered, "Oh, I'm going to enjoy being the bad guy. Call me Rick."

Esteban (Fred): "Hi, Rick, I'd like to talk to you about the holiday schedule. Do you have a minute now? It's kind of urgent."

Rick (Esteban): "Sorry, Esteban, the schedule is all set, we can't change it."

Esteban (Fred): "Well, that's one of the things I'd like to talk about, but not the only one. I'd really appreciate a few minutes of your time."

Rick (Esteban): "All right. Let's talk now."

Esteban (Fred): "Thank you. I want to ask for your help. You couldn't know this since I never told you, but February is my department's busiest month—we ship mostly to the Northern Hemisphere. Given the current vacation schedule, I will find myself severely understaffed. I am wondering if there's anything we can do about that."

Rick (Esteban): "Well, don't blame me! That's your problem."

Esteban (Fred): "Exactly, this is my problem, and I'm asking you for help. I understand that you couldn't have known because I didn't tell you."

"Wait a minute!" the real Esteban interrupted. "He could have asked! You're making me take all the heat. Rick has some 'response-ability' in this situation too, doesn't he?"

"Absolutely, but at this point I don't think it would be productive to focus on that. My taking a hundred percent responsibility does not mean he doesn't have his own hundred percent as well. Every person can take full ownership. Do you disagree that you could have told Rick and you didn't?"

"No."

"Okay, then let's keep going."

Esteban (Fred): "Exactly, this is my problem, and I'm asking you for help. I understand that you couldn't have known because I didn't tell you."

Rick (Esteban): "You should have told me."

Esteban (Fred): "Yes. It would have been a lot better if I had told you. But I didn't. So now I have this situation and I need your help. Is there something you can do to help me?"

Rick (Esteban): "We get a lot of complaints when we change schedules. My boss doesn't like that a bit."

Esteban (Fred): "Let me check if I understand. It may be possible to reschedule my department's vacations, but you are concerned that if people complain you'll get in trouble with your boss. Is that correct?"

Rick (Esteban): "You got it."

Esteban (Fred): "I see how that would be a problem for you. But what if I can guarantee that the people in my department won't complain? They are also frustrated with the schedule and would like to work during our busy month."

Rick (Esteban): "Would you put that in writing?"

Esteban (Fred): "Absolutely. What if I send you a memo, signed by all the people in my department, explaining that February is our busiest month and that we would appreciate your rescheduling vacations so that everybody is on the job?"

Rick (Esteban): "That would work for me."

Esteban (Fred): "Thanks Rick, you've been very helpful!"

"How the hell did you do that?" Esteban exclaimed. "You made me *want* to help you!"

"I can't *make* you, and you can't make Rick, do anything. But I can ask in a very compelling way. I used several techniques, but the crucial step was to stop blaming you (Rick) for the problem and focus on my contribution. That lowered your defensiveness. Then, when I asked you for help, you were much more willing to explore options with me."

"That's great, but what if Rick refuses to change the schedule after all?" Esteban added.

"Why would he do that?" I inquired.

Esteban replied laughing, "I don't know, because he's a prick!"

I challenged him: "Would he say that he doesn't want to change the schedule because he is a prick?"

"Of course not."

"So what do you imagine he would say?"

Esteban answered, "He may claim that there's a policy in place and even if all my people ask to have their vacations changed, he is not allowed to do it at this point."

"Then I would ask Rick to let you speak with the person who has the power to make an exception to the policy. This is not just for your benefit, but for the sake of the company. You could make a pretty strong case."

"Come on, Fred," said Esteban, a bit exasperated. "You know what I mean. What if he just can't change the damn schedule?"

"All right, just for argument's sake, let's say that there is an insurmountable constraint. This would be odd, because there are very few non-negotiables in business. But at the very least, the problem will not reoccur next year. You would have made it clear that February is not vacation time for your department. But more importantly, if you tried everything and couldn't change the date, you'd deal with the situation the best way you could, with as little resentment as you could. And then when you looked in the mirror you would be proud of yourself because you did your best in alignment with your values."

In any situation, the player strives to do her best to respond according to her values. The player feels secure, but not out of a naive faith that everything will work out. Her peace of mind comes from knowing that regardless of the challenge, she has the unconditional ability to respond. She may not achieve the result she desires, but she can behave righteously in the face of her trials. Her impeccable efforts yield joy, freedom, and dignity.

What was really needed was a fundamental change in our attitude toward life. We had to learn ourselves and, furthermore, we had to teach the despairing men, that *it did not really matter what we expected from life, but rather what life expected from us.* We needed to stop asking about the meaning of life, and instead to think of ourselves as those who were being questioned by life—daily and hourly. Our answer must consist, not in talk and meditation, but in right action and in right conduct. Life ultimately means taking the responsibility to find the right answer to its problems and to fulfill the tasks which it constantly sets for each individual.

VIKTOR FRANKL[5]

THE PRICE OF POWER: ACCOUNTABILITY

Taking the stance of the player is not without cost. Accepting your freedom requires that you account for your choices. Freedom and accountability are two sides of the same coin. If the devil made you do it, you don't have to explain why you did it. It isn't really you, but the devil, who actually did it. If you own your actions, you can be asked for your reasons and held accountable for their consequences. Power is the prize of responsibility; accountability is its price.

Freedom demands that you acknowledge your contribution to your problems. Contribution is not blame. In fact, the player's response-ability is at the antithesis of the victim's blame-ability. The victim tries to justify his victimhood by blaming others. There is no victim without a perpetrator. The player blames neither others nor herself. The player recognizes that she contributed to the unfolding of the situation and that perhaps she could have acted in more effective or dignified ways. The victim uses the language of "should," indicating obligation and judgment. The player uses the language of "could," indicating possibility and learning. A client of mine captures the meaning of contribution with a pithy phrase. "Whenever I have a problem," he says insightfully, "I'm around."

Blame seems like a safe haven when self-esteem is at risk. It is tempting to protect yourself by blaming others. Notice how when things get hot, your mind boils with questions such as, *Who screwed up? Who is bad? Who's wrong? Who should pay?* I learned how automatic the blame process can be by making a fool of myself in front of my kids. I was in my living room when the phone upstairs rang. I ran up, kicking a plastic cup that had been left on the stairs as I reached the top step. I got very upset. Not only did I spill purple grape juice on the carpet, I also missed the call.

I walked into the kids' room and asked in my best self-righteous voice, "Who left a cup at the top of the stairs?" A tiny voice replied, "And who kicked the cup?"

Blame obscures what's causing the problem and what can be done to solve it. When things go wrong between people, each individual owns a piece of the mess. But this is not how each of us experiences our contribution. As the saying goes, "Success has many parents, but failure is an orphan." I think the problem is totally your fault, and you think it's totally my fault. The truth is that both of us contributed to the situation. We are both response-able to find a way to make things right. Although you can take full ownership of the problem regardless of my attitude, it will be much easier to address the situation if I acknowledge my contribution as well. Besides taking the lead on recognizing your part, you can invite me to accept my contribution. If I am open, you can point out the facts of the matter, highlighting that I also did or didn't do things that contributed to the problem.

Understanding her contribution, the player can find power even in situations where she carries no blame. Let's take the case of a New Orleans resident who lost her home in the flood caused by Hurricane Katrina in 2005. Obviously, she didn't bring this disaster on herself. But taking the stance of the player, she could recognize that she is accountable for choices that contributed to the situation: for example, the choice to live in New Orleans or the choice to not buy flood insurance. There's nothing "wrong" with those choices, yet they were parts of a process that ended in a loss. This not only helps her get over her natural feeling of resignation and resentment in the face of such a loss, it also helps her plan future actions that can correct the situation and minimize the chances of its recurrence.

To claim that those affected by a problem contributed to it is not politically correct. It sounds insensitive, like "blaming the victim." One more time, contribution is *not* blaming the victim. Those who blame the victim claim that "you create your reality." "If you are suffering," they reason, "you must have brought it on yourself. If something bad happened to you, you deserved or wanted to be victimized." That is absurd. Nobody "creates" his reality alone. At the same time, nobody can relinquish responsibility for "co-creating" his circumstances. You contributed to bring about your present, and you can contribute to bring about your future.

FROM VICTIM TO PLAYER

When you take the stance of the player, you give up the hope for anything to be different than what it is. You take reality as the challenge that allows you to show who you really are and what you stand for. Whether you are talking to yourself or to others, an essential step of shifting from victim to player is to change your language from third to first person, from outside causality toward personal accountability. The language of the player includes words like "I" and addresses specific actions that you could have taken—and that you can currently take. Examples of player statements are, "I didn't back up the file," "I missed my deadline," "I lost track of time and stayed at the meeting too long," "I could not find a way to reach our profit targets without the layoffs," "I could not establish rapport with the client," or "I couldn't convince senior management to support the project."

Even when unexpected things happen, you can use the language of the player. Instead of focusing on the event, you can acknowledge that you did not anticipate the possibility. You can say, for example, "I did not anticipate that there could be a traffic jam," "I did not foresee that the weather could turn nasty," "I didn't think that our suppliers could fail to deliver on time," or "I underestimated the risk of the project."

The specific words are not crucial but the frame of mind is. Consider how the difference in the following expressions reflects a change in underlying attitude:

"It's hopeless."   "I haven't found a solution yet."
"Someone should take the first step."   "I could take the first step."
"It can't be done."   "I choose not to do it."
"You make me angry."   "When you speak that way, I feel angry."
"I have to leave."   "I want to leave."
"I don't have time (or money)."   "I prefer to focus on other priorities."

The first sentence of every pair states, "It's not up to me"; the second claims, "I am making a choice." The best way to understand this shift in attitude is through an exercise.

Recall a painful situation: an ineffective meeting, a harsh conversation, a business failure, or a personal breakdown. The best scenario is one where you believe you were treated unfairly, where you saw yourself at the mercy of other people or events that were beyond your control. Based on this situation, answer the following questions from a victim's perspective. (To accomplish the goals of the exercise you must adopt the victim's role. Make an effort to feel completely "innocent" and "wronged" by others.)

In my seminars I do this exercise in small groups. While one group member complains, I encourage the others to "help" him by sympathizing with expressions such as "I can't believe they did that to you," "That is so unfair," "They can't treat you like that," "They are so mean," "You deserve better than this." The goal is to provide what seems like "moral support" to the victim. However, this "help" is obviously unhelpful; it encourages a sense of impotence, blame, and self-righteous indignation. These comments are a life jacket made of lead that sinks the person deeper and deeper into his victim story.

Pity is an empty form of support. Nurturing the victim's feeling of helplessness, resignation, and moral outrage is a cheap way to be friendly. Just as you can buy a child's affection by giving her all the chocolate she wants or an alcoholic's affection by buying him another drink, you can buy a victim's affection by telling him he has been unfairly wronged. Chocolate, alcohol, and self-soothing explanations may bring easy pleasure, but they are ultimately destructive. Remember, your drug dealer is not your friend. Neither is your victim-support buddy. A truly caring friend offers you long-term wellness rather than immediate gratification. He blends a compassionate acknowledgment of your pain with a fierce challenge to your self-disempowering beliefs.

The questions to elicit the story of the **victim** are:

What happened to you?
Who wronged you?

What was wrong (or unfair) about what he did to you?

Why do you think he did this to you?

What should he have done instead?

What should he do now to repair the damage?

How should he be punished?

Once you have answered all of these questions, you can go on to the second round of questions. Answer them from the player's perspective. It is vital that you *refer to the same event*. The facts remain the same; what changes is your story about the situation. The purpose is to see how the player's point of view illuminates opportunities for action and learning that were hidden from you before. The story of the player is not "more true" than the one of the victim, but it is preferable because it allows you to see yourself as a contributor, capable of having influenced what happened, and capable of influencing what will happen.

The questions to elicit the story of the **player** are:

What challenge did you face?

How did you contribute (by acting or not acting) to create this situation?

How did you respond to the challenge?

Can you think of a more effective course of action you could have taken?

Could you have made some reasonable preparations to reduce the risk or
the impact of the situation?

Can you do something now to minimize or repair the damage?

What can you learn from this experience?

These questions are as useful in personal as they are in professional situations. The same way a manager can help his employees let go of a victim story, a mother can help her son. The same way a colleague can help another claim her power, a spouse can help her partner stop feeling sorry for himself and take control of a situation. The important thing to remember is that when you issue a loving challenge, love—in the form of empathy and compassion for the other's pain—comes first, and challenge—in the form of poignant inquiry to invite the other to own his power and accountability—comes second. I will explain how to lovingly receive another person's pain in chapter 5, "Authentic Communication."

A CULTURE OF RESPONSIBILITY

When I present the victim-player material to my clients, they commit to becoming players, but they raise a revealing objection. "I can change my attitude, but that won't really change things, because I'm surrounded by a bunch of victims." Furthermore, they argue that their organizations reward those who claim innocence and punish those who take responsibility. These explanations may be accurate, but they are typical victim hedges. I understand that other people can be stuck in victimhood, or that organizational systems and cultures can discourage responsibility, but waiting for other people or systems to change is a weak strategy. You can act like a player *in the face* of others choosing to act like victims, and *in the face* of a system that rewards innocence and punishes responsibility. Ultimately, you don't take the player role because it is convenient or because others will appreciate you; you take it because it is the way you choose to live.

Nevertheless, cultural challenges are significant. Recall the fundamental equation of the player: If the challenge is greater than your ability to respond, you fail; if your response-ability is greater than the challenge, you succeed. It is obviously harder to be a player in a culture that fosters victimhood. Victimhood, with its feelings of disempowerment, resignation, and resentment, is a virus that can infect every member of a group. It can acculturate or expel all "deviant" players through punishment or other forms of social sanction. There are few things that can kill a group faster than a culture of victimhood. Many executives who commit to playerhood during my workshops develop enough antibodies to remain players in spite of the system. Others succumb to cultural pressures and fall back on victimhood. Still others stay the course individually, but abandon their organizations. (When they leave as players, they do it with no blame or guilt; it is just their choice to pursue their happiness in a different environment.) Some commit to yet a fourth option: taking responsibility for changing the culture. These are the "conscious leaders."

A conscious leader goes beyond being an example of playerhood. He commits to "lowering the bar" so that others have a smaller challenge to become players. He also commits to "raising the bar" so that others find it impossibly challenging to stay in the organization as victims. In his personal interactions, the conscious leader helps others to find their own power, freedom, and responsibility. In his role as cultural architect, the conscious leader (with his conscious leadership team) gives a clear message that, "The way we do things here is the way of the player." This is a message he communicates consistently through his behavior; symbolic acts such as hiring, promoting, demoting, and firing; and implementation of formal systems such as budgeting, strategic planning, reward and recognition, etc. Consciousness of man's inherent freedom, responsibility, and power is the most important quality of a business leader; not just for the well-being of the organization's members, but for the success of the company itself.

Leadership behaviors are one of the most critical influences on an organizational culture. What matters is not what the leaders say but what they do; their actions rather than their words. If leaders display the self-righteous indignation of the victim, they encourage their followers to do the same. The political discourse of victimhood is appealing, and in the short run can produce great euphoria and a sense of community—just like a drug. The easiest way to bring a group together is to find a common enemy and blame it for the group's misery. In the long run, however, that strategy destroys the group's spirit. Only when leaders are conscious of the long-term consequences of victimhood are they willing to forgo its immediate but transient benefits. Instead of focusing the group's grief and anger on a scapegoat, the conscious leader helps the group redirect that energy toward pursuing its goals with integrity.

Unfortunately, this is not the case in most organizations—or societies. In many companies, for example, operations executives blame their sales colleagues for ruining their schedules. Sales executives blame their operations colleagues for upsetting their customers. Line executives blame staff functions for miring them in a bureaucratic maze. Staff executives blame line functions for breaking established processes and destroying organizational efficiencies. Everybody blames his manager for lack of leadership if he is hands-off or micromanagement if he gets involved. And the managers blame their subordinates for worrying only about their little fiefdoms and not following their guidance for the good of the whole.

There will always be friction in organizational life. Friction can grind the organization down or produce extraordinary energy. If executives do not operate with an overarching common vision and purpose, they will see themselves as victims. They will feel alienated from their peers and abused by decisions that constrain their individual performance. They will then retrench into turf-protecting behaviors and deal with the rest of the organization antagonistically. This behavior will communicate very clearly to everybody else that "the way to get ahead in this organization" is to adopt the stance of the victim and blame others for one's difficulties.

Thus the most important function of the leader is to encourage everyone to see him- or herself as a member of the larger system, pursuing a common vision, holding common values, and cooperating with each other in an environment of mutual support and respect. Only a conscious leader can evoke the spirit of unconditional responsibility in each of her followers and in her organization as a whole.

AL, THE PLAYER

Remember the late-arriving account executive from the beginning of this chapter? What would have happened if Al had behaved as a player rather than as a victim? Most likely, the exchange would have been quite a bit different:

John (grimacing): "You're late, Al. Again."
Al: "I'm sorry, I overstayed at the previous meeting. The CEO of the customer organization was late and everything got delayed. I felt in a bind, since my presentation was the reason for the meeting and it was a

meeting for which people had traveled long distances. If I had left at the original time, they couldn't have continued without me."

John: "It's not the meeting, Al, it's the delivery. We are still waiting for your shipment, the one that was supposed to arrive last week! Our plant is starved for parts—your parts."

Al: "I understand we have two problems: a small one, my being late to this meeting, and a much more serious one, the delay of your order. I feel fully accountable for both and would like to apologize and address them in order. Can we do that?"

John: "Whatever … "

Al: "Okay, let's start with the meeting. I'm sorry about the delay. As I said, I was nervous and didn't know quite what to do. I could have left, but that didn't feel appropriate to me. At the same time, I was troubled about staying because I knew you'd be waiting for me. If you had been one of the people in the previous meeting, what would you have liked me to do?"

John: "Stay, of course."

Al: "Even if you were late and I had another appointment?"

John: "Even if I was late and you had another appointment. But what's your point? I wasn't at that meeting; I was waiting for you here. Don't give me excuses."

Al: "You are totally right, and the last thing I want to do is to find an excuse. You were not at that meeting. But the same situation could happen with you tomorrow. So I'm asking you for a principle that I could apply to different situations regardless of the people involved. I either leave on time, come hell or high water, or I consider extending my stay when circumstances seem to call for it."

John: "Hmmm, I see your point. But it still bothers me that you left me hanging."

Al: "It bothers me too. Is there something I could have done to make the situation less bothersome?"

John: "You could have called and checked with me to see if we could delay the meeting. If I said 'yes,' then there would be no problem. If I said 'no,' at least we could have talked about our options and made a decision together."

Al: "You are absolutely right. I could have called; I should have called. In the heat of the moment, I didn't think about it. I apologize and promise that it will not happen again. Can you accept my apology?"

John: "Are you promising you'll never be late again?"

Al: "No, let me clarify, I'm promising that I will not leave you hanging without a phone call to check with you first. I hope that even that won't be necessary, but there are circumstances in which I may want to ask you for some flexibility, just like I'd ask another customer for flexibility if you needed me."

John: "All right, I accept your apology. But that doesn't address the big problem. I'm under the gun with the plant manager who's blaming me for your screwup. They can't run without those parts."

Al: "Absolutely, so let's move on to that issue. I see the great stress that we've produced. I was flabbergasted when I learned that the parts had not arrived. In fact, we shipped them more than two weeks ago. I checked into that and learned that the shipping company screwed up the paperwork and they sent the parts to another company. It will take them at least another three days to retrieve the parts and bring them over to you—"

John: "Are you saying it's not your fault?"

Al: "Not at all, I'm taking full responsibility for the delay, and explaining to you what happened. My primary concern, right now, is to see if there's anything we can do to make this mess less taxing for you."

John: "I need those parts."

Al: "I understand, and I can't deliver them to you before next Monday. But let me ask you something. Do you need the whole shipment right now?"

John: "Of course not, that's our monthly purchase. One tenth of it would get us out of this pickle if the rest of it arrives in three days."

Al: "Let me propose a deal to you. I can have a tenth of your order shipped by air this afternoon. It should be here tomorrow first thing in the morning."

John: "That could work, but how much will it cost?"

Al: "Whatever it costs, we'll pay for it. Not only that, I would not even charge you for the parts themselves. The least we can do is to give you a ten percent discount on the parts that are late. Let's just say that these new parts are that discount."

John: "Okay, so what's my end of the deal then?"

Al: "You accept my apologies and consider our relationship undamaged by this unfortunate event."

John: "Deal!"

What about John?

If Al behaves like a player, the situation improves for everybody. John gets the parts, Al keeps a customer, John's plant can operate, and Al's company recovers the good will of its biggest client. John and Al build a stronger relationship and they both feel better about themselves.

Adopting such a player's stance, however, is up to Al. What if he chose to hold on to his victim role? Is there anything John can do?

In the initial dialogue John is as stuck in the victim role as Al. This is when the notion of 200 percent responsibility can come in handy. Each participant can take full ownership and accountability for the process and the outcome of the conversation. How might things be different if Al had started in the same vein as in the beginning dialogue, but John chose to be a player, and encouraged Al to take responsibility to find a joint solution?

John: "You're late, Al. What happened?"

Al: "I'm sorry John, my previous meeting ran over. The client was late and everything got delayed."

John: "So you felt like you had to stay … "

Al: "I didn't have a choice, really. My presentation was the reason for the meeting. People had traveled long distances to attend. If I had left, they couldn't have continued without me. It would have been a big mess!"

John: "I understand. It sounds like staying was a reasonable choice, but you left me hanging, waiting for you, clueless about what was going on or even if you'd show up at all."

Al: "That was not my intention."

John: "I know. But that's what happened regardless of your intention."

Al: "Are you saying it is my fault? The CEO was late and … "

John: "No, Al, I'm not saying it is your fault. What I am saying is that you could have called me to let me know what was happening and discuss what we could do about it."

Al: "Oh, you're right. I guess I could have called. I'm sorry I didn't."

John: "I'm sorry too, but more importantly, I want to ensure that this doesn't happen again. Can we make an agreement that if either of us will be late to a meeting we'll call the other to let him know with as much advance notice as possible?"

Al: "Absolutely, you've got my commitment."

John: "Okay. I commit too. Let's consider this matter closed, then, and move to the next really big issue. Where are those parts that were supposed to arrive last week? Our plant can't run without them."

Al: "The freight company dropped the ball. They screwed up the paperwork and sent the parts to the wrong customer."

John: "So what's the deal, when can we get the parts?"

Al: "Not before next week. It will take them several days to retrieve the shipment and bring it over to your plant."

John: "Damn! We can't afford to wait that long. We need those parts now."

Al: "Sorry, but it's out of my hands. It's all up to the freight company at this point."

John: "Wait a minute, Al. Do you have any more of those parts in inventory?"

Al: "Sure. We've got plenty."

John: "Could we get enough of them to let us run the plant till next week?"

Al: "I guess so. But it would take five days to ship them over."

John: "Not by air."

Al: "Hmmm. That's an idea. It would be expensive, but I guess a lot less expensive than shutting down the plant."

John: "Al. This is a big deal for us. If you want to keep us as your client, you'll have to fly those parts to us this afternoon — on your dime. I need them here tomorrow morning."

Al: "We absolutely want you as a client. But I can't approve the extra cost without checking with my boss."

John: "No problem, there's a private phone in the next room. Come on back after you discuss it with him."

A few minutes later, Al walks into John's office with a smile.

Al: "I've called the warehouse and they are shipping those parts to you right away. Not only that, but I explained my situation to my boss and he agreed that not only should we pay for the airfreight, but we should also pay for the parts. Consider them our gesture of apology for the screwup."

John: "Thanks Al, I appreciate your company's willingness to take care of the situation."

John is entitled to anger and blame. It would be fair for him to feel wronged by Al, the shipping company, and many other things. But the life of the player is not about fairness or blame; it is about unconditional responsibility. Al is John's challenge, and as don Juan said in the epigraph, for the warrior, challenges cannot possibly be good or bad. They are just challenges.

◆

Awareness of choice is essential to personal power, responsibility, dignity, freedom, and humanity. Regardless of the situation, you can respond to your circumstances in alignment with your values. True success is not accomplishing your goals, but feeling happy and at peace. Beyond success lies the serene joy of integrity. That is why essential integrity is the heart of success beyond success.

Lamb or Lion?

In *The Way of Passion: A Celebration of Rumi,* Andrew Harvey tells a Sufi story that illustrates the difference between freedom and bondage, between submission and response-ability, between a victim and a player. A sheep and a lion represent these polarities.

Once upon a time, a pregnant lioness was looking for food. She saw a herd of sheep and attacked them. She managed to catch and eat one, but because she made a big effort when she was almost due, she died while giving birth. The lion was born an orphan, surrounded by the herd of sheep. Without knowing its identity, the young lion joined the herd and started to walk, eat, and bleat like the sheep. (He also learned to feel like a victim, to moan and to blame others for his misfortunes, as sheep do.)

One day, an adult lion came across this ridiculous scene: one of his own kind walking, eating, and bleating like a sheep. With a loud roar, the lion ran toward the sheep, dispersing them. The adult lion grabbed the young one and dragged him to a pond where he forced him to look at his reflection in the water, and said, "Look! You are not a sheep; you are like me, a lion. You are a lion, and you have a lion's strength, courage, freedom, and majesty. You are responsible for your destiny; you are the predator, not the prey." The adult lion then roared, loudly and gloriously. This made the young lion feel scared and excited. The adult lion then said, "Now it is your turn!" The young lion's first attempts were pathetic, and resembled both a bleat and a squeak. Soon, however, under the adult lion's supervision, the young lion discovered his true nature and learned to roar.

This is the roar of the player. It is the shout of recognition that arises when a human being owns his response-ability, his integrity, his freedom, and his power.

CHAPTER 3

Essential Integrity

◆

*Think only on those things that are in line with your principles and can bear
the light of day. The content of your character is your choice. Day by day,
what you choose, what you think, and what you do is who you become.
Your integrity is your destiny. It is the light that guides your way.*

HERACLEITUS

*The awakened sages call a person wise when all his undertakings are
free from anxiety about results; all his selfish desires have been consumed
in the fire of knowledge ... remember me [the Essential Truth] at all times
and fight on ... Whatever you do, make it an offering to me.*

THE BHAGAVAD GITA[1]

◆

William did everything he could to avoid meeting with his boss,
Zack. But the latest sales report dashed his hopes of keeping
the bad news contained. The revenue shortfall would impact
the bottom line of the whole U.S. operation. William needed to tell Zack
the bad news even though Zack had made it very clear that he didn't like
bad news at all.

"We will not meet the sales quota."

"Great!" Zack grunted. "What happened?"

"My team and I have been busting our asses to make the numbers, but we can't win this one. Several customers canceled their orders. With the recession, many companies have imposed buying freezes. We've tried our best to make our quota, but things are not working out."

"Oh come on, don't give me that crap. This is exactly what we talked about in that Kofman seminar, all that stuff about taking charge and not being a victim. You can't avoid responsibility! Don't blame the recession. It's you who's screwing up, and if you want to be a player, you've got to fix it!"

I had been working with Zack and his team for almost a month. Zack wanted to improve his leadership skills. After getting bad news from William, Zack thanked me in his next coaching session. He told me how helpful he found the victim-player distinction. I was pleased until I heard William's side in his coaching session. William could not hide his disappointment. "I am not a victim!" he said bitterly. "My team and I are working as hard as we can, and we are still failing. Besides allowing Zack to blame us for the recession, what good is your notion of unconditional responsibility?"

After reading the last chapter, you might have inferred that if you become a player, everything will work out just as you want it to. Once you develop response-ability, you should win contracts, get promotions, find open lanes during rush hour, and even grow younger! Life, however, doesn't work that way. There are always factors beyond your control. There are always failures. You may lower prices, offer incentives, or implement other marketing strategies. None of those actions, however, can guarantee that you will get what you want. You cannot choose to have the customers buy from you. Just as you can choose your response to the situation, so can they. They will buy or not as they choose.

"You are responsible for your life" can be a baited hook. It is true enough to sound appealing, and untrue enough to cause great confusion. As we saw in the last chapter, it is empowering to see yourself as a contributor to the problem—and thus, as a contributor to the solution. Yet it is dangerous to see yourself as sole creator of results that also depend on external circumstances. Paradoxically, assuming responsibility for results can create as much pain as avoiding responsibility for your behavior. When you choose to step up to the plate, you naturally feel that things should work out. However, even the best hitters strike out most of the time.

Zack responded to disappointing news by blaming William. How effective was his response? After their conversation, William and Zack were no closer to reaching their sales targets. They never discussed the problem and possible courses of action. Zack's "guidance" boiled down to a demand to "fix it." If William knew how to fix the problem, he would have done so already! As for their relationship, Zack and William grew more distant than ever. Trust, mutual respect, and cooperation decreased. William felt alienated and discouraged. I was not surprised to hear him say half-jokingly that he would start brushing up his résumé. Zack may have felt proud of his toughness, but it came at a high price. No leader succeeds without the commitment of his followers. At best, Zack's behavior produces grudging compliance.

To face life's challenges responsibly, you must navigate between two hazards. At one extreme lies the self-soothing explanation of the victim—"I have nothing to do with my situation." At the other lies the unrealistic omnipotence of the superhero—"I am the sole creator of my reality."

What allows you to navigate these hazards? You are most effective when you act out of essential human values. When you behave with integrity, you use the challenges in your life to express your higher self. You might not always achieve success, but you can always behave honorably. You can act in alignment with essential values, attaining the peace of mind I call "success beyond success." Essential integrity allows you to develop strength, inner peace, and self-confidence. It acts as a climbing harness, catching you when the challenges of the world prove too arduous. When you trust this harness, you feel more enthusiasm and less fear during the climb. You can take any challenge as an opportunity to grow. Essential integrity provides the secret to achieving happiness in a world where you will inevitably end up losing all your possessions—even your life and the lives of those you love.

Around 550 B.C., an oracle prophesied that the newborn son of an Indian local ruler would either be a great military leader or a great religious one. The father wanted his son to inherit his throne, so he groomed him with a life of pleasure and indulgence. Pain and suffering were banished from his sight. The child grew up in a walled palace, populated only by the sons and daughters of other noble families. The king prohibited his son from receiving any form of spiritual teaching.

One day the prince left the palace grounds. On his excursion to the outside world, he encountered sights he'd never seen before: an old man, a diseased man, and a corpse. The prince was shocked and asked his attendant to explain. "Shame on birth," replied his servant, "since to every one that is born, old age, sickness, and death must come."

The prince returned to the palace, but now his pleasure-oriented life seemed hollow. He fell into a deep depression. Neither his palace friends nor his immediate family could provide any solace; even his royal patrimony seemed meaningless.

On his second excursion, the prince saw something even more shocking: a man smiling. He wondered: How could this man smile in the face of sickness, old age, and death? This man turned out to be a spiritual practitioner. He had discovered a source of happiness beyond worldly pleasures. Soon after, the prince escaped from the palace and disappeared into the forest. He cut off his hair and exchanged his rich garments for a tattered robe. He set out to find an answer. How could a man smile in the face of sickness, old age, and death?

He practiced with various teachers, but concluded that none of them had found the answer. He decided to meditate on his own. He sat for a long time under a tree. Then, on the first full-moon day of May, he stood up and smiled. People then asked him, "Are you a god?" "No," he replied. "Are you a man?" "No," he replied. "Are you a saint?" "No, he replied." "Then what are you?" "I am awake." And so he came to be known as "the awakened one" which in Sanskrit is "The Buddha."

Prince Siddhartha's realization cannot be put in words. In fact, he told his followers that he had attained "no-thing" under the tree. But the story suggests a truth echoed in many wisdom traditions. Actualization comes only through detachment from petty desires, and through action that goes beyond immediate gratification. After all, the final outcome of your life is already determined: death. You must discover happiness in the process of living, as opposed to hoping for a different end.

Only the ethical dedication to a transcendent purpose can overcome the impermanence of existence. As George Bernard Shaw put it in *Man and Superman,* "This is the true joy in life, the being used for a purpose recognized by yourself as a mighty one ... the being a force of Nature instead of a feverish selfish little clod of ailments and grievances complaining that the world will not devote itself to making you happy."

OUTCOME VERSUS PROCESS

Think of three characters you admire. They can be real people, such as your aunt or George Washington, or mythical characters like Santa Claus or Hercules. For the purpose of our discussion, I'll work with three of my own: William Wallace (Mel Gibson's character in *Braveheart),* Viktor Frankl, and Mother Teresa of Calcutta.

Think now of the key personality traits that make each of your chosen characters admirable to you. I admire Wallace's courage and love of freedom, Frankl's resilience and dignity, and Mother Teresa's kindness and compassion.

Compare these admirable traits with the typical success markers of our culture, the kind of traits featured in *People* magazine. After doing this exercise with thousands of people, I have yet to find anyone who selected characters whose qualities were power, wealth, youth, beauty, pleasure, or fame. It is fascinating how we gravitate unconsciously and instinctively to things that ultimately mean very little to us, and how we sacrifice unconsciously the very values that ultimately motivate our behavior. We rightfully scorn executives who defraud investors, yet in our own lives we often assume that success is the road to happiness—even when success requires us to compromise our highest values. I have seen many managers indulge in political games they despised because they thought that it was necessary in order to achieve some result they desired. Perhaps they were right, and success called for a relaxation of their ethical standards. My point is that happiness requires the opposite. We cannot be happy when we betray what we value most.

Outcome attributes depend on the result of a given situation. For example, an Olympic gold medalist is a winner. Everybody loves a winner, but this exercise suggests that you would be better off focusing on *process attributes*, qualities that you reveal through your behavior. Even if an athlete does not win, we can celebrate his effort and commitment. This is not to say that winning is not important, but that winning is not the only thing that matters. I admire Wallace's courageous leadership even though he was tortured to death. We rightly celebrate firefighters and policemen who risk their lives in public service. We don't discriminate between those who survive and those who do not. All of them demonstrate a willingness to sacrifice for the safety of the community.

ESSENTIAL INTEGRITY

This distinction between *outcome* and *process* allows you to look at your actions in a different way. You can see that every action has two purposes. First, you act in order to move toward a desired result. Second, you act in order to express your values.

In the previous chapter, I said that action is your response to an external challenge; you employ your skills and resources to create a desirable future. You can evaluate your progress by examining the alignment of the intended and real outcomes; this is the measure of your *success*. In this chapter, I suggest that there is an additional standard by which to evaluate your actions. You can also look at the alignment between your behavior and your values; this is the measure of *integrity*, or success beyond success. Most people consider integrity as a particular value, akin to honesty, but here I define it as the adherence to a code of values.

Your behavior always expresses your values-in-action. Your integrity hinges on whether your values-in-action agree with your essential values. When they do, you feel pride. When they do not, you feel guilt. You can espouse lofty morals, but they are meaningless if they don't guide your behavior. Enron had an impressive code of ethics, as did Tyco, WorldCom, and many other companies involved in corporate scandals. Those codes of ethics didn't prevent executives at those companies from acting unethically. The corporations' ethical codes espoused the highest moral principles. Yet executives' behavior belied those principles. As the saying goes, "What you do speaks so loudly that I cannot hear what you say."

Are you willing to win at any cost? Before you say "yes," consider another question. What if winning requires unethical behavior? That may cause you to hesitate. Most of us recognize a dividing line between right and wrong that ought not to be crossed. However, the line is often forgotten in the midst of action. We often betray ourselves in moments of unconscious impulsiveness. In such moments, the concern for success becomes paramount, obscuring any qualms about integrity. In those moments you starkly face a question of priorities: you put integrity first and subordinate success, or you put integrity second and uphold success at all costs.

When you act with integrity you attain success beyond success. The good news is that you can guarantee success beyond success, even in a world where success is beyond your control. You can always choose to act with integrity, because you control your own behavior. No matter what others do, as Gandhi exhorted, you can "become the change [you] want to see in the world." Integrity gives you the unconditional power to express your most admired qualities and be proud of yourself. It also gives you a safety net of peace and dignity when things don't work out.

Consider this story about Barry, a plant manager in the auto industry. Barry and his team wanted to improve the quality of a truck assembly line. After analyzing the production process, they identified a problem: Some machines were not performing within specifications. The team adjusted the machines. Did this yield higher quality? Unfortunately, it did not. The improved process revealed that the defects originated in another plant. Barry approached the other plant manager with the data, but his colleague rebuffed him. Barry had no authority to impose his will on his colleague. Despite his team's effort, Barry's trucks' quality remained substandard.

On the outcome level, Barry and his team failed. They did not attain the quality improvement they wanted. On the process level, the story is different. They experienced disappointment, but they also experienced pride. Team members worked hard to address the problem and acted in line with their values. They did their best. This satisfaction enabled them to accept the (momentary) failure without becoming dejected. Soon, they began looking into alternative means to address the quality problem. Barry and his team continued pursuing success beyond success.

When I tell this story in my seminars, people always ask if Barry and his team found a solution. The more important question is whether acting with essential integrity in pursuit of success beyond success increases your ability to achieve ordinary success. The answer depends on the time span: in the short term, not necessarily; in the long term, absolutely. Respecting essential values imposes constraints on your behavior, constraints that do not affect those who disregard those values. Thus, the person without scruples appears to have more degrees of freedom than the person with scruples. If the former can "win" by breaking rules that the latter feels bound to respect, it is more likely that he will carry the day.

During a soccer match between Argentina and England, the famous Diego Maradona illicitly scored a goal by pushing the ball with his hand. The referee thought he'd used his head so he counted the goal as legitimate. The English were enraged; the Argentineans were doubly elated. Getting away with the violation made the goal extra cool. At the end of the match, Maradona boasted that it was not his hand but "the hand of God" that pushed the ball. I felt embarrassed. The next day I shared my disappointment with an Argentinean friend of mine. "What do you think Maradona should have done?" he challenged. "Tell the referee that the goal was invalid," I answered. "But that would have hurt Argentina!" (I assume he meant the team, not the country, but fans often confuse these things.) "Yes, it would have hurt the team's chance of winning the match.

But Argentina was much more hurt by the team's lack of integrity—and the fans' celebration of it."

According to logic, you cannot do better by having fewer choices. However, human beings are not computers, and sometimes more choice means worse outcomes. If you are a smoker trying to quit, for example, you would be better off not having cigarettes available. If you are navigating close to enchanting sirens, you'd be better off tied to a mast. Similarly, if you want sustainable success, you'd be better off abstaining from unethical strategies. In the long term, the virtuous pursuit of excellence achieves more real success than the unbridled pursuit of success.

Imagine that Maradona was a CEO who used accounting gimmicks to boost reported profits. Imagine further that he got away with it and increased the market value of his company. Suppose that he never got caught and bragged about it to his management team. What message do you think his team would get? "Honesty is for suckers. To get ahead in this organization you've got to do whatever it takes. You may lie, cheat, and steal as long as you don't get caught." What are the odds that this company will succeed in the long term with such a corrupt culture?

Moreover, the ultimate success is what wise men have called a "good life." Such a life has always been associated with spiritual integrity, not with material success. One of Socrates' main teachings, for example, is that to a man who preserves his integrity, no real long-term harm can ever come. The uncertainties of this world are such that anybody can be stripped of his possessions and thrown into prison unjustly, or crippled by accident or disease; but these are chance happenings in a fleeting existence that will soon end. Provided your soul remains untouched, Socrates claimed, your misfortunes will feel relatively trivial. Real personal catastrophe consists in the corruption of the soul. That is why he argued that it does a person far less harm to suffer injustice than to commit it.

[Socrates] was the first [philosopher] to teach the priority of personal integrity in terms of a person's duty to himself, and not to the gods, or the law, or any other authorities … It is a priority that has been reasserted by some of the greatest minds since … Jesus said: "What will a man gain by winning the whole world, at the cost of his true self?" And Shakespeare said: "This above all: to thine own self be true."[2]

There are some important differences between success and integrity. Success is in the future. It is the outcome of a process that takes time and depends on factors beyond our control. Integrity is immediate and unconditional. Every time we act, we are either in alignment with our values or we are not. We choose whether or not we are aligned. When it comes to integrity, we can always be players. No one can take that away from us.

THE MARSHMALLOW EXPERIMENT

It is one thing to say that we can choose to act with integrity; it's another thing to do it. The difference between saying it and doing it boils down to a single word: discipline. Discipline allows you to regulate and direct your energy toward your goals in alignment with your values. Discipline is the capacity to maintain awareness and choose consciously in the face of instinctual pressures. The self-control to subordinate immediate gratification to long-term objectives is essential for success beyond success. An experiment conducted with a group of four-year-olds at Stanford University highlights the importance of discipline.[3] The researchers put each child in a room, seated at a table with a marshmallow on it, and made the following offer: "You can either have one marshmallow now or two marshmallows in five minutes."

Fourteen years later, after the children had graduated from high school, the researchers compared those who had immediately eaten one marshmallow to those who had waited. The children who had eaten quickly appeared to be far more attached to immediate success. They frequently lost control in stressful situations, grew irritated, and fought more often. They often succumbed to temptations that derailed them from their studies and other objectives. By contrast, the children who had waited for the second marshmallow averaged 210 points higher (out of a possible 1,600) on their SATs, the college entrance exam.[4]

When the children — now adults — joined the workforce, the differences grew even more pronounced. Those who had held out for two marshmallows proved more adept at developing intimate relationships, demonstrated more intellectual capacity, and showed greater self-control in frustrating situations. The children who ate a single marshmallow tended to be loners, less reliable, and incapable of postponing gratification. When confronted with stressful situations, they displayed little tolerance or self-control.

I am sure that all the children, patient and impatient alike, wanted to do well, to be successful and happy. But here's the paradox: What seems to make you feel good in the moment makes you feel terrible in the end. This "marshmallow logic" can be seen in alcoholism, credit card debt, gambling, and so many other dysfunctional behaviors of individuals and groups.

For thousands of years, human survival depended on fast reactions. Our ancestors, the humanoids who won the reproductive race, survived because of their ability to react quickly. They bypassed the slowest part of the nervous system, the conscious deliberative mind. In situations of emotional intensity, your thinking brain gets short-circuited and your instinctual brain takes over. It pushes you toward pleasure and away from pain. As an individual, you need discipline because you are genetically programmed to respond instinctually to immediate risks or opportunities in your environment.

Discipline is essential for organizations as well. In his study of companies that went from "good to great," Jim Collins found that the key common factor was the existence of disciplined people producing disciplined thoughts and taking disciplined actions. Disciplined companies responded to challenges effectively; they were able to maintain flexibility on a tactical level while remaining firmly anchored in their core mission and values. Both on a personal and an organizational level, discipline is a direct consequence of conscious choice and response-ability, the capacity to enact a course of action that is congruent with our purpose and ethics.

In the midst of a crisis or a phenomenal business opportunity, an organization without discipline operates unconsciously, guided by fear or greed. Often, what looks appealing can lure you down a deadly path. How can you remain open to new information (and the consequent temptations) without deviating from the virtuous path? Homer suggests an answer as he describes how Odysseus dealt with such "fatal attraction."

Odysseus was about to sail past the Sirens' island. The Sirens were famous for their irresistible songs, which attracted sailors toward deadly reefs, where they sank with their ships. To avoid disaster, Odysseus had all his shipmates plug their ears with wax, but because he wanted to hear the Sirens he kept his ears unplugged. He ordered his men to tie him to the mast and ignore any orders he gave, to avoid dragging them to perdition. This restriction allowed him to expose himself to temptation without losing himself in it.

Organizational seas are filled with sirens. Some of their songs say, "If you want to make this sale, don't tell the customer that you can't make the delivery date." "If you want to get the loan, don't tell the bank that you have an offshore subsidiary where you've parked your debt off the balance sheet." "If you want to raise the stock price, 'adjust' the books to capitalize expenses, turning them into assets." Other songs say, "If you want that promotion, don't help the other candidate—or even better, sabotage him." "If someone does not support your ideas, think of him as an enemy and get him out of your way by whatever means possible." "If you want to save face, never recognize your errors and blame others for them." The lamentable litany of fraud, lies, and ethical breaches we find in the news every day suggests that many managers cannot resist these sirens' songs.

Covering your ears with wax is not practical. You need all your senses to navigate the treacherous currents of change. To what mast can you tie yourself in order to stay on the straight and narrow when the sirens start to sing? The only lasting safety that I have found is a total commitment to essential values such as respect, honesty, freedom, and love. When you are fully conscious, you know that these values are the key to happiness and peace, to self-esteem and dignity. When the enchanting songs seduce you, you get lost. Without a fundamental commitment to essential values, a commitment that might seem irrational to your irrational mind in the moment of tempta-tion, you will sink without remedy—probably bringing your organization with you.

WHAT ABOUT SUCCESS?

When I present this material to business audiences, people object that suc-cess beyond success removes the motivation for success. I still remember an intense conversation I had some years ago with Hank, a hard-nosed execu-tive from the oil industry. "This is crazy!" he challenged me, almost jumping out of his seat. "You are telling us that it's okay to fail as long as we do it nicely. That is bullshit. It is not okay to fail. If you fail enough, you go out of business. In the real world you don't get 'marshmallow points' for trying your best. You've got to deliver. No excuses."

Like many business people, Hank thought that if you feel satisfied with your behavior, regardless of the outcome, you will stop striving. He worried that if people focused on success beyond success they would disregard suc-cess. Without the drive to succeed, he imagined that complacency would gain the best of him, his employees, and even his children and spouse. This may be why many managers do not acknowledge their employees—and why many parents do not praise their children. For those who fuel their engines on the fear of failure, the focus on integrity threatens to leave them "run-ning on empty." They doubt that anyone can function without the carrot of achievement and the stick of frustration.

Let me be clear. I am *not* advocating that success is unimportant, that failure is okay, or that we should feel good about missing our goals. In fact, one of my essential values is excellence: a commitment to use my resources fully, doing my best to accomplish the outcome I seek. I believe it's impos-sible to act with integrity without pursuing excellence. What I am asserting is that if you want to live a "good life" you must *subordinate* success to integrity, not vice versa.

Integrity is a better guiding principle than success on two counts. First, integrity implies excellence, so it encourages full dedication to the mission at hand: that is, to win. There is no loss of energy or loss of focus on the task. Second, integrity provides a wider interpretation than success. Whereas success tends to focus on the local subsystem and the short term, integrity focuses on the systemic long-term consequences. Myopic lust for winning the battle creates a strategic blindness that can lose the war.

Reality is complex and ever-changing. It is impossible to "manage" such a system through logical models. There are too many variables. You can use technical tools to get some intuition on the behavior of the system, but you can never comprehend the full implications of external events and your own behavior. That is why integrity, with its simple set of practical principles, is so valuable. Since the beginning of humankind, people have been struggling to find rules of behavior that foster higher and higher levels of success. Integrity represents a summary of human wisdom accumulated over thousands of years.

Some say that my teaching is nonsense.
Others call it lofty but impractical.
But to those who have looked inside themselves,
this nonsense makes perfect sense.
And to those who put into practice,
this loftiness has roots that go deep.

LAO TZU, *TAO TE CHING*

THINK BIG

A value-based approach counteracts the myopic tendencies of self-centered behavior. One of the most puzzling systemic paradoxes is that coherent and rational individual behavior often produces incoherent and irrational systemic behavior. Most people believe that when every element of a system performs at its local best, the system performs at its global best. Not so. Individual intelligence often leads to collective stupidity. If you optimize the sub-systems, you sub-optimize the system. Systems theory teaches that in order to optimize a system, you must sub-optimize its sub-systems.

Let us see how this works in a soccer game. The objective of each team is to win. Each does this by scoring more goals than the other. To accomplish this objective, a team organizes itself into two sub-teams, offense and defense. The sub-objective of the offense is to score goals; the sub-objective of the defense is to prevent the opponent from scoring. Let's say that the coach of the team is a business school graduate who learned about management by objectives and performance-based incentives. He defines a compensation system where the offense receives payment in direct proportion to the goals they score, and the defense in inverse proportion to the goals they allow.

If the incentive system works, the team will end up defeating itself. Think about it. The offense would rather lose a game 5 to 4 than win 1 to 0. The defense would rather lose 1 to 0 than win 5 to 4. Even if the team is losing, players on the defense would be reluctant to leave their positions to help the offense score; vice versa for the offense helping the defense if the team is winning. While each sub-team tries to optimize its sub-objective, it sub-optimizes the team's objective.

Substitute "operations" for "defense" and "sales" for "offense," "revenues" for "scoring" and "costs" for "preventing the other team from scoring," and you understand how conflicts arise within organizations. I worked with a chemical company mired in such a conflict. The R&D department had developed a special kind of lubricant. The engineering department wanted to take time to improve the production process. The sales department wanted to turn the product over to production immediately, so they could bring it to market at the earliest possible date. Both departments argued their case. "A quick launch will improve sales," said the one. "An efficient process will reduce production costs," replied the other. Both teams had lost sight of the larger question: What would be best for the company?

To address this question it is necessary to understand the system's goal. The company does not exist to optimize speed or efficiency. Nor does it exist to maximize revenue or to minimize costs. Let's say that the goal of an organization is to fulfill its mission, acting in alignment with ethical and legal standards. In the case of a for-profit company like my client, this means to make as much money as it can, within legal and ethical boundaries, in the present and in the future. Once everybody accepts this, people realize that their primary goal is *not* to succeed as sales people or production people, but to succeed as *company* people. That is, to win the game as a team. There is still an important discussion to have, but now it is not a conflict of *ends* between two sub-teams, each trying to optimize their sub-goal. Now it is a discussion of *means* in the context of a *cooperative* effort.

When the chemical company executives focused on the global objective, they began to work with, rather than against, each other. I facilitated a meeting where the two groups tried to reach a consensus on what to do. I will describe this process in detail in chapter 6, "Constructive Negotiation." As they explored the situation, they discovered a policy constraint that was the core of the conflict: The engineering department could only work on process improvements before the operations department began production. Once the refineries started to work, it was very difficult to modify the production process. This rule made sense for mass-marketed products, but it was not relevant at the early stages of this innovative product. The executive committee, made up of the heads of R&D, Engineering, Operations, and Sales, had established the rule and had the authority to change the rule. It was decided that Operations would start production with the current process in a small refinery, while Engineering worked on improving the process that would be implemented in the larger refinery six months into the future.

When people in an organization forget their common ground, business goes poorly. Information does not flow, decisions tend to protect sub-organizational concerns, and performance suffers. Systemic myopia does not just create problems at the task level. Interpersonal relationships become strained and conflicts crop up everywhere. Furthermore, individuals feel tremendous stress. Instead of trusting fellow employees, they grow wary of them. Who wants to have an enemy covering his back?

In order to improve global efficiency, people need to look beyond local efficiency. Individuals, teams, functions, geographies, and any other sub-organizations need to see themselves as members of a larger community.

This takes awareness, discipline, and integrity; it often requires eschewing local short-term success and committing to systemic long-term success. What is the relationship between this kind of success and success beyond success? To answer this question we need to delve deeper into what motivates us.

WHY DO YOU WANT WHAT YOU WANT?

Think of something you want: a new car, more free time, an office with natural light, a higher salary. Ask yourself the following question: "If I got that (new car, free time, office with natural light, salary increase), what would I get that is even more important to me than that (new car, free time, etc.) itself?" For example, I want to write this book. My question would then be, "If I write this book, what would I get that is even more important to me than writing the book?" One answer is, "I would help people be more effective and act with integrity in business."

Next, ask yourself the same question again using the answer to the previous question: "If I got to help people be more effective, what would I get that is even more important to me?" My second answer might be, "I would participate in the development of a more conscious society."

Take this answer and ask the same question again and again, until you cannot come up with any further underlying reason for wanting what you want. (In my case, a possible sequence may be, "to fulfill my mission in life," "to feel that my life is meaningful," "to realize true happiness.") After doing this exercise with hundreds of people, I have found that no matter how disparate the beginning, most inquiries converge on a practically universal set of values: truth, happiness, fullness, freedom, peace, and love.

You can verify the fundamental nature of these qualities by reversing the inquiry. Ask yourself, "If I lived truthfully, feeling happy, full, free, at peace, and in love, what would I get that is even more valuable for me than being true to myself, feeling happy, full, free, at peace, and full of love?" This is an awkward question. If you think about it, you'll find that nothing is more valuable than these things. Truth, happiness, fullness, freedom, peace, and love are not means to a further end; they are *the ultimate end.*

Success, defined as obtaining something we want, is notably absent from this list of values. Without denying its importance, success, like all external results, is an intermediate goal on the way to a superior objective, such as happiness. One question alone is sufficient to prove this: "What would I obtain through success that is even more important to me than success itself?"

Don't take my word for it. See what you come up with for yourself. I am not imposing my set of values on you, claiming that it comes from some external human or divine authority. I am inviting you to explore what is ultimately meaningful to you, and to act in a way that satisfies that ultimate concern moment by moment. Human beings have been investigating how to play the game of life for thousands of years. Everybody who has taken such an investigation to its conclusion has come up with a very similar ethical recommendation: "Do not focus on egocentric cravings, and express your highest virtue in every action." Coincidentally, this echoes the optimizing principle of systems thinking I presented above. It also parallels a dictum of game theory: "In order to win the game, you must be willing to not win the sub-games. If you try to win the sub-games, you will lose sight of the goal and probably lose the game."

Seek refuge in the attitude of detachment and you will amass the wealth of a spiritual awareness. Those who are motivated only by desire for the fruits of action are miserable, for they are constantly anxious about the results of what they do.

They who have renounced their selfish attachment to the fruits of their action live in wisdom. Neither agitated by grief nor hankering after pleasure, they live free from lust and fear and anger.)

Those who are deluded become attached to the fruits of their action. Performing all actions for my sake [the Essential Truth] and without expectations, act free from the fever of the ego.

THE BHAGAVAD GITA[5]

CONSCIOUS BUSINESS

WINNING THE REAL GAME

Consider chess. The goal of the game is to checkmate your opponent. In order to achieve this goal you follow different strategies. One is to take the pieces of your opponent and prevent her from taking yours. (This is a super-simplification, just to make a point.) Taking your opponent's pieces and protecting yours is a sub-goal, valuable only as a stepping stone toward the goal of checkmate. You need to stay conscious of this hierarchy of goals to play effectively. Your best strategy may be to sacrifice a piece; that is, to give it up for the sake of positional advantage. "Sacrifice" comes from the Latin *sacrificium*, which means "to make sacred." When you make a sacrifice, you relinquish a lower goal in order to pursue a higher one.

If you forget the hierarchy of goals you will make stupid mistakes. You may become so intent on taking your opponent's pieces that you end up committing "sacrileges": that is, giving away a positional advantage that is more valuable (to win the game) than the pieces you take. To play chess consciously you need to keep in mind the hierarchy of means and ends. You make sacrifices and avoid sacrileges.

What is the ultimate goal of human life? Happiness. Aristotle called happiness the "highest good" because it is the end of all means. You seek other basic goods such as money, fame, or power because you think they will make you happy, but you want happiness for its own sake. Everything you do—work, play, pray, study, marry, have children—is a search for happiness.

To live consciously you need to keep this hierarchy in mind. You make sacrifices and avoid sacrileges. You value money, fame, and power insofar as they are means toward happiness. You work, play, pray, study, or start a family in order to promote your happiness. You decide, for example, how much time and energy to devote to professional versus family life, assessing how your choices would affect your happiness. Rather than "balance" work and family, you would seek to "integrate" them as complementary aspects of a good life.

Beyond choosing what to do, the conscious pursuit of happiness entails choosing how to do what you do. You can spend time with your family, but the result of this choice will be very different if you connect with them lovingly than if you remain cold and distant. Spending time with your family will not make you happy; spending time loving your family will. The way you do any activity is more important for your happiness than the activity itself. Philosophers and sages of all traditions have devoted great efforts to study which behaviors lead to happiness; they call them "virtues." Psychologists have found six universal virtues, endorsed by almost all religious and philosophical traditions, to be at the core of a happy life: wisdom, courage, love, justice, temperance, and transcendence.[6]

If you engage in business consciously, you never forget that business success is not the goal. Business success is a means toward your happiness. You do business to live (happily), you don't live to do business. Most people don't link business with happiness; they think of business as a necessary evil. However, business is one of the most important strategies through which human beings pursue happiness. Customers buy something because they believe it will contribute to their happiness. Employees work because they receive material and psychological compensation that furthers their happiness. Shareholders invest because they expect a return that will make them happy. The value of a business, then, is measured by its ability to contribute to human happiness.

If business is to become a true means toward your happiness, you need to pay attention to the way you do business. Most people believe that happiness is an outcome, a result that accrues to the winner. This is just not true. Although the outcome is important, happiness depends more on the process. Happiness comes from integrity rather than success, from behavior in alignment with essential values rather than winning or losing. If you want to do business consciously, you need to enact the universal virtues of wisdom, courage, love, justice, temperance, and transcendence and seek success beyond success.

While people are built to work, most jobs are not built for people. What employers from the pharaohs to modern TQM managers have been primarily concerned about is not how to tailor a job so as to bring out the best in the workers but rather how to get the *most* out of them. So one of the intriguing paradoxes of the human condition is that while surveys indicate that about 80 percent of adults claim that they would continue to work even if they had so much money that they didn't have to worry about having more, the majority can hardly wait each day to leave their job and go home.

MIHALY CSIKSZENTMIHALYI[7]

OUTSIDE IN OR INSIDE OUT?

Imagine that you just received a hundred million dollars. Before you get too happy, you should know that research has found that many people who suddenly come into big money end up alienated from their families and their friends, very unhappy, and eventually go broke! In any case, you got your hundred million dollars. You took two years off, traveled the world, celebrated in style, and because of your prudent investments, you now have a hundred and twenty million dollars. What will you do with your life now? Take a moment, or an hour, to think about it. This exercise allows you to examine your true desires, free of financial fears.

Many people respond that they would change their activities very little or not at all (some of the hardest-working business leaders hold fortunes far exceeding a hundred million dollars). Other people imagine creating new organizations that could serve society. Out of the thousands of people whom I have asked this question, no one has ever answered, "Nothing." On the contrary, when people feel relieved of their financial constraints, even in their imaginations, they experience a rush of enthusiasm. Instead of feeling their fears assuaged, they now feel the freedom to do what they really love. Instead of seeing business as a vehicle to get the material wealth that they do not have, they see business as an opportunity to express the creative energy bursting out of them.

This is a radical shift in perspective. Let us call the first perspective, the one that starts with lack and scarcity, "living from the outside in," trying to fill a black hole of emptiness with stuff from the outside. Let us call the second perspective, the one that starts with fullness and abundance, "living from the inside out," manifesting in the world the infinite value that flows from within. Living from the inside out is an overflowing inner richness that wants to express itself by creating something that transcends the small self. Living from the outside in is a sense of emptiness, a feeling of lack that wants to soothe itself by filling itself with material, psychological, or even spiritual objects.

Any activity can be done inside out or outside in. It is possible, for example, to play tennis out of lack. In this case, the athlete would be trying to prove that he is "good" by winning. His focus is not to do his best to win, but to beat his opponent. He feels that winning shows that he is better: not just a better player, but also a better person altogether. A tennis player operating from lack, with no scruples and hell-bent on winning at any cost, might attempt to distract or hurt his opponent in order to get an advantage. (There is a famous case of a young French player whose father used to put sleeping pills into the water bottles of his son's opponents—until one of them fell asleep driving his car after the match and suffered a fatal accident.) This disgraceful behavior is an indictment of the player, not of the game. Tennis as an activity does not encourage these actions. Lack-based foul play is not due to tennis but to the confused mind of the outside-in player.

It is also possible to play tennis out of fullness. In this case, one would seek to express the skill, the emotional fiber, and the human possibility that one unconditionally *is*. A tennis player operating from fullness would not seek to prove his value—it would be so obvious to him that it would not require any external validation. He would not need to destroy his opponent to quiet his fears. Such a conscious player would still put his heart and soul into the game, playing to win. He would strive to win not because the result was that important, but because his very essence called him to give 150 percent of his energy to the task. That is the spirit of excellence.

It is also possible to play the game of business from the outside in or from the inside out. A lack-based competition is a game of scoundrels. In desperation, these people turn the natural hierarchy of means and ends upside down, sacrificing the higher (morality, consciousness) to the lower (satisfaction of biological impulses and primitive psychological urges). Their only goal, unrestricted by any ethical considerations, is to make money. This is the typical behavior of a criminal organization or Mafia. Fullness-based competition, on the other hand, is a game of ladies and gentlemen. Ladies and gentlemen keep their priorities straight, taking lower means, such as making money, as a path to higher ends, such as happiness, peace, and freedom.

A striking illustration appears in *The Bhagavad Gita*, one of the most sacred books of Hinduism. The *Gita* tells the story of Prince Arjuna, besieged by doubts as he faces members of his own family on a battlefield. Torn between the desire to do his duty (fight) and to not harm his relatives (leave), he turns to his charioteer, the divine teacher Krishna, for advice. In one of the most beautiful pieces of mystical poetry ever written, Krishna tells Arjuna to go to battle and fight with all his might, but he instructs him to make it an offering to the divine, not a satisfaction of his egoistic desires. In other words, Krishna commands Arjuna to focus on the process and release the outcome. In blazing words, Krishna suggests that virtuous behavior is more important than life and death itself. "He who is free from selfish attachments, who has mastered himself and his passions, attains the supreme perfection … Free from self-will, aggressiveness, arrogance, anger, and the lust to possess people or things, he is at peace with himself and others … All his acts are performed in my service … Make every act an offering to me [the Essence of Value]; regard me as your only duty."[8]

Krishna warns Arjuna that those who do not heed his call, those who remain selfishly attached to the outcome of their efforts, will turn "demonic and inhuman." They will fall into a "dark hell" of "hypocrisy, arrogance, conceit, anger, cruelty and ignorance." "Hypocritical, proud, and arrogant, living in delusion and clinging to deluded ideas, insatiable in their desires, they pursue their unclean ends. Although burdened with fears that end only with death, they still maintain with complete assurance, 'Gratification of lust is the highest that life can offer.'"[9] These are the selfish individuals that the British philosopher John Locke had in mind when he wrote, "… [I]n matters of happiness and misery … men come often to prefer the worse to the better; and to choose that which, by their own confession, has made them miserable."

In a letter to philosopher Henry Geiger, psychologist Abraham Maslow reflected on his clinical experience:

I have concluded that over the course of a lifetime—in the proverbial long run—the probability is approximately five to one that evil will be punished [almost eighty-five percent]. That virtue also will be rewarded seems to have a probability of only about six to five [fifty-five percent], but it is nevertheless greater than mere chance [fifty percent] … The real key issue is that punishment and reward are largely intrapsychic, that is, relating to one's sense of happiness, peacefulness, and serenity and to the absence of negative emotions like regret, remorse, or guilt. So, as far as external rewards are concerned, these are apt to come in terms of basic-need gratification for belongingness, feeling loved and respected, and generally inhabiting a more platonic world of pure beauty, truth, and virtue. That is, our rewards in life are *not* necessarily apt to be in terms of money, power, or social status of the ordinary sort.[10]

FRICTION PROVIDES TRACTION

To demonstrate our skill, we need a challenge. All competitive games rely on this principle. Take video games for example. When you master a certain level, your reward is a more difficult level. Then you are challenged again and again. Studying both great athletes and ordinary performers, Mihaly Csikszentmihalyi found that we perform at our best when we are in what he calls the "flow zone" between the anxiety of a task that is too challenging and the boredom of one that is not challenging enough.

Let us return to the exercise involving your admired characters. First, consider whether they followed the philosophy of success beyond success. Mother Teresa, Viktor Frankl, and William Wallace were inspired by something beyond success. Consider how this philosophy enabled them to confront daunting odds and persevere with greatness. Frankl had little hope of surviving in Auschwitz. Wallace had little hope of escaping from prison. Mother Teresa had little hope of saving the lepers of Calcutta. But all of them stuck to their values.

Consider the situations that revealed the traits you admire in your characters. What opportunities allowed these qualities to shine forth? As every fiction writer knows, characters need adversity to demonstrate greatness, challenges that push them beyond their everyday existence. Wallace faced abuse by the English. Frankl faced the Nazi death camps. Mother Teresa faced extreme poverty and disease. The very difficulties they confronted afforded them the possibility of displaying their essential qualities. Although they appeared to be curses, they were in fact blessings.

It may come as a shock to discover that some of the best opportunities to display values are challenges that the characters cannot overcome. Admirable characters may fail, but they fail gloriously. In *Braveheart*, Wallace cannot escape. As he prepares to die, he spits out the narcotic given to him by the English princess. He refuses to blunt his mind to the pain of horrible torture. He remains conscious, able to shout "FREEDOM!" with his last breath. Frankl didn't escape the camp or free his fellow prisoners. Yet, his inevitable and harrowing situation provided him with the ultimate platform to demonstrate his dignity and compassion—not only through his activities in the camp, but also for the rest of his life as a therapist. A journalist asked Mother Teresa how she could stay committed to work with the destitute and sick, "You know you can't save them. They will all die." She replied, "Your strength falters because you see only poor sick people. My love endures because I see Jesus Forsaken in his distressing disguise."

Heroes require extraordinary adversity to show their mettle. They need challenges that let them prove that they are not just fair-weather sailors. They need a fierce storm to show that they are able to navigate gallantly.

Their virtue lies in their response to the situation, not in the outcome. They may not be able to bring their boat safely to port and they may even perish in the rough seas, but that is irrelevant to their virtue.

Analyzing myths from different civilizations, anthropologist Joseph Campbell discovered that every culture tells similar stories about virtuous characters. These stories are variations of a basic plot that he called "the hero's journey." "The standard path of the mythological adventure of the hero is a magnification of the formula represented in the rites of passage: separation-initiation-return ... A hero ventures from the world of common day into a region of supernatural wonder: fabulous forces are there encountered and a decisive victory is won: the hero comes back from this mysterious adventure with the power to bestow boons on his fellow man."[11]

Campbell argues that the universal repetition of this plotline reveals generic aspects of the human psyche. It can be very enlightening to look at your life experiences as heroic journeys. Although less fantastic, your stories are no less fraught with challenges and opportunities to express your greatness.

When we win it's with small things,
and the triumph itself makes us small.
What is extraordinary and eternal
does not *want* to be bent by us.

... Winning does not tempt that man.
This is how he grows: by being defeated, decisively,
by constantly greater beings.

RAINER MARIA RILKE, "THE MAN WATCHING"[12]

YOUR LEARNING EXPERIENCE

Think of a life situation in which you grew dramatically, a "stepping stone" in your path that shaped you, bringing you to be the person you are today. Such a learning experience is typically a story of challenge, a trial, an overcoming of adversity. Consider now the initial moments of that story as the challenge began to unfold. How did you feel?

I've asked thousands of people to do this exercise in my seminars. Almost without exception they report emotions such as fear, anxiety, chaos, disappointment, shock, surprise, anger, hurt, pain, bewilderment, discomfort, concern, and so on. It makes perfect sense. To overcome adversity, we first need to encounter it. We need to come face-to-face with the naked hardship of life. At this moment, some of us may feel like saying, "Damn!"

Now reflect on the end of your story, when you moved through the challenge and reached the other side. How did you feel then? Most people report feelings of gratitude, peace, satisfaction, freedom, pride, hope, trust, and happiness. Interestingly, the more upset people felt at the beginning, the better they felt at the end. These stories work like slingshots: The more stress you bear, the more power you get. Standing at the end of a learning experience, people look back and realize that what they cursed as a damned moment was really a blessed one. The facts remain the same, but the interpretation changes. Adversity can be an ally, an opportunity to show greatness.

These learning stories have a gratifying end. You overcame challenges and gained self-knowledge and wisdom in the process. There is a temptation to attribute the good feelings to such success. As we have seen, however, true joy does not come from winning but from dignified struggle. Many stories do not have such happy conclusions. Sometimes you fail and you just feel sorrow. I suggest that you think of such stories as works in process, journeys that you have not yet finished. You can tell that they are not complete because they have not yet yielded their wisdom.

You can learn from every situation. You are unconditionally response-able. You can express your values in the face of any circumstance. As poet David Whyte says, the soul can grow from any experience. The strategic mind tells us that we need to be in control to be safe. "The soul says something more radical and frightening to us, wholly unlike the soothing reassurances of the strategic mind. Out of the silence the soul startles us by telling us we are safe already, safe in our own experience, even if that may be the path of failure. Soul loves the journey itself. The textures and undulations of the path it has *made* through the landscape by hazard and design, are nourishing in themselves."[13]

Not long ago, I had one of these wonderful and infuriating learning opportunities. I had a meeting with the senior executives of a European firm that was considering engaging my company's consulting services. Although the meeting was going well, one of the executives was behaving quite antagonistically. He challenged me bluntly: "This material is soft stuff and does not apply to the hard business world." I tried to understand his position by asking him several times to express his concerns, but I did not succeed. He simply repeated his initial statement.

I wanted this job. I grew afraid that this man would make me lose it. I started to prepare my rebuttal. I wanted to show this turkey that he didn't know what he was talking about. I wanted to make a fool of him in front of everybody. As I opened my mouth, I realized that I was about to say something I would later regret. "This guy is not my enemy," I thought. "I'm upset because he doesn't seem to want to work with me, but that's no reason to get nasty. He is just doing what he thinks is right." I shut my mouth and took a deep breath.

I looked at the executives and said, "I'm not sure if this material is suitable for your company at this time. That is for you to decide. I believe that to succeed in business, a company needs to make the best possible use of its people. I also believe that a culture of responsibility, integrity, and humility, coupled with skills in communication, negotiation, and coordination, supports a high-performance organization, one that yields exceptional results. My offer is to help you develop leaders who are capable of creating such a culture. If you think that this offer is not the best value for your money, you should not work with my company."

The meeting continued much more pleasantly and the conversation ended well. As I later recalled the episode on the airplane, a smile of satisfaction spread across my face. I had done the best I could and held my tongue when I was ready to lash out.

In the end, the company decided not to hire our services. From a business standpoint, I had failed. That hurt. I like winning, just like anyone else.

At the same time, I had remained true to my values. I did not achieve my outcome goal, but I achieved my process goal. I offered our services to a client by presenting the value I thought we could add to their business in the most appealing way I could. Beyond this, I could only respect the client's free will. The week following the client's decline, I had a meeting with my partners. I told them the story with sadness. They shared my sorrow but said with pride, "Oh well, success beyond success."

There is an animal called an *ushghur,* a porcupine.
If you hit it with a stick, it extends its quills
and gets bigger. The soul is a porcupine,
made strong by stick-beating.
So a prophet's soul is especially afflicted,
because it has to become so powerful.

A hide is soaked in tanning liquor and becomes leather.
If the tanner did not rub in the acid,
the hide would get foul-smelling and rotten.

The soul is a newly skinned hide, bloody and gross.
Work on it with manual discipline,
and the bitter tanning acid of grief,
and you'll become lovely, and *very* strong.

If you can't do this work yourself, don't worry.
You don't even have to make a decision,
one way or another. The Friend, who knows
a lot more than you do, will bring difficulties,
and grief, and sickness,
as medicine, as happiness,
as the essence of the moment when you're beaten,
when you hear *Checkmate* …

RUMI, FROM "CHECKMATE" [14]

ZACK AND WILLIAM RELOADED

At the beginning of the chapter, we saw Zack wield the notion of unconditional responsibility as a weapon of shame and manipulation. He focused exclusively on success. How would the conversation change if he aspired to lead his team with a philosophy of success beyond success? How would things be different if he wanted to address the business problem with excellence, but was also intent on enhancing his relationship with William, helping him grow and express his highest virtue? To show the unconditional nature of these goals, I will portray William as being much more discouraged than he appeared to be in the first encounter.

William: "We will not meet the sales quota."

Zack: "Tell me more."

William: "Several customers canceled their orders. With the recession, many companies have imposed a buying freeze."

Zack: "Ouch! That hurts. I'm sure there's a lot of distress in the organization about this."

William: "You bet. We're all very disappointed. It's a horrible situation."

Zack: "Indeed. I'm disappointed as well."

William: "Yeah, it's awful."

Zack: "Oh well, it is what it is. I'd like to work with you and focus on what we can do about this. Do you guys have any plans?"

William: "There's nothing we can do! The recession is not our fault."

Zack: "Of course the recession is not your fault, but that doesn't mean that there's nothing we can do. The rain is not our fault, but we open umbrellas to stay dry… "

William: "What do you mean?"

Zack: "We are up against a great challenge, the recession, the buying freezes, and all that. It seems to me that we have a chance to show our true colors as we face this challenge and do the best we can to respond to it."

William: "But what can we do?"

Zack: "I don't know, but 'what can we do?' sounds like the perfect starting question. Maybe we can gather the team to brainstorm on recession strategies. What do you think?"

William: "We've already thought long and hard. We couldn't come up with a solution to increase sales."

Zack: "I understand, and I appreciate how tough the situation is. However, I want to look beyond sales increases—although I would certainly like some of those! I'm thinking that perhaps we can find ways to improve other aspects of the business such as reputation, customer service, cost reduction, or quality. We might come up with ways to use sales resources for marketing and building relationships with our customers that will yield fruit in the next upswing of the economy. Let's think of what we need to do so that even if we can't improve sales we can still be proud of ourselves."

William: "I like it. It will shake off this feeling of doom and get us thinking along much more productive lines. I'm getting a bit tired of all the moaning and groaning about the economic situation. Hey, I have an idea! What if we invite some of our customers to put their heads together with us? They might think of things we could do to help them in this recession. I'm sure they're hurting as much as we are."

Zack: "That's a great idea!"

Working for a leader who focuses on success beyond success is a great boon. This, however, depends on the leader. Now let's switch places. Let's assume Zack does not change his ways. Is it still possible for William to pursue success beyond success?

William: "Zack, we will not meet the sales quota."

"What's the matter?"

William: "Things have gotten very tough out there with the recession. Our customers are not buying. We have tried several things to keep our sales up in spite of the buying freezes, but we haven't succeeded."

Zack: "Are you blaming the recession? You sound like a victim."

William: "No, I'm not blaming the recession. I'm explaining to you that we have not been able to respond effectively to the challenge of the recession."

Zack: "Well, if you are a player, you should be able to solve the problem."

William: "I don't know exactly what you mean by 'player,' but I don't see how responsibility can guarantee success. My team and I are doing all we can, holding ourselves to the highest standards of effort and integrity. But we have not found a way to meet our sales commitment."

Zack: "It's nice to know you're working hard, but you don't get extra points for effort. I expect results."

William: "I understand, and I want to give you results. I am meeting with you because I'm concerned that we won't reach the numbers."

Zack: "Look, this is an important quarter for us. The analysts are breathing down our neck since we lowered our projection last quarter. If we don't even meet the reduced expectations, our stock price will take a big hit."

William: "I know. And I'm doing my best to deliver the numbers you want, but I can't fabricate them."

Zack: "Can't you? What if we 'ship' stuff out and recognize the revenue this quarter and then 'return' it next quarter when the economy turns up? It wouldn't be the first time we resort to 'ghost sales' to satisfy the Wall Street crowd."

William: "Yeah, I've heard stories about that. But I think it would be a bad thing to do. For starters, it's not only against company policy; it's illegal. If we're found out, we will have to worry about a lot more than the financial analysts. But even if we were able to get away with it, I still wouldn't want to do it. I would feel like I'm lying to our bosses, to the investors, and to anybody who looked at our financial statements. I couldn't live with myself."

Zack: "You don't have the guts to take some risks?"

William: "No Zack, this is not about risk. It's about integrity. I'd rather miss our estimates honestly than appear as though we reached them through deception."

Zack: "Are you for real? This is the dog-eat-dog world we're talking about, not a fairy tale where good guys win. I need someone who'll do anything to win."

William: "Sorry Zack, then I'm not your man. I will not cross certain
boundaries, even if that's the only way to win."

William may be fired for standing up to his boss. Even if he keeps his job,
he may still suffer for his ethical choice. There are no guaranteed external
rewards for behaving ethically. The only guarantee is that, even with the
pain of injustice or the loss of his job, William will be able to look in the
mirror and feel proud of what he sees.

Unconditional integrity has the power to transform situations that seem
like a curse into a blessing. The lotus, sacred in the East, grows amid the
stench of the swamp. In fact, the foul waters provide nourishment for the
plant and allow its beauty to blossom. Similarly, life's adversities can provide
nourishment for the heart and allow it to bloom. The Western voice of Antonio Machado also speaks to the power of the human heart:

> Last night, as I slept,
> I dreamt—blessed illusion!—
> that there was a hive
> humming within my heart;
> and the golden bees
> were working there
> turning ancient heartaches
> to white combs and sweet honey.
>
> Last night, as I slept,
> I dreamt—blessed illusion!—
> that it was God who was
> within my heart.

"LAST NIGHT AS I SLEPT"[15]

Once you relax your attachment to success and commit to success beyond
success, you cannot be swayed by external conditions. Focusing on essential
integrity makes you happier, more peaceful, and more courageous. Furthermore, it provides you with the support to take a leap of consciousness, to

transcend your own particular way of interpreting the world and embrace others. We will turn to that prospect in the next chapter as we explore the development of ontological humility.

The way in which a man accepts his fate and all the suffering it entails, the way in which he takes up his cross, gives him ample opportunity—even under the most difficult circumstances—to add a deeper meaning to his life. He may remain brave, dignified and unselfish. Or in the bitter fight for self-preservation he may forget his human dignity and become no more than an animal. Here lies the chance for a man either to make use of or to forgo the opportunities of attaining the moral values that a difficult situation may afford to him.

VIKTOR FRANKL[16]

CHAPTER 4

Ontological Humility

◆

We do not see things as they are.
We see things as we are.
THE TALMUD

Beauty in things exists in the mind which contemplates them.
DAVID HUME

If ... we are wise enough to base our self-esteem not on being "right"
but on being rational—on being conscious—and on having integrity,
then we recognize that acknowledgment and correction of an error
is not an abyss into which we have fallen
but a height we can take pride in having climbed.
NATHANIEL BRANDEN[1]

◆

Edward throws the financial report on the table. "This is a disaster! I can't bring it to the board. It's shameful."

"What?" reacts Christina, surprised and furious. "It's a perfectly good report! My team spent the last five days preparing it."

"You wasted five days. It's of no use at all. It's too long, badly written, and incoherent. The conclusions are not clear and they sound indecisive. How many times do I have to tell you how important these reports are? Call your team and rewrite it immediately. I need something acceptable for the meeting tomorrow."

Edward leaves the room and Christina collapses in her chair.

"What a jerk!" she grumbles. "Nothing is good enough for him. I have no clue what he wants."

Edward believes the report is a "disaster." Christina believes the same report is "perfectly good." Edward left the room furious with Christina. Christina stayed in the room equally furious with Edward. Sound familiar?

Disagreements like this one are common in boardrooms—not to mention family rooms—around the world. They are notoriously frustrating and painful. Predictably, these conversations rarely improve things. In fact, they generally worsen problems and damage relationships. They hurt people, making them less eager to work and live together. In this case, both Edward and Christina walk away upset. Edward is convinced that Christina is careless. Christina is convinced that Edward is a jerk.

Both Edward and Christina can enjoy recounting the episode indignantly to their respective friends. That perverse gratification, however, doesn't change the fact that neither one gets what he or she wants. After this conversation, Edward lacks his report and Christina lacks the satisfaction of a job well done. Furthermore, I wouldn't expect either result to improve any time soon. Edward hasn't told Christina what he expects and Christina has no idea how to satisfy Edward's needs.

While problems like this one emerge in our interactions, we sow their seeds with our own individual attitudes and beliefs. Edward's aggressive style has more to do with his internal thoughts and feelings than with Christina's report. Christina's defensiveness has more to do with her self-esteem and poise than with Edward's comments. As I showed in chapter 2, every result depends on how able we are to respond to the challenges that we face. Edward and Christina posed challenges to each other that exceeded their respective capacities to respond. Therefore, what ensued was an unproductive exchange that kept the most relevant information locked inside each person. Without sharing that information, the job will not get done, the relationship will deteriorate, and everybody will suffer.

In chapter 2, I explored how we can confront challenges with responsibility, adopting the self-empowering attitude of the player. In chapter 3, I considered how we can remain grounded in integrity when dealing with forces beyond our control. In this chapter, I want to present an effective way to approach situations in which people disagree about what is going on and what to do about it. I hope you will learn how to create alignment, trust, and mutual understanding when people hold differing perspectives.

People see the world differently. The way in which you deal with such differences defines you as a "controller" or a "learner." Controllers claim to know how things are, how they ought to be, and what needs to be done. They give a lot of orders and ask very few questions. Learners are curious and humble, less certain about how to interpret what is going on and what to do about it. They are more inquisitive than directive. They tend to consider others' perspectives instead of imposing their own.

In times of change, the learners will inherit the Earth while those attached to their old certainties will find themselves beautifully equipped to deal with a world that no longer exists.

ERIC HOFFER

Controllers stake their self-esteem on being right—or at least convincing everybody that they are. They manage situations by imposing their opinions on others and claiming that these opinions are "the truth." They feel satisfied when they have eliminated all opposing views and everybody agrees with them. They believe that they see things as they are, and that whoever does not see things in the same way is wrong.

Learners stake their self-esteem on staying open—and inviting everybody to share their views. They seek to manage situations by consensus. They feel at ease presenting their opinions to others as reasonable assessments and inviting others to present their different opinions in a spirit of mutual learning. They believe that they see things as they appear to them, and that their view is only part of a larger picture.

CAN YOU SEE IT MY WAY?

Jean Piaget, the Suisse developmental psychologist, conducted a revealing experiment. He met with a series of children and handed each a wooden block that they were allowed to examine. The block was painted green on one side and red on the other. Sitting face-to-face with the child, he held the block between them with the red side toward himself and the green side toward the child. Piaget asked the child to identify the color he or she saw. The child always answered correctly, "Green." Then Piaget would ask a penetrating follow-up question. "What color do you think I see?"

Most children younger than five years old answered, "Green." They proved incapable of recognizing that the person across the table could see something different than they did. Older children gave the correct answer. They understood that while they saw green, the researcher saw red. These children demonstrated that they had developed a sense of perspective, the ability to appreciate a situation from another's point of view.

After fifteen years of consulting work, I'm sad to report that many executives have never learned this basic lesson. They never question the absolute validity of their own perspective. They assume that if they think that a report is a disaster, the report must be a disaster. They see the proverbial green paint on their side of the block and assume that everybody else's side must be green as well. Often more than forty-five years old, these executives behave as though they have had forty years of experience in being five-year-olds. Their development has stalled because of their ontological arrogance.

My five-year-old daughter, Michelle, says she doesn't like broccoli because it's yucky. In fact, the opposite is true. Michelle calls broccoli "yucky" because she doesn't like it. She doesn't see it that way, of course.

She thinks that anyone who likes broccoli has no taste: a typical case of ontological arrogance. Ontology is the branch of philosophy that studies the nature of reality. Ontological arrogance is the belief that your perspective is privileged, that yours is the only true way to interpret a situation. While ontological arrogance is normal, even endearing in children, it is much less charming in adults—yet unfortunately, it is almost as prevalent.

Ontological arrogance by both Christina and Edward has led to a complete breakdown in communication. Of course, they do not see it that way. Christina says that Edward is a jerk. But the same logic that applies to Michelle and her broccoli applies to Christina. Christina calls Edward a "jerk" not because he is, but because *she* can't figure out how to work with him. Edward thinks of Christina as "careless" not because she is, but because *he* can't figure out how to work with her.

In charged situations, most of us assume we see things as they are; that is not so. We actually see things as they appear to us. Check out the logic for yourself. When was the last time you met an "idiot" who thought exactly like you? Do you believe people disagree with you because they are idiots? Or do you call them "idiots" because they disagree with you?

The opposite of arrogance is humility. Humility comes from the Latin word *humus*, meaning ground. A humble person does not see himself as above others; he does not pretend to hold a privileged position. Ontological humility is the acknowledgment that you do not have a special claim on reality or truth, that others have equally valid perspectives deserving respect and consideration. There are many ways to look at the world, and each way has its bright and its blind spots. Only from the perspective of ontological humility can you accommodate that diversity and integrate it into a more inclusive view. Ontological humility makes sense intellectually, but it is not the natural attitude of the human being. It requires, at least, the cognitive development of a six-year-old.

… [W]hat things *are* independently of our modes of perception and thought is something of which we cannot form any conception.

On the one side we have the world of things as they appear to us—what Kant calls the world of phenomena. This is the world of possible knowledge for us. But all the forms this knowledge takes are subject-dependent. On the other side there is the world of things as they are in themselves, what Kant calls the noumenal world. Its mode of existence has nothing to do with the particular ways in which we register things. But to this realm, for that very reason, we have no means of access.

BRYAN MAGEE[2]

WHAT YOU SEE IS WHAT YOU GET (NOT WHAT IT IS)

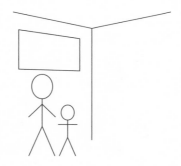

Consider the following image:

You probably see two people looking through a window. That's the common answer given by Westerners. When African villagers look at this image, however, they see something entirely different. They see a mother and her son taking refuge from the sun under a palm tree.

The image can be seen in two different ways, each as valid as the other. Yet we rarely see both possibilities. We may oscillate between one perception and another, but this requires effort. It is possible, although even more challenging, to see the two images simultaneously. But we normally interpret things in one way and unconsciously exclude other possibilities—and not just when we look at stick figures.

A company's comptroller examines last year's financial statements and she sees a stable, successful business. The marketing vice-president looks at the same documents and sees a stagnant company. A board member believes the financials prove that the CEO is failing. One investor sells his shares based on the reports. Another investor buys those shares. The financial statements are the same, but each person interprets them and reacts to them differently.

The Native Americans have a useful saying. "You can't judge a man until you've walked a mile in his moccasins." Similarly, we can't communicate effectively until we consider the world from another person's point of view. In the course of our development, human beings transcend the childish notion of the single-perspective world and grow into an acceptance of multiple views. This is a developmental challenge that demands surrendering one's monopoly on the truth, an accomplishment that many people never achieve.

So how can you accommodate divergent views on multi-colored blocks, broccoli, financial reports, and life in general?

You need to understand that your perceptions are conditioned by your particular way of seeing. Other people can have different and equally valid perceptions derived from different and equally valid ways of seeing. Ontological humility does not mean abdicating one's own perspective. It is perfectly humble to state that some circumstances are "problematic," as long as you add, "for me." That is an explicit acknowledgment that the same circumstances may not appear problematic "to you." Humility is compatible with asserting yourself; your views are perfectly valid. Humility is incompatible with obliterating others; their views are equally valid.

We live in a meaningful world. Our experiences are significant, because our minds are constantly interpreting our perceptions. We don't just process information like a computer. We make sense of our world and develop an understanding of what is going on inside and outside ourselves. We "make" such sense in our minds; we don't acquire it from the outside. We'll call our sense-making systems *mental models.*

Your mental model is your own particular set of deeply ingrained assumptions, generalizations, beliefs, and values. They allow you to make sense of the world you experience and operate effectively in it. For example, when a client describes a problem, I use my mental model to understand his situation. The meaning is not in the sounds I hear, but in the images, memories, feelings, and ideas that my client's utterances trigger in my mind.

Different mental models create different interpretations, feelings, opinions, and actions. If another consultant with a different mental model heard the same story from my client, he would understand things differently. He may focus on things that I found irrelevant, and discard information that I found significant. That in itself does not create difficulties. The problem arises from ontological arrogance, when I assume that *my* truth is *the* truth. Arrogance leads me to claim that my way of making sense is the *only* reasonable way of making sense of the client's story. Ontological humility requires that you understand mental models and how they influence people's experiences and actions.

There's an old story of two clerics arguing about how to do God's work. In the spirit of conciliation, one finally says to the other, "You and I see things differently, and that's okay. We don't need to agree. You can do God's work your way, and I'll do God's work His way."[3]

DISSECTING MENTAL MODELS

We use four types of filters to organize and make sense of our experience: biological, linguistic, cultural, and personal.

Biology

We act as if we perceive the world as it is, yet scientific evidence suggests that this is not the case. The range of human hearing, for example, is rather limited. Dogs hear high-pitched notes that elude our register. Elephants hear low ones. Cats and owls see well at night, while human nocturnal vision is quite poor by comparison. We humans, like all other animals, have physiological limitations that determine our perceptions. We only experience what fits our nervous system.

That which eludes perception also eludes response. A dog can answer to an ultrasonic whistle, but a person cannot. A bat can navigate a cave in pitch-black conditions, but a person cannot. Our biology does not just determine the range of possible experiences; it defines the range of possible actions.

If the doors of perception were cleansed
everything would appear to man as it is, infinite.
For man has closed himself up,
til he sees all things thro' narrow chinks of his cavern.

WILLIAM BLAKE, FROM "THE MARRIAGE OF HEAVEN AND HELL"

Language

We naively assume that we experience things as they are and then apply a label to them. In fact, language determines our experiences as much as our raw sense perceptions do. At a fundamental level, we don't talk about what we see. We see only what we can talk about.

Imagine that a telephone appears in a small hamlet in sixteenth-century England. You're standing next to a farmer looking at the object. It makes a noise. Both you and the farmer see the object and hear the noise, but that's where your shared perceptions end. You hear "a phone ringing," while the farmer simply hears a strange noise. If you ask the farmer to "pick up the telephone," he would probably stare blankly at you.

We don't need to travel in time to illustrate this point. An accountant sees things on a balance sheet that an engineer does not. The engineer sees the same numbers, to be sure, but he does not know the language that the accountant uses to interpret those numbers. Similarly, an engineer can read a circuit design that is incomprehensible to the accountant. The accountant sees the same lines on the paper, but he does not know the language that the engineer uses to interpret those symbols. Shared language allows us to live in a shared world, communicate, and coordinate our actions.

> We cannot see anything until we are possessed with the idea of it, and then we can hardly see anything else.
>
> HENRY DAVID THOREAU

Culture

Shared experiences forge shared perspectives. Corporations, families, nations—all groups—develop habitual patterns of interpretation and action. As time progresses, these shared practices become established as the group's culture. Edgar Schein defines the culture of a group as "a pattern of basic assumptions—invented, discovered, or developed by a given group as it learns to cope with its problems of external adaptation and internal integration—that has worked well enough to be considered valid and, therefore, to be taught to new members as the correct way to perceive, think, and feel in relation to those problems."[4]

Professions operate as cultures. Members of a professional community share more than technical expertise and language; they share a world-view. In the auto industry, for example, vehicle designers are well known for their aesthetic sense. Automotive engineers focus on functionality. Procurement executives focus their attention on low cost. Each of these professionals sees the vehicle, and the business, from a different perspective. What shows up for designers as an aesthetic thing shows up for engineers as a mechanical thing and for procurement executives as a financial thing.

A culture is a double-edged sword. On the one hand, it simplifies the transmission of effective coping mechanisms. On the other hand, it limits the exploration of new mechanisms. As the practices are handed down to new generations, they become orthodoxy. Instead of being "the ways in which our group has responded effectively to the challenges of the past," they become the "only correct ways of responding to the challenges of the present and the future."

In a famous experiment of the '70s, researchers put four monkeys in a cage that contained a ladder leading to a bunch of bananas hanging from the ceiling of the cage. When the first monkey touched the ladder, the researchers hosed all the monkeys with cold water. Soaked and confused, the monkeys tried to reach the bananas again, but whenever one of them touched the ladder, all were "punished." Soon enough, the monkeys learned the lesson: The ladder was "taboo." The researchers then exchanged one of the "experienced" monkeys for a new one. As soon as he entered the cage, the new monkey started toward the ladder. Before he could touch it, the other monkeys pulled him down. After a few repetitions, the new monkey abandoned his attempts. The researchers then exchanged another of the experienced monkeys with a new one. Before long, none of the original monkeys remained. Yet the lesson endured: No monkey ever climbed the ladder. (Incidentally, had any of the second-generation monkeys tried, they would have succeeded. Researchers did away with the water hose early in the experiment.)

In a 1996 survey by PricewaterhouseCoopers, almost half of the respondents listed differences in operating philosophy as the most troublesome post-deal difficulty. Moreover, cultural differences were reported to have incurred substantial costs in lost business opportunities. The same year, a management survey by the *Wall Street Journal* indicated that a majority of its respondents reported that culture was the main obstacle they encountered in implementing change. "Invariably," concluded the authors, "culture appears at the top of everyone's problem list. Cultural differences in operating style, customer relations, and communications represent formidable obstacles to post-merger integration."[5]

Personal Circumstance

Each of us is a unique blend of race, sex, religion, nationality, and family. We each carry characteristic memories. We think that our history belongs in the past, but that is not the case. Our history informs our understanding of the present and the decisions and actions through which we shape our future. We reap what we sow, not just materially but also mentally.

If a boy spends his childhood cowering in front of an authoritarian father, for example, he may find himself, as an adult, cowering in front of his boss. If a girl grows up in a nourishing environment, she is much more likely to view a new manager with an open perspective. Members of non-dominant groups are acutely sensitive to diversity issues to which members of the dominant culture are completely oblivious. Our history predisposes us to see and feel certain things more than others. It may have been decades since I suffered frostbite in my toe, but I still feel it ache every time a cold front moves through.

Personally, I had the curse (as well as the blessing) of living under a military dictatorship. The government pursued a policy of exterminating political opponents. Meanwhile, the regime publicly denied everything. My childhood left me with an acute sensitivity to intolerance and denial. It is not a coincidence that I chose a line of work in which I help people find their essential integrity and respect each other unconditionally.

All four of these filters—biology, language, culture, and personal circumstance—shape our mental models. These mental models, in turn, condition our perceptions, thoughts, feelings, and actions. They lead us to associate with certain people and not with others; to think in certain ways and to reject others; to undertake certain actions and not even consider others; to decide what is acceptable and what is not. Because of the tremendous power of mental models, we can only live within them. That is to say, we live in *our* experiential reality, the reality that shows up in *our* interpretative space. Because of our diverse backgrounds, my experiential reality is never quite the same as yours. Each of our mental models is unique. We live in the same objective world, but because of the differences in our mental models, we each experience and make sense of this world in dramatically different ways.

We don't recognize our mental models; they are transparent and invisible to us. We see the world through them, but we don't see them. They are like colored glasses. While we are all equally blind to our colored glasses, each one of us has glasses of a different color. If I am seeing green, oblivious to the fact that I am looking through green-colored glasses, I will believe that green must be the intrinsic color of reality. If you see red, you must be wrong. Of course, you will hold the exact opposite belief since you are seeing the (colorless) world through your invisible red-colored glasses.

Controllers want to prove that their perspective is the correct one. That proves that they *are* right—as a matter of self-worth, not just of accuracy. Controllers equate being right with being effective. They can't imagine not knowing and still being competent. Blinded by ontological arrogance, they don't want to see others' perspectives for fear that theirs will be disproved and their self-confidence will be taken away. Unfortunately for them, in most interpersonal situations, the question is not, "Are you right or are you wrong?" but "Do you want to prove you are right, or do you want to be effective (i.e., have a productive conversation)?"

Ontological humility means that you recognize and validate your and the other's mental models. When you realize how pervasive and powerful these filters are, it is obvious that calling someone an idiot because they see things differently is, well, idiotic. (Of course, that's just *my* humble opinion.) It is tempting to stop there and let each person think whatever he thinks, but you have a business to run. To work efficiently, you need to do more than accept everybody's views. You need to create a shared map of the situation that will enable you and your counterparts to get things done together. How can you unify multiple perspectives? How can you integrate different views? How can you include others, seeing diversity as an opportunity to grow?

No Problem

When we face a threat to our effectiveness and well-being, we say that "we have a problem." We talk about problems as if they were objects, like toasters or televisions. That may explain why we spend so much time arguing about what "the real problem" is. These discussions are unproductive because they are based on a false premise; there is no such *thing* as a problem.

When someone talks about a "problem," she isn't describing an external reality, but rather expressing a concern about her well-being. There is no problem without someone who finds a situation problematic: that is to say, someone who does not like what she imagines the situation will bring. It is perfectly possible for different people to hold different assessments of the same situation. A tooth cavity, which is problematic for me, is a business opportunity for my dentist.

I AM OKAY, YOU ARE OKAY

Let's look at two opposite mental models and their consequences. The first one, based on ontological humility, we will call the *mutual learning* model. The second one, based on ontological arrogance, we will call the *unilateral control* model.[6] I've used these models, originally developed by Chris Argyris and Donald Schön, to help many of my clients shift from acting like controllers to becoming learners. As they make this shift, people stop fighting to prove that they hold the ultimate truth and start working to integrate everybody's perspective.

The mutual learning model is based on three assumptions:

My rationality is limited. My mental model conditions my perceptions and interpretations. My point of view is always partial. As a result, I can't claim any certainty about how things are or how they will be in the future. My beliefs are just hypotheses—always subject to disconfirmation.

Other perspectives are complementary. Since other people operate with different mental models, they may see things that I do not. They can provide additional data that can better inform my assessments. As a result, I'm eager to understand other people's views, especially when they disagree with my own.

Errors are learning opportunities. A defect is a treasure. Like a symptom that reveals an underlying illness and enables its treatment, a mistake is an opportunity to examine and improve the process that created it.

These three assumptions determine five strategies:

Define goals and strategies consensually. When facing a challenge, open your goals and strategies to negotiation. The more inclusion, the more wisdom—and the more buy-in. This does not require that you abdicate authority. You can request permission from the group to make tie-breaking decisions when consensus can't be reached in a reasonable time. (More about this in chapter 6.)

Win with others. Implementation takes collaboration and flexibility. Consider that every person can provide information to help you achieve your objectives. Support and respect those who see things differently from you. If you find their views convincing, adopt them. Changing your mind is a sign of openness and strength.

Share your views and listen to others' views. Share your data, concrete examples, opinions, and ideas with others so that they can reach their own conclusions. Create conditions for open conversations so that others feel invited to do the same with you. Encourage mutual inquiry.

Maximize internal commitment through free and informed choices. Provide maximal information and minimal coercion to help others decide how to satisfy their needs and interests. Encourage people to take responsibility and accountability for their choices.

Accept feelings as valid. Recognize that humans are emotional beings and that feelings are critical components of our behavior. Consider all feelings valid and worthy of investigation. (More about this in chapter 8.)

A group enacting these strategies will find its prevailing mood to be one of excitement and possibility. People will be pleased to feel in control. They will respond to the organization with loyalty and responsibility. There will be a high level of cooperation and commitment to excellence.

Mistakes will be swiftly corrected and processes continuously improved. People will be more concerned about correcting than concealing errors. They will respond to disappointing results immediately and use them as a learning opportunity. Specific problems will be solved through brief and concrete discussions. Responsibility will replace blame. There will be freedom to explore new ideas and try them without bureaucratic delays. People will challenge obsolete beliefs and feel empowered to innovate.

The ultimate consequences of the mutual learning model are every leader's dream: effectiveness, flexibility, innovation, high quality and profitability, low costs and employee rotation, competitiveness, continuous improvement, and personal and organizational growth. Yet for all its obvious benefits, the mutual learning approach is not the prevailing one in our society. Instead most of us pursue a different model, one that Argyris and Schön call *unilateral control.*

Although nonhuman issues such as statistics, flow charts, finances or high technology ... are obviously essential to managing a successful business, companies are not failing because they lack this technical knowledge: *their failure is with people.* We seem unable to learn that workers will not do high quality work much more because of the way boss-managers treat them than because they do not understand the technical or statistical aspects of what they are asked to do.

WILLIAM GLASSER[7]

I'M OKAY ... YOU'RE NOT!

I have compared mental models to eyeglasses. Mental models are invisible, I said, because you look *through* them. This suggests that if you pull the glasses away from your nose and look *at* them, you will see how they color your perceptions. Distance gives you perspective, letting you decide whether you want to continue wearing the glasses. Mental models may operate like glasses, but they are more like eyes. You can't take them off without great trauma. Your way of seeing the world has become so ingrained that you don't even think of it as a way. For you, it is *the* way.

One of the hallmarks of ontological arrogance is that you don't distinguish your identity from your opinions. You assume that your thoughts and your self are one and the same. If someone disagrees with your opinion, he disagrees with you. As a result, anyone who challenges your perspective is challenging your image and self-esteem. This makes disagreements quite contentious. Any confrontation becomes a mortal combat in which you must defend your identity—usually by destroying whoever threatened it. Ontological arrogance leads directly to unilateral control.

Like the mutual learning model, the unilateral control model is based on three assumptions:

I am perfectly rational. My point of view is objective; it's not blurred by emotion or influenced by personal concerns. I see things as they are. No mental models filter my perception.

Others are not. Unfortunately, most people aren't fully rational. They are closed-minded and attached to their ideas, which are frequently wrong. They don't see and, worse yet, don't even want to see the truth.

Errors deserve punishment. Whenever something goes wrong, somebody must accept the blame. The person responsible ought to be punished. Fear of failure promotes success.

These assumptions lead to five strategies:

Define goals unilaterally. Don't waste time trying to define common objectives. Impose the "right" goals (that is, your goals) and the "right" strategies (that is, your strategies) to achieve them.

Win over others. Implementation takes determination. Hold on to your goals and strategies and overcome any opposition. Changing your mind is a sign of weakness. Cooperate with people who help you achieve your objectives. Undermine those who don't.

Manipulate information. Present only facts and opinions that support your argument. Hide information that opposes it. The only relevant information is that which helps you convince others that you are right and they are wrong.

Use external motivation. Threaten people with dire consequences if they don't follow your instructions, and reward them if they do. Maintain an environment of fear and submission.

Suppress feelings. Emotions are a distraction. Good work is a product of hard thinking, not feeling. Expressing emotions is evidence of incompetence and weakness.

The unilateral control model looks reasonable to the ontologically arrogant. They assume that their perspective is obviously right, so they are sure that those who disagree with it are obviously wrong. The most expeditious way to get things done is to convince or remove those who disagree. In the short term, this strategy may seem useful, but it never yields good results in the long term.

In a unilateral control environment, people behave in defensive, inconsistent, controlling, and manipulative ways. They are guarded and fearful, looking to band with "allies" in opposition to "enemies." They withhold relevant information, thoughts, and feelings. This leads to hypocritical relationships and repressed conflicts that surface as underhanded political maneuvering. Periodically, public outbursts destroy the facade of peace and harmony. These emotional explosions are so counterproductive that they reinforce everybody's belief in the need to avoid all open confrontations, which leads to even more repression and covert power games.

Interpersonal and group relationships become defensive. Group dynamics calcify and the focus turns to winning and losing instead of collaborating and learning. There are antagonism, mistrust, miscommunication, risk aversion, conformity, and compliance to external norms. There is no internal drive or commitment to a common vision. Motivation is low and people do the minimum necessary to keep from being fired.

People experience fear, stress, and anger. The prevailing mood is anxious, cynical, and resentful. People feel demoralized by their inability to control (or even understand) their destiny. They respond with rebelliousness or submission to those who manipulate them. There is no collaboration or enthusiasm. The drive to succeed is nonexistent.

Errors escalate and multiply. People are more concerned about covering up their mistakes than correcting them. These mistakes build until they explode into crises. Far more energy is focused on laying blame than on solving problems. People keep secret, self-validating theories based on private arguments rather than share them publicly. Vagueness and abstractness in communication lead to misinterpretation, misunderstanding, and lack of coordination.

There is minimal freedom to explore new ideas and possibilities. Conformism, low energy, and inertia are the norm. Calls for adaptation and innovation go unheeded as people withhold solutions that might challenge established beliefs and norms. The default tendency is to think "within the box" rather than expanding beyond traditional boundaries.

Authoritarianism prevails. There is no cooperation in defining goals and setting strategies. Without a shared vision and purpose, people act apathetically, submitting to groupthink, conservatism, and risk aversion. People feel disempowered. Compliance requires constant policing by a punishing authority.

The ultimate consequences of the unilateral control model are simple and devastating: ineffectiveness, inflexibility, lack of innovation, low quality, high costs, high personnel rotation, lack of competitiveness, obsolescence, negative profitability, escalating crises and, finally, organizational collapse.

[The] relationship [between a manager and employee] is far more like that between the conductor of an orchestra and the instrumentalist than it is like the traditional superior/subordinate relationship. The superior ... cannot, as a rule, do the work of the supposed subordinate any more than the conductor of an orchestra can play the tuba. In turn, the ... worker is dependent on the superior to give direction, and ... to define what the "score" is for the entire organization, that is, what are standards and values, performance and results. And just as an orchestra can sabotage even the ablest conductor—and certainly even the most autocratic one—a [team] can easily sabotage even the ablest, let alone the most autocratic, superior ... employees have to be managed as if they were *volunteers.*

PETER DRUCKER[8]

WHO WANTS TO BE A CONTROLLER?

If unilateral control is so deadly and mutual learning so powerful, why don't we all embrace mutual learning? Why don't we drop our ontological arrogance and adopt an attitude of humility? It seems like an obvious choice. Yet the vast majority of people don't make it. Many individuals, particularly those in authority, are perfect examples of unilateral control.

The unilateral control model has automatic defense mechanisms. Its immune system is set to destroy anything that threatens its beliefs and assumptions. Without even thinking about it, controllers suppress any information that contradicts their mental model. Thus, they operate according to the unilateral control model without even realizing it. They spend their days manipulating others while still considering themselves open and curious.

Changing from unilateral control to mutual learning goes against social conventions. We live in an arrogant culture. Since early childhood you are conditioned to feel worthy only when you win. You learn to save face and to prove that you are right. If you fail, you feel like a failure. No wonder you cling to the unilateral control model even when it proves ineffective. In fact, you never experience it as being ineffective. You only notice other people opposing you, and then you blame them for your difficulties. That confirms, in your controller mind, that you need to push harder and impose your will on "those idiots who don't know what the hell they are talking about."

Of course, you'd never call them "idiots" to their faces. One of the basic premises of the unilateral control model is that you must act as though you are not trying to unilaterally control others. When this duplicitousness takes over the culture, the organization goes crazy.

Many organizations have implicit paradoxical codes of conduct. Some of the typical messages in these cultures are:

Keep others informed, but hide mistakes.
Tell the truth, but don't bring bad news.
Take risks, but don't fail.
Beat everybody else, but make it look as if nobody lost.
Be a team player, but what really matters is your individual performance.
Express your independent ideas, but don't contradict your boss.
Be creative, but don't deviate from the rules.
Promise only what you can do, but never say "no" to your boss's requests.

Ask questions, but never admit ignorance.
Think about the global system, but you'd better optimize your own
    sub-system.
Think long-term, but you'd better deliver immediate results.
Follow all these rules, but act as if none of them exist.

Many organizations seem hell-bent on pretending that what is happening is not really happening. To survive, employees have to accept that they are not experiencing what they experience. This puts them in impossible contradictions. Furthermore, they have to act as if these contradictions don't exist, which makes it impossible to discuss or change them. It is not surprising that stress and apathy run rampant. Repressing reality is at the core of mental illness.

"You should say what you mean," the March Hare went on.

"I do," Alice hastily replied; "at least—at least I mean what I say—that's the same thing, you know."

"Not the same thing a bit!" said the Hatter.

"Why, you might just as well say that 'I see what I eat' is the same thing as 'I eat what I see'!"

LEWIS CARROLL, *ALICE'S ADVENTURES IN WONDERLAND*

ORGANIZATIONAL DEFENSIVE ROUTINES

Chris Argyris and Donald Schön found that when managers are asked how they would behave under certain circumstances, the answer they usually give is their "espoused theory," a model for action consistent with their explicit values. Most managers claim to behave according to the mutual learning model.

However, observing the behavior of thousands of managers, Argyris and Schön discovered that the way managers claim to behave is considerably different from the way they actually do behave. The authors call the true guidelines a manager uses to take action "theory-in-use." Most managers behave according to the unilateral control model.[9]

These managers' theory-in-use is incompatible with their espoused theory. If they want to maintain their behaviors, this divergence must remain hidden; once exposed, it becomes unsustainable. That's why in a duplicitous environment people are damned if they try to obey the contradictory messages and damned if they try to expose the contradictions. "If [individuals] do not discuss the defensive routines [the inconsistencies between espoused theories and theories-in-use]," writes Argyris, "then these routines will continue to proliferate … If they do discuss them, they will get in trouble."[10]

Individuals aren't the only ones with contradictions between their espoused theories and their theories-in-use. In *The Neurotic Organization*, Manfred Kets de Vries and Danny Miller present some of the most common corporate gaps between declarations and actions; "We are good citizens of this community" (while we pollute the town's lake); "Our workers have autonomy" (while we fire anyone who questions authority); "Quality is paramount" (while we sell defective products); "People are our most important asset" (while we let go 50 percent of our employees every year).

Argyris explains that defensive routines are strategies that enable individuals and organizations to avoid embarrassment, allowing them to ignore the inconsistencies between their words and their actions. In an organizational defensive routine:

The manager gives a contradictory order (or two different managers give contradictory orders).
The manager makes his order undiscussable.
The manager makes the undiscussability of his order undiscussable.

For instance, a supervisor tells a worker that whenever he detects a defect, he must immediately stop the production line and report it. The following day, another supervisor tells the worker that when there is a rush, he should report any defects but shouldn't stop the line. If there is no clear standard of when "there is a rush," the worker is trapped: If he stops the line, he will get in trouble; if he doesn't stop the line, he will also get in trouble. If he tries to get his supervisors to resolve the contradiction, he will also get in trouble. "We are too busy to solve *your* problems. Deal with it!"

Defensive routines wreak havoc on an organization. De Vries and Miller found that "double-bind communications thwart the emergence of mutual confidence and initiative. Anger is aroused, conflicts are suppressed, and an atmosphere of false consensus is encouraged. To subordinates, it seems easier just to give in. Paralysis of action becomes quite common."[11]

Although inconsistencies are inevitable, they are also manageable. Organizational life is too complex to avoid contradictions. Inconsistencies are a fact of life, but not sufficient to create organizational defensive routines. The fundamental trigger for the defensive routine is not the contradiction but its undiscussability. Consequently, the best strategy to deactivate a defensive routine is to make it discussable. A culture of mutual learning, in which people are open to discussing their behaviors, is the best antidote against organizational defensive routines.

LET'S TALK ABOUT IT

Shifting a culture of unilateral control is extremely challenging because it doesn't look like a culture of unilateral control. A controller assumes that, just as he does, others identify with their own opinions and will construe any disagreement as a personal attack. So he tries to defeat them, politely, looking as though he is not disagreeing with them. He doesn't want to risk upsetting or embarrassing others, so he doesn't present his differing views openly. He looks for subtle ways to win the argument without ever having a frank discussion. If he can't do this, he tries to get his way through intimidating behavior. So it is very unlikely to see disconfirming information coming to the surface in a unilateral control environment. When it does, it is quickly suppressed.

A sales executive named Mark approached me after a seminar and asked me to help him deal with a delicate situation he had with his administrative assistant, Sally. Mark explained to me that Sally was very difficult and was unwilling to follow instructions. Mark was so frustrated that he wanted to fire her, but after hearing my presentation on unilateral control and mutual learning, he began to have doubts. He wondered whether he was behaving in an arrogant and controlling way and not giving Sally a fair chance. He wanted to look at the situation from a more learning-oriented perspective and consider other options.

I asked Mark to give me some data to support his assessment of Sally. He explained that she never asked him any questions and made decisions on her own without checking with him. Specifically, he spoke about how she was managing the preparations for a sales convention scheduled to take place in two months. Sally was relatively new to the job and this was the first time she was organizing a meeting of such magnitude, Mark reported, yet she insisted on doing the whole thing herself. Mark feared things would go awry if he could not advise Sally and oversee the preparations. However, whenever he tried to engage her in a conversation about how things were going, he felt she rebuffed him with a nonchalant "Everything is okay."

"Have you shared your concerns with Sally?" I asked Mark.

"That would be like telling her I don't trust her! It would be disrespectful," he replied. I asked the natural follow up question: "Is it more respectful to fire her without giving her a chance to correct her behavior?" An awkward silence ensued. Mark could see my point, even if he couldn't quite embrace its ramifications. I told him that he could work things out with Sally, but first he needed to lighten up. As it turns out, the most powerful solvent of ontological arrogance is not will, but humor.

OUT OF ARROGANCE

Two explorers are walking across the African savanna. Suddenly, a lion appears. The first explorer takes off his knapsack, takes a pair of running shoes out of it, and puts them on.

"What are you doing?" asks the second explorer.

"I'm preparing to run," says the first.

"Don't be stupid, you'll never outrun the lion."

"I don't need to outrun the lion," says the first, "I only need to outrun you!'"

The heart of every joke is its unexpected turn. You assume the explorers are pitted against the lion together. The punch line destroys your assumption. It spoils the automatic interpretation you had created in your mind. When you laugh, you make a confession: "I believed that things were one way, but clearly they aren't." What seemed like a fact turned out to be nothing but a mistaken inference. A good joke reveals the unbearable lightness of being (real). It shows you that your idea of the world is not the real world.

Laughter is a sure sign of shifting from arrogance to humility. When you observe your mental models without attachment, you lighten up. You stop taking yourself so seriously. You relax your opinions and lose the smug notion that your views are obviously correct. This undermines your natural conceit and opens you to curiosity and wonder. As the punch line shakes your self-confidence and shows you that your interpretation of the first part of the joke was not right, you intuit that your whole life could be a "joke" in which the world is permanently shaking up your ill-conceived certainties. Humor is the royal road to ontological humility.

When you fall prey to ontological arrogance, you say pompous things like, "Listen to me, this is the way things really are, I know what I'm talking about." You become overly serious, blind to the filters of your mental models. In this sentence, the term "really" is nothing more than a request for obedience. "You must surrender to reality," your arrogant words imply, "I am just explaining to you what reality is." Expressions such as "really," "objectively," "the truth is," and "obviously," followed by an opinion, are a sure sign that you are operating in the unilateral control model. But there's hope. You can notice your rigidity, remember to loosen up, and take yourself less seriously.

When you laugh you get a full dose of ontological humility. But turning ontological humility into mutual learning interactions takes some work. You need to learn to express your views and receive other people's views with honesty, respect, and humility. You need to learn to do this not just with other learners but, more challengingly, with the large number of unilateral controllers that surrounds you. In fact, when you try mutual learning, you will discover how many unilateral controllers work with you! How can you express yourself with ontological humility without being overwhelmed by those who feel totally certain of their opinions? How do you assert what you think without overwhelming those who think differently?

A gentleman knocks on his son's door. "Jaime," he says, "Wake up!"

Jaime answers, "I don't want to get up, Papa."

The father shouts, "Get up, you have to go to school!"

Jaime says, "I don't want to go to school."

"Why not?" asks the father.

"Three reasons," says Jaime, "First, because it's too dull; second, because the kids tease me; and third, because the teachers hate me."

The father replies, "Well, I am going to give you three reasons why you *must* go to school. First, because it is your duty; second, because you are forty-five years old, and third, because you are the headmaster."

ANTHONY DE MELLO [12]

Let's go back to Mark and his problem with Sally. I asked him whether he thought that Sally could manage the upcoming convention by herself.

"No!" he said. "She doesn't have the necessary experience."

"Why don't you just tell her that you are concerned about her trying to organize the convention alone because this is her first time?" I asked. "That doesn't attack Sally, it just means you believe that she doesn't have enough experience to do a quality job all by herself."

Mark agreed with my logic, but he still resisted speaking so openly to his assistant. He did not want to "put her on the spot" and "make her defensive."

I pointed out to Mark that those were his fears and they had nothing to do with Sally. I encouraged him to role-play with me what it would be like to engage Sally in a mutual learning conversation. He agreed to do the experiment. We proceeded to play out the interaction several times, until Mark felt comfortable enough to talk to Sally. (I will describe the techniques I taught Mark in the next three chapters.)

Two days later, I got a call from Mark. He was ecstatic. He told me that he had had one of the best conversations of his life. Not just because of what happened in the exchange, but because of what he had learned about himself. Mark openly told Sally that he was worried because he believed that she did not have enough experience to organize the sales convention all by herself. He explained that he appreciated her effort and initiative, but would like to be more involved in helping her and supervising her efforts. In response, Sally started sobbing. She confessed to Mark that she was worried sick because she felt that he had dropped this huge project on her lap, and that to prove that she was worthy of her job she had to do it all without help. She was stressed and anxious, but fearful that if she asked Mark to get involved he would think that she was incompetent.

Mark was flabbergasted. He saw how he had created a story about the situation that featured Sally as rebellious and non-cooperative and him as kind and generous; a story where he wanted to help but she spurned it. This story wasn't the truth; it was just a story—and not a helpful one. When Mark dared to test his interpretation, he got disconfirming information; his story fell apart. With his new understanding, planning for the convention was not a problem any longer. Moreover, Mark's stronger relationship with Sally improved their ability to work together across the board. He was astonished by the ramifications. "I wonder in how many places I am doing the same thing," he told me. "Assuming that I know what's going on, when the truth is that I don't have a clue. I wonder how much of my life I am spending in my own dream world."

The key shift in Mark's thinking was going from "You don't know what the hell you are doing and you're too stuck up to accept my help" to "I'm concerned that without prior experience you will not be able to organize this alone. I would like to help and supervise you as you do this for the first time." The first thought is a perfect example of a toxic opinion: an opinion disguised as a fact. To communicate with ontological humility and support mutual learning, you need to distinguish facts from opinions and to express your opinions productively.

Nan-in, a Japanese master during the Meiji era (1868–1912), received a university professor who came to inquire about Zen. Nan-in served tea. He poured his visitor's cup full, and then kept on pouring. The professor watched the overflow until he no longer could restrain himself. "It is overfull. No more will go in!"

"Like this cup," Nan-in said, "you are full of your own opinions and speculations. How can I show you Zen unless you first empty your cup?"

ZEN PARABLE

TOXIC OPINIONS

A fact is objective. You are awake. This chapter is number four. It's snowing. You experience facts through your senses. Other people could also experience the same facts through theirs. Facts are public; they refer to the mutually observable world. To report a fact you can use sentences of the type, "S (subject) is P (predicate)." The subject of your statement of fact is the sensible world. In this chapter's opening dialogue Edward could have stated, "The report is eighteen pages long." Christina could have stated, "My team worked five days on the report." These are simply facts with no evaluations attached to them.

An opinion is subjective. I believe you should go to sleep. I find this chapter interesting. I think this is a great day for skiing. You form opinions in your mind. Other people cannot read your mind. Your opinions are private; they do not refer to the mutually observable world, but to your ideas about it. To express your opinions you can use sentences of the type, "*I* think that S is P," or "S is P for *me*." The subject of *your* opinions is always *you*. In the opening dialogue Edward could have stated, "This report is too long for my purpose in the meeting." Christina could have stated, "I thought this was the type of report you needed." These statements are Edward and Christina's opinions. They may be truthful or deceptive, but they are not true or false in any objective sense.

You observe facts and form opinions all of the time. When you meet someone, you don't just observe what clothes he is wearing. You make assessments about him based on (what you think of) his clothes. Having opinions is not a choice; you are constantly and automatically evaluating everything that concerns you. Many of these opinions are useful. Many others, however, are toxic.

An opinion is toxic when it masquerades as a fact. Because of its sentence structure, a toxic opinion appears as an expression of fact. For example, "Broccoli is yucky" or "Edward is a jerk." These judgments pretend to be something more than opinions. They use the language of facts. You can make them even more misleadingly factual by adding words such as "really," "truly," and "objectively." For example, "This job is really difficult," "The real problem is that you are stuck on doing it your way," "Your behavior is truly despicable," "Objectively, San Francisco is the best place to live."

The problem with toxic opinions is that they make a claim to describe objective reality. Thus, differing toxic opinions lead to conflict. If I prefer to live in San Francisco and you prefer to live in New York, we have a difference of opinion. If I say "San Francisco is the best place to live," and you say "New York is the best place to live," we have a conflict.

This is exactly the toxicity of ontological arrogance. The controller, oblivious to his mental models, experiences his opinions as true descriptions of the public "real" world. He will not say, "I don't like broccoli" or "I don't know how to work with Sally," two first-person statements. He will make third-person statements claiming to describe how things *are* instead of how *he* thinks about them.

Toxic opinions create confrontations. Expressing them rarely improves matters. If Christina tells her boss he's a jerk, she'll end up on the street.

In the movie *Liar Liar*, Jim Carrey's character gets himself in a world of trouble for speaking his toxic opinions left and right. Some people like to think there's value in being brutally honest, but toxic opinions always turn out to be more "brutal" than "honest." Sharing these opinions destroys efficiency, hurts relationships, and creates animosity.

Keeping toxic opinions to yourself is not much better. When you control your tongue, you stuff the toxicity in your mind. If you simply withhold your toxic opinion while taking it as the truth, you will end up causing the same (or worse) problems in the long term. When you hide relevant information—including opinions and feelings—problems remain hidden, relationships become superficial and hypocritical, and you compromise your integrity. Worse yet, the other person can usually "smell" your toxic opinions behind your facade of politeness. To maximize effectiveness, deepen relationships, and live authentically, you must "refine" these toxic opinions and extract the truth at their core. Even the most unconscious and impulsive opinions contain very important information.

A man whose axe was missing suspected his neighbor's son. The boy walked like a thief, looked like a thief, and spoke like a thief. But the man found his axe while he was digging in the valley, and the next time he saw his neighbor's son, the boy walked, looked, and spoke like any other child.

TRADITIONAL GERMAN STORY

EFFECTIVE OPINIONS

Some people believe that observations are good and opinions are bad. I disagree. Opinions are essential to making decisions. What makes the difference is whether you express your opinions effectively or toxically.

Observations are simply true or false. We can verify that the chair is either red or not. Similarly, we can observe whether the report is either eighteen pages long or not. Opinions, on the other hand, can't be compared to an external world. I can observe with my own eyes that Marco is in his office, but when you tell me that Marco is "in trouble," I can't use my senses to verify it. Effective opinions distinguish clearly between verifiable and non-verifiable statements.

The first condition of an effective opinion is that you *own* it. You must acknowledge that it is *your* opinion as opposed to *the* truth. This creates "space" for the coexistence of multiple perspectives and lowers defensiveness. Instead of asserting, "The plant is inefficient," you can say, "I believe that the plant is operating inefficiently." Instead of, "You're wrong," you can say, "I think that you're wrong." Instead of, "The meeting is boring," you can say, "I find the meeting boring." Instead of, "We are wasting time," say, "It seems to me that we are wasting time."

That's a first step, but it won't get you very far. If you consider Bob an idiot, you're not going to refine your toxic opinion simply by saying "Bob, I *think* you are an idiot." In order to fully own your opinions, you need to examine your thinking more closely and realize that you call someone an idiot when you disagree with him or you don't understand his reasoning. What you need to change is not just your speech but your *thinking*. Instead of thinking that Bob is an idiot, you need to convince yourself that you are calling Bob an "idiot" in your mind because you are irritated. You are irritated because you disagree with his ideas or you don't understand where he is coming from. Then you can honestly say, "Bob, I disagree with your argument; and here is why ... " or "Bob, I am not following your train of thought; what makes you think that ... ?"

The second condition of an effective opinion is that you explain your reasoning. Upon request, you must be able to provide the facts and the desires that support your assessment. Opinions arise from comparing objective conditions with subjective desires. For example, you would think that a snowy day is "great" if you hoped to ski, but "terrible" if you hoped to sunbathe.

If you refine your opinion, even if the other doesn't share your interests, she will understand your reasoning. For example, if Edward were to say, "An eighteen-page report is not something I can use. I need a summary that can be read in no more than five minutes," Christina may disagree with Edward asking readers for only five minutes of their time, but not with the fact that the report is eighteen pages long and that most people cannot read eighteen pages in five minutes.

The third condition of an effective opinion is that it points to a desirable change in the task (solving the problem), the relationship (enhancing cooperation and trust), and the well-being of all participants in the conversation. Effective opinions trigger actions that would not occur otherwise. Edward doesn't gain anything by arguing that Christina's work is a disaster. He needs a report that he feels comfortable presenting to his board. His toxic assessment of Christina's work is more likely to prevent him from getting it.

What could he do differently?

EDWARD AND CHRISTINA RELOADED

Christina and Edward's interaction can be more productive if at least one of them acts as a learner and displays ontological humility. Let us see first how a skillful Edward could maximize task effectiveness, maintain and even enhance the relationship with Christina, and act honestly and respectfully.

Edward approaches Christina's desk. "Can we talk about the report for a second?" he asks.

Christina: "Of course. What do you think of it?"

Edward: "I'm sorry but it doesn't fit my needs. I know you worked hard on it and I value your effort. Actually, I think most of it is okay but there are some things I want you to change."

Christina: "I'm sorry to hear that. I did my best to meet your requirements. I was hoping you'd be pleased with the outcome."

Edward: "I understand, and once again, I do appreciate your effort. Even though there are some problems with the draft you prepared, the good news is that we have time to correct it. If you change the format, summarize the first two sections, take out some questionable numbers, and include disaggregated information on regional results, I think it will be just right for what I need. When do you think you can work on it?"

Christina: "Right away. I know how crucial your board meeting is, so this report is my top priority. It would be very helpful to me if you could give me more details on the changes you want. I'd really appreciate it if you could give me ten minutes of your time to go over what I've done so far."

Edward: "I'd be delighted. I really appreciate your willingness to take care of this right away. Let's go to the conference room. We can use the large table to work side by side."

As the person in authority, Edward has more power to modify the situation. Christina, however, can also take 100 percent responsibility and be a player—even if Edward behaves unskillfully.

If Christina adopted the stance of the learner, she could improve the conversation dramatically:

Edward throws the financial report on the table without ceremony. "This is a disaster! I can't bring it to the board. It's shameful."

"I'm sorry, Edward," says Christina in a calm voice. "I obviously missed the mark with your requirements."

Edward: "You certainly did! This is of no use at all. It's too long, badly written, and incoherent. The conclusions are not clear and they sound indecisive."

Christina: "I understand how you'd be frustrated. I'm disappointed myself that after working so hard the result is not satisfactory to you."

Edward: "You wasted your time!"

Christina: "That's what it seems like at this point. However, I wonder if there's anything I can do to improve this report so you can use it. Perhaps we can salvage some of the work my team and I did."

Edward: "I sure hope so. I need this report for the board meeting in two days. Call your team and rewrite it right away. I need something acceptable by tomorrow."

Christina: "That's exactly what I was planning to do. Now to make sure that the rewrite is useful to you, I need some help from you."

Edward: "What do you need?"

Christina: "Ten minutes of your time. It would make a huge difference if you could go over the report with me and tell me as specifically as possible what you don't like about it and what you would like us to do instead. I'm sure that with a better understanding of what you want we can have it ready for you by tomorrow."

Edward: "I can't do it now. I'm late for a meeting."

Christina: "Could you do it after that meeting?"

Edward: "I guess so. I have some time over lunch."

Christina: "What if I order some food for you and we discuss the rewrite of the report over lunch?"

Edward: "Tell you what, you get me some sushi and I'll show up at noon."

Christina: "You got it."

Many of us hide our truth because we can only think of unproductive and hurtful ways of expressing it. Others just blurt it out, taking pride in their brutal honesty. Many of us suffer at the hands of people who express their truth in toxic ways. Others of us get blindsided by situations we were never told about before—because someone did not want to "hurt" us. The root cause of all this pain is ontological arrogance.

Ontological arrogance is stiff and hard. Ontological humility is flexible and supple. When people are aware of how mental models affect their experience and how others' perspectives can contribute to a richer understanding of a situation, they operate in the spirit of mutual learning. They are able to address difficult situations with effectiveness, while deepening their relationships and enhancing the quality of each other's lives.

In the next chapter, we will consider how to express and elicit all perspectives in the spirit of mutual learning. We will turn difficult conversations into opportunities to communicate with authenticity and respect.

Men are born soft and supple;
dead, they are stiff and hard.

Plants are both tender and pliant;
dead, they are brittle and dry.
Thus whoever is stiff and inflexible
is a disciple of death.
Whoever is soft and yielding
is a disciple of life.
The hard and stiff will be broken.
The soft and supple will prevail.

LAO TZU, *TAO TE CHING*

CHAPTER 5

Authentic Communication

◆

We tend to see ourselves primarily
in the light of our intentions,
which are invisible to others,
while we see others mainly in the light of their actions,
which are visible to us.

J.G. BENNETT[1]

You want the truth!?
You can't handle the truth!

JACK NICHOLSON, IN *A FEW GOOD MEN*

◆

Sharon ran the human resources department of a telecommunications company. Her boss, Patricia, proposed a change in the company's benefit policy that Sharon found unfair and a move certain to destroy employee morale. Sharon wanted to share her frank opinion about the new proposal without offending her boss. After much internal debate, she requested a meeting with Patricia, who didn't respond for a week. Finally, she invited Sharon to her office. What follows is a description of their conversation. The right-hand column reports the conversation as you might have heard it if you'd been there. The left-hand column reveals what Sharon thought to herself but never told Patricia.[2]

What Sharon thought but did not say	What Sharon and Patricia said
This is a bad idea. We need to kill it now.	**Sharon** Hello, Patricia. I'm glad we have a chance to discuss the changes in the benefits plan.
You have to leave? I've waited a week for this meeting! You are avoiding me.	**Patricia** Hi, Sharon. We need to hurry because I have to leave soon. Edward (the CEO) wants to see me and he may call any minute. What do you need from me?
These people trusted us; we made a commitment to them.	**Sharon** Changing benefits could be a big deal, people will be upset—
The finance guys! You are all ears for the accountants, but you're deaf when it comes to HR. You just want to squeeze the maximum profit out of people. Don't you see the emotional turmoil that this change will bring?	**Patricia** Yes, I know, but we need to do it. Healthcare costs are going through the roof, and our pension liabilities are killing us. We can't match our foreign competitors' costs. The finance guys have determined that we've got to reduce our overhead to stay viable.
We're talking about human beings, not pieces of furniture. We can't mess with their lives like this! This is just wrong.	**Sharon** It could cause a real uproar if we don't handle it well. Maybe we—
I hate it when you interrupt me. The benefit plan is not changing for the best. The announcement isn't the issue—the decision is the issue. Once again, I'm the one giving the bad news, and everybody's gonna want to shoot the messenger.	**Patricia** I agree. The announcement is up to you. Say whatever you need to say, as long as you explain that the benefit plan will be changed for the best. I don't want to seem insensitive, but we have to make difficult decisions and we need to adjust our costs to international standards. Just explain this so they understand.
This is just wrong.	**Sharon** Okay, but what about the commitment we made to the employees—
What agreement? We don't have an agreement. I don't know how long I can keep working for this company …	**Patricia** (*interrupting as the telephone rings*) That's Edward calling. You'll have to excuse me. Thanks for your comments. I'm glad we reached an agreement on this. Send me the draft on the announcement ASAP.

Reading the right-hand column, it is easy to see that Patricia and Sharon didn't have a conversation, but instead had overlapping monologues. Sharon never expressed her concern with the new plan; Patricia never heard it. We know from reading the left-hand column that Sharon walked away feeling confused, hurt, and resentful. She will at best prepare a halfhearted announcement, which won't help much with morale. We don't know Patricia's unshared thoughts and feelings, but my guess is that she too left the conversation unsatisfied, feeling as bad as Sharon. An already strained relationship has reached new lows.

In a coaching meeting with me, Sharon related the details of this exchange, along with her frustration. She felt trapped in an impossible bind. "I know that I need to discuss this with Patricia, to tell her what I really think," she reflected, "but when the moment arrived I hid my truth. I knew that there was little hope of scrapping the plan unless I revealed my misgivings, but if I shared my real opinion I probably would accomplish little other than exacerbating my bad relationship with my boss." I listened sympathetically. I've encountered many similar situations and they do seem untenable. We are damned if we say what we think—and damned if we don't.

Exchanging valid information is the first step in any cooperative effort. It is impossible to create a shared understanding of a situation without an honest disclosure of all sorts of information, from basic facts to opinions, feelings, interests, and desires. Sharon's frustration reflects a paradox. It is precisely at times when communication is most vital that our conversations break down most dramatically.

What would the consequences have been if Sharon had revealed the contents of her left-hand column? Is it possible for her to express herself honestly without hurting her relationship with Patricia and her career? Is it possible for any of us? In this chapter, I will explore these questions and identify some ways to capitalize on the creative potential of difficult conversations.

Anytime we feel vulnerable or our self-esteem is implicated, when the issues at stake are important and the outcome uncertain, when we care deeply about what is being discussed or about the people with whom we are discussing it, there is potential for us to experience the conversation as difficult ... If we try to avoid the problem, we'll feel taken advantage of, our feelings will fester, we'll wonder why we don't stick up for ourselves, and we'll rob the other person of the opportunity to improve things. But if we confront the problem, things might get even worse. We may be rejected or attacked; we might hurt the other person in ways we didn't intend; and the relationship might suffer.

DOUGLAS STONE ET AL., DIFFICULT CONVERSATIONS[3]

DIFFICULT CONVERSATIONS[4]

Every conversation has three aspects: the task, which I identified in chapter 1 as the It or impersonal dimension; the relationship, the We or interpersonal dimension; and the self, the I or personal dimension.

The *task* conversation focuses on the issue at hand. Patricia and Sharon, in the previous example, needed to address a change in the benefits policy. Most difficult conversations involve disagreements about what is going on, what has led things to be the way they are, why it happened, what should happen next, and who should do what to make it happen. There are also questions about who said what, who did what, and why people said or did what they said or did. Who acted right? Who acted wrong? Who should be praised? Who should be reprimanded?

The *relationship* conversation focuses on the emotional bond between the participants. Implicitly, Patricia and Sharon were addressing the nature of their connection and their feelings for each other. Most difficult conversations involve doubts about the way we relate to each other. Typical questions are: Are we close? Are we aligned? Do we have a common purpose? Are we cooperating? Can we trust each other? Do we respect each other? Have there been betrayals or breakdowns that threaten our relationship? How do I feel about you? How do you feel about me? What should I do about you and your feelings? What should you do about me and my feelings?

The *self* conversation focuses on people's identity and self-esteem. Patricia and Sharon were each attempting to validate their own feelings and establish themselves as "good people." In difficult conversations people feel that their sense of identity and esteem is at risk. Questions include: How am I feeling? What does this situation mean to me? Are my feelings okay? What does it say about me? Should I speak up or keep them to myself? What will others think of me? How will that affect my well-being?

A "difficult conversation" is difficult because we feel threatened in the three aspects of task, relationship, and self. Our automatic reaction is defensive, and that brings out the worst in us: the ontologically arrogant controller. We are certain that we know what is really happening and what needs to happen. Our certainty, however, is false.

On the level of task, the situation is always far more complex than any one of us can see. Not only are there relevant facts that one of us knows and the other doesn't, there are relevant thoughts and feelings that we have not shared with each other. Each one of us, however, thinks that he knows everything he needs to know to fully understand what is going on. Our goal becomes to prove to the other that "I am right and you are wrong."

On the level of relationship, unspoken assumptions and expectations can lead each of us to feel disappointed and resentful toward the other. When criticism meets defensiveness, it turns into contempt. We end up alienated from each other and lose all sense of solidarity. We conclude that it would be useless to discuss things openly, since we are clearly at odds. We suppress our feelings and avoid talking about the relationship.

On the level of self, we feel embarrassed and threatened when our self-image is challenged. We fall into what David Burns calls "polarized thinking," an all-or-nothing logic that assumes that we are totally competent or totally incompetent, totally good or totally bad, totally worthy or totally unworthy, without any middle ground.[5] Thus, anything less than perfect is awful and anything less than praise is an insult. We strive to protect our identity, claiming that we are absolutely right and the other is absolutely wrong. (The other, of course, feels equally threatened and behaves equally defensively, creating an irresolvable situation.)

The difficulty of the conversation increases because of the way in which each one of us attributes intentions to the other. Intentions are invisible to others; each one of us, however, thinks that "I know (because I can infer with certainty) what you intended," and that "you cannot know (because you are taking things the wrong way) what I intended." So, our goal becomes to tell the other that what she did was bad, and that what I tried to do was good; therefore she needs to take the blame and commit to fixing things.

Under these conditions, it is no surprise that the conversation turns into an argument in which I think you are the problem (you are wrong, selfish, naive, stubborn, controlling, irrational, etc.), while you think that I am the problem. Each one of us makes sense of the situation according to his mental model and believes that his interpretation is "the truth." These conditions prevent us from questioning our ideas and exploring the other's ideas with genuine openness.

MAKE IT EASY

To improve these conversations we need to change our assumptions and our behavior. In regard to the task, we need to assume that each one of us can provide significant information to the other. Thus, our goal becomes to explore each other's reasoning, to understand why we think what we think. We need to assume that we have contributed to the current situation and explore our role in it.

In regard to the relationship, we need to realize that cooperation stems from solidarity, not self-righteousness. Mutual trust and respect are at the core of every productive interaction, so the feelings we have for each other are fundamental to a successful conversation. These feelings are not always productive, so before we can jump into a task we need to address our own feelings and the other's. We will discuss how to do this in detail in chapter 8, "Emotional Mastery." But let's establish here that we need to address everybody's feelings with equanimity and compassion before getting to problem solving.

In regard to the self, we need to understand that the psychological stakes are high, that there are serious identity issues at play. We need to expand our view of ourselves and realize that no simple all-or-nothing label can describe who we are. Thus, the goal is to act in alignment with our essential values, focusing on integrity as the only way to experience true self-esteem. We need to stop all the "controller" attempts to achieve self-worth through proving that we are right and the other is wrong.

> A human life is an ongoing process that involves a constantly changing physical body as well as an enormous number of rapidly changing thoughts, feelings, and behaviors. Your life therefore is an evolving experience, a continual flow. You are not a thing; that's why any label is constricting [and] highly inaccurate ... Abstract labels such as "worthless" or "inferior" [or "worthy" or "superior"] *communicate nothing* and *mean nothing.*
>
> DAVID BURNS[6]

To deactivate the negative attribution of intentions, we need to accept that we can only know the impact that others' actions have had on us, but we cannot know what intentions they had when they acted the way they did. Similarly, we can only know what we were thinking when we took some action, but we cannot know what impact our actions had on others. In a productive conversation, the goal is to let others know what impact their actions had on us, and inquire as to what led them to act the way they did. Conversely, we need to inquire to learn what impact our actions had on them, and to reveal the reasoning behind them.

As Stone *et al.* argue, there are two mistakes in terms of discussing intentions. First, is that "we make an attribution about another person's intentions based on the impact of their action on us. We feel hurt; therefore they intended to hurt us." We feel cheated, thus they intended to cheat us. "Our thinking is so automatic that we aren't even aware that our conclusion is only an assumption." Second, is that we believe that our good intentions heal a hurtful outcome. We try to clarify our intentions in a way that prevents us from hearing the impact that the other person experienced—regardless of our intentions. When they say, "Why were you trying to hurt me?" they are really communicating two separate messages: first, "I know what you intended," and second, "I got hurt." When we are the person accused, we focus only on the first message and ignore the second in our attempt to defend ourselves. ("You let me down!" "Well, I didn't mean it!")[7]

In order to avoid the escalation of negative attributions and emotions, it's necessary to understand, acknowledge, and validate the impact of our actions on the other before even beginning our attempts to clarify our intentions.

Before we get into specific strategies to handle difficult conversations, let us find some poignant examples.

WHAT WE THINK VERSUS WHAT WE SAY

Take a moment and think about a difficult conversation you've had recently. It may have been with a coworker, manager, spouse, or friend. Just make sure you pick an exchange that went poorly: an argument with the sales manager about customer relations or a fight with your spouse about taking out the garbage. The goal here is to transform your rotten conversation into something useful and valuable, so the worse the conversation was, the better it will be for the exercise.

Reading this chapter may be instructive, but you'll get a lot more out of the material if you actually do the exercise. This requires more effort, but the return on investment is phenomenal. Thousands of people have found that writing down the conversation gives them perspective. Objectifying a personal experience is essential to understanding the material as it applies to your own life. As I mentioned in the introduction, theoretical mastery without practical skill-building counts for very little in this world. And the only way to build skills is to exercise in a safe practice field under the guidance and support of a coach.

CONSCIOUS BUSINESS

Take a blank sheet of paper and write a paragraph describing the context of your lousy conversation. What relevant events preceded it? What problem triggered it? Where did it take place? Who took part? What were your thoughts and feelings at the start? What did you imagine the other person's state of mind to be? What were you trying to achieve? Why was that important to you?

Next, draw a line down the middle of another sheet of paper. On the right-hand side, write down the dialogue that took place as accurately as you can. Avoid interpretations or additional remarks; just write down people's actual words. When you're finished, imagine handing the sheet of paper to the other person. Consider whether the person would accept that what you've written is fair and accurate.

When you have finished recreating the dialogue, turn your attention to the left-hand column. Write down all of the thoughts and feelings that you experienced but did not express. Leave aside for now what you imagine the other person was thinking or feeling. Focus on the thoughts and feelings that went through your mind as the conversation progressed. (Your case should look something like Sharon and Patricia's at the beginning of this chapter.)

Now it is time to examine the impact of your conversation more closely. Take out a separate sheet of paper and answer each of the following three questions.

How did the conversation affect the issue under discussion?
How did the conversation affect your relationship with the other person?
How did the conversation affect your state of mind and well-being?

Read over the words in your left-hand column. Imagine that you had given voice to all of those comments exactly as you wrote them. Then answer these next few questions.

How would sharing the material from the left-hand column have affected the issue under discussion?
How would sharing the material from the left-hand column have affected your relationship with the other person?

How would sharing the material from the left-hand column have affected
your state of mind and well-being?

If you are like most people who have done this exercise, you had very good
reasons for not sharing this material. Hiding your true thoughts and feelings,
however, has negative consequences as well. Take a moment to consider
them by answering the following questions.

How did not sharing some of your thoughts and feelings affect the issue
under discussion?
How did not sharing some of your thoughts and feelings affect your
relationship with the other person?
How did not sharing some of your thoughts and feelings affect your state of
mind and well-being?
One final question: What do you think was in the other person's left-
hand column?

SHARON'S ANSWERS

I asked Sharon these same questions about her exchange with Patricia.

"How did the conversation affect the issue under discussion?"

"It didn't. Patricia didn't even hear my concerns. I'm sure that the new
benefits policy will make a lot of people unhappy. My guess is that any cost
savings will be dwarfed by productivity losses."

"How did the conversation affect your relationship with Patricia?"

"Relationship? What relationship? Patricia and I don't have any relationship. It's just a polite front that we both keep up for each other. I'm sure we'd
both be happier if we never had to deal with each other again."

"How did the conversation affect your state of mind and well-being?"

"It was awful. I was mad at Patricia for being so insensitive, but I was also
mad at myself for being a coward. I never said what I really thought. I made
that lame excuse about the announcement. What bullshit! It's not about the
announcement, it's about the decision."

"How would sharing the material from your left-hand column have affected the issue under discussion?"

"It wouldn't have changed anything. If I had said exactly what I felt, I would be out of a job for nothing. They would simply implement the policy without me."

"How would sharing the material from the left-hand column have affected your relationship?"

"It would have destroyed whatever semblance of relationship Patricia and I have. It would have been a total breakdown."

"How would sharing the material have affected your state of mind and well-being?"

"I would have felt ashamed of myself. My left-hand column was disrespectful. It was incompatible with my ethical standards of respect for others, even Patricia."

"How did not sharing some of your thoughts and feelings affect the issue under discussion?"

"We never addressed the real issue. Patricia thinks I can write an announcement that satisfies her needs, but I can't. I think this will create a lot of problems for Patricia, for me, for the employees, and for the company."

"How did not sharing some of your thoughts and feelings affect your relationship with Patricia?"

"It is very frustrating. Every time I think of Patricia, I cringe. I imagine she enjoys working with me as little as I enjoy working with her."

"How did not sharing some of your thoughts and feelings affect your state of mind and well-being?"

"It didn't work. I'm angry. I have my job, but I don't really want it—except for the money. I feel like a hypocrite."

"What do you think was in Patricia's left-hand column?"

"My guess is that she is hoping to get through this change without any big blow-ups with the union. I'm sure she'd like my help and is upset that I seem to oppose her. I bet that she got her marching orders from Edward, and is trying to do what she was told. She's probably worried that Edward will get upset with her if she raises any issues to him. Perhaps she even had a left-hand column conversation with Edward similar to the one I had with her! Wouldn't that be something?"

YOUR PRIVATE WASTE SITE

When I do this exercise, I usually discover that my left-hand column is full of ugly stuff. There are harsh opinions and broad generalizations; I also find intense emotions such as fear, anger, and anxiety. Sometimes, I'm surprised to discover feelings of gratitude and affection in my left-hand column. I've worked with numerous clients who report similar discoveries. We regard these as "positive" feelings, yet many of us feel uncomfortable and vulnerable expressing them. Intimacy is often as frightening as conflict.

Still, the bad stuff usually outweighs the good stuff. For some people, this comes as a big surprise. Can you really carry such wild thoughts and feelings? Yes. Do other people have similar thoughts and feelings? Yes again. The left-hand column exercise reveals a vast territory that rarely comes to light. For most of us, however, this is not news. We are quite aware that we are withholding critical information; we are also aware that other people are withholding emotions and thoughts as well. Yet, we insist on acting as if nobody is doing this, as if we don't all have our own densely packed left-hand columns.

It reminds me of Hans Christian Andersen's tale, "The Emperor's New Clothes." A couple of rogues persuade the emperor to buy clothes woven of a magic cloth. These are special clothes, the rogues assure the emperor, so special that they are invisible to anyone who is stupid or unworthy of holding their current office. Of course, the emperor sees no clothes, but not wanting to be exposed as unworthy, he pretends to see them. All of his attendants and the rest of the population pretend to see clothes, too. No one wants to look stupid. But not everyone is afraid. During a parade, a little boy sees the emperor and cries out, "He's naked!" We can go on acting as if we are all wearing fine linens—or we can be brave enough to speak the truth, to admit that we are naked.

It would be convenient to erase our left-hand columns, but it is impossible. Just as we cannot choose to avoid a headache or cough, we cannot choose what to think or feel. If we could, we would never choose to think unhappy thoughts or feel miserable feelings! A life without negative thoughts seems appealing, but that's not the way our minds work. No conscious decision makes an idea appear; no conscious decision makes it disappear. In fact, it usually works precisely the opposite way. The harder you try to get thoughts and feelings out of your head, the more they stick; the harder you try to ignore them, the more they demand attention.

If we want to improve our interactions, we need to find a way to deal with our left-hand columns. But that's not easy to do. These thoughts and emotions are often quite unpleasant, sometimes even nauseating. Exploring your left-hand column is like discovering toxic waste in your mouth. You can't ignore it, but what can you do with it? It often feels like there are two choices: Either spit it out or swallow it.

"Spitting out" the left-hand column has serious side effects. We all know the relief that comes from finally unloading on an irritating colleague. It feels good to tell him what we really think! Yet, just like dumping toxic waste, these "raw" thoughts and feelings pollute the psychosocial environment of your relationships and your own well-being. Dumping triggers aggression and antagonism; it hinders problem solving and destroys mutual respect.

On the other hand, "swallowing" toxic thoughts and feelings is hardly a panacea. Silence helps avoid immediate confrontations but it does not generate solutions. Hiding relevant information makes it impossible to discover and address difficulties. While a real conflict remains hidden, people spend an immense amount of time discussing tangential issues. Interpersonal relationships suffer. Meantime the toxic waste sits in the belly. This is a metaphor, but it turns out to carry some scientific truth. Medical literature is filled with studies linking repression to migraines, hypertension, anxiety, depression, and other illnesses. Every time we swallow toxic thoughts and feelings, we literally hurt ourselves.

And to top it all off, the toxicity comes out anyway! We can only repress intense thoughts and feelings for so long. At some point, the waste has to come out. Usually, it's in the form of anger directed toward the wrong people at the wrong time. Since we can feel safe around our loved ones, we feel free to hurt them. We swallow resentments at work and spit them out at home.

We face what I call a "quatrilemma," that is, a quandary with four horns. We cannot control the appearance of toxic thoughts and feelings in our mind. If we express our toxic thoughts, we create a lot of damage. On the other hand, if we don't express them, we also cause great harm. Finally, we cannot really hide our thoughts and emotions for long. We may be able to keep them inside, but their essence oozes out in counterproductive ways. Just as we can make a reasonable guess about our counterpart's left-hand column, so can they.

How can we escape the four horns of this dilemma? There is an old Jewish saying: "Whenever you are offered two equally bad alternatives, choose a third."

More than any time in history mankind faces a crossroads. One path leads to despair and utter hopelessness, the other to total extinction. Let us pray that we have the wisdom to choose correctly.

WOODY ALLEN

TOXIC WASTE PROCESSING

There's an old fable about three men who come across a poisonous tree. The first man worries about the tree's risk to others. "Let's destroy it before someone eats its poisonous fruit," he says. The second man is wiser. He sees the first man's point, but he wonders whether it's necessary to cut down the tree. "Let's not cut it down," he says, "but build a fence around it so nobody is poisoned." The third man is wiser still. He says, "Oh, a poisonous tree. Perfect! Just what I was looking for; I'll gather its fruit and use it to prepare medicine."[8]

If you don't want to dump the "poison" of your unspoken thoughts and emotions into your conversations and you don't want to swallow it, what do you do? You can refine it. Just as refineries transform crude oil into fuel, we can transform our left-hand column to support task effectiveness, healthy relationships, and self-integrity. The same thoughts that destroy communication when dumped or stuffed can be refined to energize more effective, relational, and honorable conversations.

The first step to processing toxic thoughts is *awareness*. Simply the act of writing a left-hand column promotes consciousness. It provides a chance to separate ourselves from our thoughts and consider them objectively. This is not always easy. If you consider yourself to be a forgiving person, you may be shocked to discover a cesspool of resentment in your left-hand column. Perhaps you don't want to accept the shadow part of you that hates your boss. You want to cross that statement off your sheet. But if you ignore your darkness, you will not be able to bring it to the light of awareness.

On the other hand, accepting the part of you that hates your boss does not mean you have to indulge that part. You don't have to—nor should you—go tell off your boss. Instead you merely need to accept that you carry that judgment. That acceptance is simple, straightforward, and powerful. Part of the left-hand column's power comes from our unwillingness to acknowledge it. When you befriend these thoughts and feelings, they are instantly weakened. It is similar to a diplomatic axiom: Keep your friends close and your enemies closer.

The second step is assuming *unconditional responsibility*. As we discussed in chapter 2, even though you can't choose what shows up in your left-hand column, you can choose how to respond to that material in alignment with your values. You can choose to distill and express your thoughts and feelings with integrity. As a player, you look honestly at your left-hand column and ask yourself, "How am I contributing to this ineffective conversation? How can I invite the other's truth and offer mine in a respectful and honest way?"

Going beyond the present conversation, your player voice also asks, "What mistakes have I made? What mixed intentions have I enacted? How have I contributed to the problem?" The more you own your part of the situation, the more balanced you will feel during the conversation, and the more you will be able to listen with respect and compassion.

Unless you abandon the polarized thinking that says, "I'm totally competent or totally incompetent, totally good or totally evil, totally worthy or totally unworthy," assuming responsibility will threaten your identity. Acknowledging that you are always a part of the problem means that you are not perfect, which in "all or nothing" logic implies that you must be awful. Feeling so vulnerable about your identity, you will not accept any ownership. When faced with negative information about yourself, you will become defensive; you will deny or justify any involvement.

When you adopt the player stance, you no longer feel at the mercy of your automatic defensive routines. You gain insight into how you are using them and how they hold a kernel of truth. For example, if my left-hand column is filled with jealous statements about my boss, I can realize that my boss has something that I want. That does not imply any wrongdoing on my boss's part. Assuming responsibility, on the other hand, does not mean that I am solely responsible for the situation. It does not preclude my conversation partner from owning her contribution. Just because I realize I am jealous of my boss doesn't mean my boss can't realize that she feeds that jealousy to support her feeling of superiority.

The third step is to strive for *mutual learning*. As we saw in chapter 4, we frequently operate within the unilateral control mode, trying to "win" conversations, showing others that we are right while they are wrong. In order to communicate anything from your left-hand column effectively, it's essential to remind yourself that its content is not "the truth," but just your judgments and interpretations. You need to express them humbly, aiming for mutual understanding.

When we shed our desire to control others we can focus on how to work better together, share information, and achieve our goals. If you go into a meeting determined to force the other to abandon his ideas, the conversation will go much differently than if you enter the meeting eager to explore the best way you both can figure out to take care of your needs.

As Kerry Patterson and his coauthors state:

> … Conversations often go awry not because of the *content*
> … but because others believe that the painful and point-

ed content means that you have a malicious *intent*. How can they feel safe when they believe you're out to do them harm? Soon, every word out of your mouth is suspect.

Consequently, the first condition of safety is *Mutual Purpose*. Mutual Purpose means that others perceive that we are working toward a common outcome in the conversation, that we care about their goals, interests, and values. And vice versa. We believe they care about ours. Consequently, Mutual Purpose is the entry condition of dialogue. Find a shared goal and you have both a good reason and a healthy climate for talking.[9]

Without mutual purpose, the conversation degenerates into an unproductive argument.

Preparing for the Conversation

There are five mutual learning purposes in a difficult conversation:

First, *learning their story*. Exploring the other person's perspective is always helpful. What information do they see that we missed or don't have access to? What past experiences influence them? What is their reasoning for why they did what they did? What were their intentions? How did our actions impact them? What do they think we are contributing to the problem? What are they feeling? What does this situation mean to them? How does it affect their identity? What's at stake?

Second, *expressing your views and feelings*. Your goal should be to express your views and feelings with clarity, honesty, and respect. You hope that the other person will understand what you are saying, and perhaps be moved by it, but you can't count on that. What you can do is present to the other, as productively as you can, what you want them to know about your views, intentions, contributions, feelings, and identity issues. You can share your story.

Third, *addressing the situation together*. Given what you and the other person have each learned, what would improve the situation going forward?

Can you brainstorm creative ways to satisfy both of your needs? Where your needs conflict, can you use equitable standards to ensure a fair and workable way to resolve the conflict?[10]

The fourth step is to *create a respectful context* for the conversation. The right conversation within the wrong context is the wrong conversation. You can choose the perfect words, but they will likely fail if you say them with anger or they are received with distrust. Before you initiate a conversation, take some time to ground yourself in your values. Before getting into the content, spend some time creating a productive context of mutual respect with others.

Patterson *et al.* point out: "While it is true that there's no reason to enter a ... conversation if you don't have Mutual Purpose, it's equally true that you can't stay in the conversation if you don't maintain Mutual Respect ... As people perceive that others don't respect them, the conversation immediately becomes unsafe and comes to a screeching halt. Why? Because respect is like air. If you take it away, it's all people can think about. The instant people perceive disrespect in a conversation, the interaction is no longer about the original purpose — it is now about defending dignity."[11]

The final preparatory step is to *ensure that you have a proper setting* for the conversation. Is the physical environment conducive? (It is difficult to have a good conversation standing in the cold, or without privacy.) Does everyone have enough time to discuss the issue? Is everyone ready to have a frank discussion? Does everyone know the background of the conversation? Are there any significant issues (such as external distractions, potential interruptions, etc.) that need to be addressed before everyone can engage in the substance of the conversation?

Creating the right setting is always a worthwhile investment. When people are in the right mood, the conversation flows, and problems dissolve almost miraculously. When they are not, it is impossible to have a productive interaction.

Something we were withholding made us weak
Until we found out that it was ourselves

CONSCIOUS BUSINESS

We were withholding from our land of living,

And forthwith found salvation in surrender.

ROBERT FROST, FROM "THE GIFT OUTRIGHT"[12]

MEETING IN THE KITCHEN

Let's switch metaphors.

There is a fundamental difference between people bringing cooked foods to a potluck versus everyone bringing ingredients and preparing the meal as a group. Through our work transforming the left-hand column, we've learned how to make tasty dishes that appeal to a wide range of people. I tend to like my enchiladas spicy, but I've learned that you don't, so I ease up on the cayenne pepper when preparing my offering for the potluck. Similarly, you like to make salad, but you've learned to keep the dressing on the side, so each of us can decide exactly how much he or she wants. These insights and habits are healthy and productive and will no doubt result in more enjoyable potluck dinners, not to mention business meetings.

But we have higher aspirations. As business colleagues and family members, we don't just want to learn how to share pre-made dishes in the dining room; we want to pile into the kitchen and whip up one fantastic feast together. This presents its own set of challenges. How do we tell each other where the ingredients are? How do we decide whether to use your pasta recipe or mine? Is it possible for us to create new recipes together? For that work, we need a different set of skills.

We will focus on cultivating two skills that I call productive expression and inquiry. These skills are the skeleton key to authentic communication. "Expression" concerns how we present our opinions, feelings, and needs respectfully, while "inquiry" concerns how we help the other to express her opinions, feelings, and needs.

When two noted family therapists examined couples in the throes of heated discussions, they noted that people fall into three categories: those who digress into threats and name-calling; those who revert to silent fuming; and those who speak openly, honestly, and effectively. After watching dozens of couples, the two scholars predicted relationship outcomes and tracked their research subjects' relationships for the next ten years. They had predicted nearly 90 percent of the divorces that occurred. Over time, couples who found a way to state their opinions about high-stakes, controversial, and emotional issues honestly and respectfully remained together. Those who didn't, split up. [13]

SPEAKING YOUR TRUTH

Productive expression is a way to present your viewpoint to others as effectively as you can. You are not trying to convince anyone that you are right; you are helping others to understand why you think the way you do. Productive expression creates an opportunity for others to question and contribute to your thought *process* instead of discussing its final *product*. Productive expression helps reveal and resolve differences in knowledge (by sharing information), reasoning (by sharing needs, standards, and logical inferences), and purposes (by sharing objectives). When you express the underbelly of your reasoning, you may feel vulnerable. There's good reason for that. Just like the boy who calls out that he sees the emperor naked, you are exposing your thoughts to others' scrutiny. That is why in order to commit to productive expression, you need to be brave. You must love the truth more than you love saving face.

Here are some guidelines for productive expression:

- **Find common ground.** Describe the problem in a way that feels true for both sides. Avoid judgments that can trigger the other's defensiveness. Mediators call the story that honors both "my story" and "your story" "the third story." This third story is usually presented as a difference between the parties. Say, for example, that I believe it is best to expand our retail chain nationally, while you believe that it is best to go international. I can begin by saying, "I want to talk about our expansion plans. My sense is that we see things differently. You believe it would be best to invest our capital in opening new stores in other countries, while I believe it would be best to open new stores within our country. I'd like to learn more about how you see things and explain to you how I am seeing them. Does this seem useful to you?"

- **Provide facts.** Remember that concrete examples and illustrations are the common ground on which to build with your partner. Communicate the observations (facts) that support your reasoning and the standards against which you compare them. Provide concrete examples and illustrations. Consider the difference between announcing, "Our help desk sucks!" and saying, "Last week, only sixty-five percent of the calls to our help desk were taken within five minutes." (See chapter 4 for an extended discussion on facts versus opinions.)

- **Own your opinions.** Your opinions are what you think, not the objective truth. They come from partial information; others may have different ideas that are equally valid. Can you accept that you may have something to learn from the conversation? If not, consider revisiting our discussion on Ontological Humility. It's a lot easier for the help desk manager to listen if you say, "I am troubled by the complaints I have received from customers and would like some help to improve the situation," than if you accuse him with, "This is unacceptable!"

At the heart of better communication is the self-statement. *A self-statement puts the responsibility for your emotional experience squarely on your shoulders. It is the one single, easy-to-learn skill that can most dramatically improve the communication. ...* Self-statements always begin by using the subject "I" to discuss a problem. They exist in opposition to their nemesis, "you" statements. A *"you" statement puts the responsibility for your emotional discomfort on your partner, never on yourself.* "You" statements are communications of criticism, blame, and anger. In "you" statements, your emotional experiences and negative behaviors are always presented as being an appropriate response to the irresponsible or hurtful action of someone else. "I" statements decrease the emotional reactivity of the system. "You" statements increase the emotional reactivity and interpersonal tension.

JOHN W. JACOBS[14]

- **Recommend actions.** Productive conversations thrive on specifics as opposed to generalities. Connect recommendations for action with your interests and concerns. In the help desk case, for example, you could suggest, "I would be happy to lend a hand sending some of my administration people to you during peak hours. You could train them so that they can reduce the burden on your operators." At the same time, don't forget your humility! Other people may have information that changes your perspective. Stay flexible. If the help desk manager told you that training would take his people off the phones during critical times, you may need to consider other options.
- **Ensure comprehension.** Many communication problems stem from the practical challenge of understanding each other, so ensure that people follow your reasoning. Give them a chance to clarify questions. Ask them, "Does this make sense?" or "Can I clarify anything further?" Invite responses to your expression. Ask questions like, "What do you think about this?" "Do you have different information?" "Do you see any gaps in my reasoning?" "Did you reach a different conclusion?" "Have I addressed your concerns?" "Can you think of other ways of looking at the problem?"
- **Accept challenges.** When you encourage feedback, you will get challenges. Remember that alternative views do not weaken your argument; they reorient you from unilateral control toward mutual

learning. Avoid the temptation to become defensive before you understand the other's perspectives.

Consider two scenarios for discussing a hiring decision with your fellow executive committee members. You could announce, "We should hire George instead of Louise." Or you could follow the suggestions above and say something like this: "I'd prefer to hire George instead of Louise. I met with both of them, read their résumés, and spoke to their references. George impressed me as being the most qualified. He has a graduate degree in organizational behavior and has worked as a workshop leader for the last fifteen years. Louise has been successful as a consultant in designing training programs, but she has never worked as a facilitator. That is why I believe George is the better candidate. On the other hand, I have based my opinion on few observations and many assumptions. There may be other reasons that Louise would be more useful to us than George. I'd like to know what you all think."

Humility does not mean giving up your point of view. Your purpose is to explore the situation together, not to abandon your perspective. Imagine that despite your humble, generous comments, one of your coworkers gets aggressive. "What do you mean George is better than Louise?" she might say. "You're totally wrong; Louise is the candidate we need!" It is possible to remain open and curious without giving up your view. You can clarify humbly yet firmly: "I did not mean to say that George is better than Louise. I'm sorry if it came across that way. What I meant to say is that given my information, I thought that George would work out better for us than Louise. And of course, I may be totally mistaken about that. It sounds to me like you have a different perspective."

You can then turn the conversation to an investigation of why the other thinks that Louise would be better for your company than George. To fulfill that task, you will need to use productive inquiry.

ELICITING THE TRUTH FROM OTHERS

We spend so much time focusing on how to express ourselves that we often overlook what is perhaps the most crucial part of any conversation: listening to other people. Productive inquiry is a way to learn about other people's reasoning. It can not only help them express what they are thinking, but also why they are thinking it. When we inquire productively, we create a climate of collaboration. We can reveal and resolve differences; we can relate effectively and work together toward a common purpose.

The core of productive inquiry is not a technique, but an attitude. Productive inquiry requires a profound openness and receptivity, a commitment to listening with total attention. This can only come from a strong desire to understand the other person, to discover her world with appreciation and respect. The ability to pay attention is inversely proportional to the need to be right. The more concerned you are about proving you are right, the less energy and patience you will have to inquire into and truly hear what the other person has to say. The less the other person feels received and appreciated, the less he will be willing to listen to you and engage in a productive conversation. As the saying goes, "I don't care how much you know until I know how much you care."

I have found it of enormous value when I can permit myself to understand another person. The way in which I have worded this statement may seem strange to you. Is it necessary to *permit* oneself to understand another? I think that it is. Our first reaction to most of the statements which we hear from other people is an immediate evaluation, or judgment, rather than an understanding of it. When someone expresses some feeling or attitude or belief, our tendency is, almost immediately, to feel "That's right"; or "That's stupid"; "That's abnormal"; "That's unreasonable"; "That's incorrect"; "That's not nice." Very rarely do we permit ourselves to *understand* precisely what the meaning of his statement is to him. I believe this is because understanding is risky. If I let myself really understand another person, I might be changed by that understanding. And we all fear change. So as I say, it is not an easy thing to permit oneself to understand an individual, to enter thoroughly and completely and empathetically into his frame of reference. It is also a rare thing.

CARL ROGERS[15]

While good inquiry is fundamentally an attitude, there are some practical guidelines for promoting it in the midst of a conversation:

- **Stay open.** Full engagement involves your body, not just your mind. Hold a relaxed posture, do not cross your arms, maintain eye contact, and don't forget to breathe. Body language is even more crucial when listening. If you are looking elsewhere (at a book, a computer screen, or TV), it is nearly impossible to connect with the speaker. Keeping your body focused and open helps to establish rapport.

- **Be quiet.** Do not interrupt or "finish" other people's sentences. This demonstrates poor attention, impatience, and lack of respect. Listen with interest and curiosity without hurrying the speaker. For some people this feels like a waste of time. This opinion is usually based on an arrogant assumption ("I already know what I need to know"). Even if others' ideas seem flawed to you, allowing their free expression is essential to creating a constructive context.

- **Summarize.** After the person has finished, summarize what you heard in a way that encourages the other to take ownership of her opinions. I call this a "detox summary" since it can refine a toxic statement into a productive one. This summary shows that you have paid attention and that you want to understand the other person. It also provides a chance for the person to present his views again if he is not satisfied with the way you have expressed them. For example, if someone tells you, "This work is useless, it has to be redone." You can restate, "I understand that this doesn't serve you and that you want it redone," and then inquire, "What is it that you don't like? What changes would make it more useful to you?" Alternatively, if someone says to you, "It's impossible to work like this!" You can restate, "I hear that you find it difficult to work in these conditions," and then inquire, "What things are getting in the way? What can I do to help you?"

- **Acknowledge and validate.** Let the other person know that you find his feelings reasonable, and that they matter to you. This acceptance relaxes identity questions about the legitimacy of his feelings. Validation entails pointing out that his thoughts and feelings are (at least partially) right; that there is a kernel of truth in his story. It is crucial to communicate to the other person that you want to understand what he feels, and that you think that he is a person worthy of attention. You could say, "I see that my email upset you, and I feel sorry about that. I understand how I came across as overly critical and chastising. I realize now that my tone was not very collegial." Only after feelings and identity issues have been settled is it possible to start addressing the task.

- **Don't prosecute.** Use inquiry to understand and learn, not to prove you are right and others are wrong. Ask open-ended questions that promote expression. You may feel defensive when the sales manager announces that customers hate your service, but remember that you may not know the facts and the reasoning that led to his conclusion. You could ask, "What evidence suggests to you that customers are dissatisfied with our service?"

- **Ask for permission to counter.** Don't begin counter-arguing without the speaker's consent. You may be anxious to respond to the speaker, but restrain yourself. Make sure she has finished expressing her position before you present alternative information or areas of disagreement. You can say, for example, "I'd like to show you some information that you haven't taken into account. Are we ready to move to a dialogue? Or are there other things you'd like to present first?"

With these tips for pursuing productive inquiry in hand, let's return to the hiring case that pits George against Louise. You've proposed hiring George and you've used productive expression to present your case. That didn't stop a colleague from jumping down your throat. Instead of steamrolling your colleague or coaxing her into understanding why you are right, you want to find out the reason she is opposed to your proposal.

You could say, "Hmmm, I see that you disagree with my assessment. You believe that Louise is more suitable for this job than George is. I'd like to understand what leads you to believe that."

"Louise seems to be much more mature," she tells you.

"How has Louise demonstrated her maturity to you?" you might ask, "and how do you think that Louise's maturity would improve her ability to do the job?"

By asking these questions, you have not abandoned your contention that George is the best person for the job, but you are orienting yourself to learning more about the situation. Louise's resume mentioned that she had served as a consultant, but you didn't know that she supervised a staff of twenty employees. After productively inquiring, you learned this. With this additional information perhaps you will change your mind. On the other hand, you may still believe that George is the best candidate. At that point you can sincerely say, "I hear your arguments and, although I think they are reasonable, I'm not persuaded." You could propose that her desire to get a more experienced person for the job may be met by having George go through a six-month apprenticeship. Discussing the hire at this deeper level is much more collaborative and potentially much more productive. It is akin to the difference between bringing a meal to a potluck and cooking something together. Of course, you and your colleague may still disagree. We will study how to conduct a constructive negotiation in the next chapter.

◆

Productive expression and inquiry are two sides of the same coin. When we express our ideas productively, we implicitly answer the questions that someone using productive inquiry would have asked. When we inquire about someone's ideas productively, we implicitly help him express himself productively. This implies that it only takes one skillful person to improve the quality of a conversation. Incidentally, using terms such as "expression," "inquiry," "observations," "opinions," or "mental models" is not necessary.

When we act skillfully, others simply feel we are having a good conversation, not suspecting that we are using any technique.

In some situations, however, it may be beneficial to tip our hand and explain the principles of productive expression and inquiry. This is safe because expression and inquiry are not tools to use *on* but *with* others. That is the essential difference between a collaboration tool and a manipulation tool. A manipulation tool is most powerful when I have it and you don't. For example, in order to coerce you, it is best if I have a weapon and you don't. A collaboration tool is most powerful when we both have it. If we are trying to solve a problem together, it is best if we both know how to express our views and inquire into each other's. Productive expression and inquiry aim to produce a "good" conversation where everyone understands and treats one another with respect. It is like a game where no one wins or loses.

VERBAL SELF-DEFENSE

Usually, conversations don't feel like dances. They feel more like hostile exchanges. It only takes one person employing these techniques, however, to turn these challenges into productive conversations. This requires some degree of self-mastery. Despite knowing all the techniques, it is easy to get baited by an aggressive opponent and lose your balance.

The best way to examine such an attack and response is to illustrate it. So consider the following dialogue between me and a hypothetical reader of this book. For the purposes of our exercise, let's assume the reader doesn't particularly like what he's read.

Reader: "Fred, your book stinks. It's a piece of junk."
Fred: "I'm sad to hear you didn't like it. What didn't you like about it?"
Reader: "I didn't like anything! Not a single page is any good. It is a waste
  of paper. Poor trees, they died for nothing."
Fred: "I see that you think my book is a complete waste. I'm sorry to
  hear that; I was hoping you'd find it useful. Can you tell me what was

missing that would have made it more valuable to you? It'd be very useful for me to know so I can try to improve the next edition."

Reader: "Don't even try. It's a lost cause. There's no way to fix it."

Fred: "You believe that it's impossible to improve?"

Reader: "Really, it's so bad that there's no way to *not* make it better. However, even if you improve it 100 percent, it will still be a waste. The best thing to do would be to take it off the bookshelves and burn every copy. That way you may be able to salvage the little that remains of your reputation."

Fred: "I see that you definitely don't like the book. Fortunately, there are people who have a different opinion. Thank you for your suggestion, but I prefer to risk leaving it as it is and trust that those who find it useful will use it and those who don't will give it to their library."

Reader: "That's such a rip-off. How do you dare ask people to pay for something like this?"

Fred: "I understand that you consider it a rip-off. If I thought it was a rip-off, I'd do as you say, but I don't. I've made an honest effort and I believe it deserves to be evaluated by the reader. Anyway, as it's my book and my skin that are at stake, I'll make what I consider the best decision. I will continue selling the book as is."

In this example, I was able to engage an aggressive partner without losing my balance. At the same time, I didn't get much else out of the exchange. Let's imagine another critic who starts equally aggressively but may be willing to share some constructive criticism.

Reader: "Fred, your book is horrible."

Fred: "I'm sorry to hear you don't like it. What was it you didn't like?"

Reader: "It's bullshit. You have all these pie-in-the-sky statements about how wonderful corporate life could be. That's a pipe dream. Nothing you say makes any sense in the real world."

Fred: "So you consider it inapplicable? Hmmm, that worries me, as I wanted to write something practical, something that would help people work more effectively and make a difference."

Reader: "Well, you failed. It's too boring to be worth anything as science fiction, but it is equally fantastic."

Fred "Can you give me an example?"

Reader: "Sure. Take your idea of responsibility. You keep blaming the victim! How can anyone be responsible for others mistreating them? If my boss yells at me, that is not my fault."

Fred: "Thank you for being so specific. I understand your disagreement, and I see things just the way you do."

Reader: "Then why did you write all that crap about being unconditionally responsible?"

Fred: "I wrote it because I wanted to make a different point than the one you got. Perhaps I need to revise my language since it led you to interpret me as saying something I do not mean to say."

Reader: "So what is your point?"

Fred: "That when your boss yells at you, that is not your fault. And that when your boss yells at you, you've got a choice as to how to respond. You can yell back, swallow your anger, ask some questions as to why he's upset, or do something else. My point is that you are not a robot with preprogrammed responses. You have the ability to respond. That's what I mean by response-ability in the face of a set of circumstances."

Reader: "That's not what you said."

Fred: "I understand that my writing didn't convey that message to you. I appreciate you bringing it up. I'll go back and review the text to see if I can clarify it further. Thanks for the input."

Reader: "Of course, I'm here to help."

It is possible to engage a hostile critic without matching them in kind. Productive advocacy and inquiry not only prevent you from losing your balance; they can also uncover a wealth of information. In the preceding example, I learned that a section of my material was not particularly clear to my critic. If he couldn't follow the argument, it is likely that other people whom I will never meet would have trouble following it as well. By engaging my critic, by seeing beyond his aggressive stance, and instead focusing on the core information he was attempting to convey, I can produce a better book.

◆

How would things change in this chapter's initial dialogue if Sharon used the productive advocacy and inquiry skills?

The first change would be internal. Sharon would abandon her insistence on getting Patricia to stop the change in benefits. She'd see that as an attempt to exert unilateral control. She would not renounce her desire to keep the current benefits policy, but she would aim to share her concerns with Patricia in the interest of helping her make a fully informed decision. She would also inquire about the reasons motivating Patricia, so she could understand the full picture herself.

Let's assume that although Sharon objects to the new benefit plan, she won't quit over the issue. In this new scenario, Sharon has spent some time setting a productive context for this meeting, so pay attention to her thoughts in the left-hand column. As I said above, it is impossible to change what appears in our left-hand column. It is possible, however, to develop an attitude shift when going into a conversation, promoting humility over arrogance. This change modifies the way in which we interpret the world, triggering very different reactions that lead to a very different left-hand column.

What Sharon thought but did not say	What Sharon and Patricia said
I'm glad we are finally meeting. We need to address this before it becomes a serious problem.	**Sharon** Hello, Patricia. I'm glad we have a chance to discuss the changes in the benefits plan. I am concerned about their impact on employee morale.
You have to leave? That's a problem. I need at least twenty minutes to talk about this. Perhaps it would be best to come back later.	**Patricia** Hi, Sharon. We need to hurry because I have to leave soon. Edward (the CEO) wants to see me and he may call any minute. What do you need from me?

What Sharon thought but did not say	What Sharon and Patricia said
I don't want to rush through this discussion. A poorly planned decision could bring about some pretty bad consequences for all of us.	**Sharon** I understand that Edward has priority. In order to help you with this, however, I'd need about twenty minutes of your time. I'd like to understand your goals for the change and alert you about some possible negative consequences I foresee. If this is not a good time, perhaps we could schedule something later.
That would work for me. This conversation is my highest priority.	**Patricia** Actually, I'd appreciate the time to prepare for my meeting with Edward. What if I call you when I finish my meeting with him? I should be done in an hour at most.
I'll be waiting for your call.	**Sharon** That would work for me. I'll be waiting for your call. Thanks.
Oh well, at least you called. I hope we can have our twenty minutes now.	*(An hour and a half later)* **Patricia** Sorry I'm a little late, the meeting ran over.
I don't understand how these changes make sense. The reduction in benefits will probably upset people and hurt employee morale.	**Sharon** No problem. You have asked me to prepare an announcement about changes in the benefits policy. I looked at the proposed changes and realized I don't understand the reason for them. It would help me a lot to understand the logic behind them.
That's a scary thought. I guess there's not much point in high morale if we are not competitive. I don't know if I believe the story of the finance people, but I don't have the information to second-guess them. If this were my company, I wouldn't change the benefits package, but it is not my company. On second thought, if this were my company, perhaps I would change the benefits package just like Edward and Patricia are suggesting.	**Patricia** Healthcare costs are going through the roof, and our pension liabilities are killing us. We can't match our foreign competitors' costs like this. The finance guys have determined that we've got to reduce our overhead to stay viable. If we don't, sooner or later we'll go out of business. I imagine that there will be a backlash when we announce this. Nobody likes to give up benefits that they counted on. That's why I need your help in explaining the situation and minimizing the hit on morale. We need everybody's efforts to stay competitive.

What Sharon thought but did not say	What Sharon and Patricia said
I need to be convinced before I can write something compelling that will be convincing to others. It is difficult to make sense of complicated financial arguments. I'll need some help from you and the people who did the analysis.	**Sharon** I understand now. I don't like it, but I understand it. If you give me a choice between losing my job because the company goes out of business and reducing my benefits, I'll take the latter. I think the rest of the people will feel the same. The key will be to make a strong case that our competitive situation is untenable without these changes.
I can try, but I'll need some help.	**Patricia** Right. We're counting on you to make the case.
I want Brian, but his boss won't give him the time to work with me unless you ask. I need your help in order to get Brian's help.	**Sharon** I think I can do it, but I need some help from the finance people who did the analysis. I need them to explain the situation to me in lay terms so I can explain it to our employees. Can I get you to ask Brian to work with me? He seems to be the most patient of them.
We'll see. Jeff is not famous for his helpful disposition. But I'll leave dealing with him up to you. Just get me Brian.	**Patricia** Absolutely. I'll talk to Jeff tomorrow morning. I'm sure he'll be happy to let Brian work with us. How long do you think you'll need him?
I hope it doesn't take me a full day to understand the analysis. People will only give me five minutes to explain it to them. I hope it's relatively simple to grasp and convey.	**Sharon** It's hard to say at this point. But I'd be very happy if I can work with him for a day, and then have him check my announcement to make sure I am presenting the financial argument correctly.
It looks like the situation is as serious as they say. Edward tends to move slowly.	**Patricia** You got it. I will get you Brian tomorrow. Edward wants to move fast on this and at the last staff meeting he told all of us that this is a top priority.
Well, this conversation went a lot better than I expected …	**Sharon** Thank you, Patricia. I appreciate your help.
So do I.	**Patricia** Thank you, Sharon. I feel much more relieved now than an hour ago. I want to do this as painlessly as we can.

When you and I speak our minds, we may discover that our ideas are not so far apart. Or we may discover that we have a lot of disagreements. That's one of the main reasons why many of us hide our truth. We want to avoid conflicts. No wonder. We view conflicts as negative affairs that hamper effectiveness, strain relationships, and damage people. But we can do better. In the next chapter, we'll take these techniques and apply them to a structured negotiation process.

If you don't know the kind of person I am
and I don't know the kind of person you are
a pattern that others made may prevail in the world
and following the wrong god home we may miss our star.

For there is many a small betrayal in the mind,
a shrug that lets the fragile sequence break
sending with shouts the horrible errors of childhood
storming out to play through the broken dyke.
And as elephants parade holding each elephant's tail,
but if one wanders the circus won't find the park,
I call it cruel and maybe the root of all cruelty
to know what occurs but not recognize the fact.

And so I appeal to a voice, to something shadowy
a remote important region in all who talk:
though we could fool each other, we should consider—
lest the parade of our mutual life get lost in the dark.

For it is important that awake people be awake,
or a breaking line may discourage them back to sleep,
the signals we give—yes or no, or maybe—
should be clear: the darkness around us is deep.

WILLIAM STAFFORD, "A RITUAL TO READ TO EACH OTHER" [16]

CONSCIOUS BUSINESS

CHAPTER 6

Constructive Negotiation

◆

*In the creative dispute, the persons involved are aware
of the other's full legitimacy. Neither loses sight of the fact that
they are seeking ... to express the truth as they see it.
In no way is either person reduced by this.
Such a confrontation, within a healthy atmosphere of
love and genuine relatedness, enables each individual
to maintain a unique sense of self, to grow authentically
through real communication with other persons,
and to realize the worth of simplicity and directness in relationships.*

CLARK MOUSTAKAS[1]

"Love" is the radical respect of the other as a legitimate other.

HUMBERTO MATURANA

◆

Peeople are going to die!" screamed Bruce, the chief vehicle engineer. "I don't give a damn about your fuel economy numbers. This vehicle is already too light. If we take out any more mass, we might as well call them rolling coffins."

Larry, the executive for regulatory affairs, shook his head. "You may not give a damn, but the government does! If our fleet doesn't meet the CAFE standards for gas mileage, there will be hell to pay."

"You're going to have to get your compliance from some other vehicle," said Bruce. "This one is barely crashworthy as it is. Don't bother me any more. Get out of my face!"

"Listen, you jerk, your vehicle is not going into production unless I sign off on it. If you don't make it lighter you might as well kiss its ass good-bye … "

While Larry and Bruce "discuss" what to do about the new launch, their company racks up about ten million dollars in lost revenue and extra costs each day. No wonder tempers are growing short and sparks are flying. Both men are pursuing noble goals. Bruce wants to save lives; Larry wants to comply with the government's emission standards. Yet neither is able to get what he wants without the help of the other. Despite the high stakes, a timely resolution seems impossible.

Conflicts are often messy and unproductive. When we clash in a professional or personal relationship, it is easy to find damage in the three areas we have discussed throughout this book: the impersonal, the interpersonal, and the personal. In regard to the task, a poorly handled conflict threatens our ability to coordinate actions and produce good results. In terms of relationships, unresolved disputes lead to resentment, distrust, and complete breakdown. Finally, a mismanaged conflict can hurt people emotionally, spinning them off into despair, self-doubt, or rage.

It is easy to understand why people assume that conflicts are inherently destructive; however, the energy of conflict is not inherently destructive. The negative consequences that we observe daily stem from our inability to manage conflicts constructively. To live full productive lives we need to learn how to handle conflicts: Avoidance is not an option.

Wherever there is life, there is conflict. Every life form, from the single-cell amoeba to the gigantic blue whale, experiences conflict. Conflict arises wherever there are needs and scarce resources to satisfy them. Plants compete for light and soil; animals compete for food and mates. Human needs extend far beyond food, shelter, and sex. We want power, attention, fame, love, and material wealth. We want a happy family, a big house, a good job, and a corner office. But there are only so many corner offices in any given building. So what do we do? We compete.

We don't have a choice as to whether we face conflicts; we can only choose how to respond to the unavoidable conflicts we experience. Conflicts can fuel grudges and misunderstandings, as in the exchange at the beginning of this chapter, or they can become opportunities to collaborate, deepen relationships, and express integrity. In this chapter, I will examine the nature of conflict and introduce a process of *constructive negotiation*. This technique for resolving disputes not only yields practical solutions to the problems at hand but also addresses the personal and interpersonal concerns of the conflicting parties.

TYPICAL APPROACHES TO CONFLICTS

There are no difficult conflicts. There are only conflicts we don't know how to resolve. As I explained in chapter 2, taking responsibility means recognizing that our inability to deal with a situation is derived not only from the situation itself, but from our skill as well. We call the situation difficult when we don't know how to respond to it. When we say that conflicts are detrimental to task, relationship, and self, we are saying that our approach to them fails on all three counts. Here are some typical approaches to conflict along with their inherent drawbacks.

Denial. Some people find conflicts so threatening that they decide to deny their existence. They try to pretend the conflicts away. Denial implies acting as if everything is all right when it actually is not. A manager in denial, for example, views his staff as a mutually supportive team when in fact destructive power struggles are the norm. This is akin to ignoring the dangers of crossing a cliff-ridden mountain pass. You can set off on the trail with your eyes squeezed shut while you reassure yourself that you are safe, but you shouldn't be surprised if you end up falling into an abyss.

Avoidance. Some people are willing to see conflicts, but they do everything in their power to steer clear of them. In the face of tense situations, they withdraw. An avoiding manager knows his team is consumed by power struggles and responds by never holding staff meetings, so that no one has to face anyone else. Avoiding cliffs may be better than falling off them, but it creates its own problems: Few paths remain eligible, and those that are open often require lengthy detours.

Surrender. When some people discover that their desires conflict with those of others, they give up. This eliminates the overt confrontation, but it never works. The person surrendering does not get her needs met. Sooner or later this causes resignation and resentment, which not only ruin the person's mood but also undermine her relationships and jeopardize the work product. A surrendering manager tries to please everyone by flip-flopping on decisions in order to keep the peace. Surrendering is like camping at the edge of the cliff. You keep meaning to cross the chasm, but instead you keep deciding to pack up and go home.

Domination. Some people try to impose their desired solution at any cost. Initially, this strategy yields positive results on the task level, but it always causes major damage to relationships and it personally hurts those whose needs aren't met. If people are unhappy and relationships suffer, external achievements will be short-lived. Furthermore, this approach often prevents the "winner" from exploring possibilities that could yield an even better result for him. A dominating manager pushes through his proposal to cut spending without asking for input, never learning that one of his employees knows a way to cut costs more effectively. The dominator climbs up and down steep mountains using unnecessarily difficult routes. Companions get dragged along, unsuccessfully trying to tell him that there's a shortcut nearby.

Escalation. In this variation on domination, the person operates behind the scenes. He attempts to impose his will by lobbying an authority figure behind his counterpart's back. This combines all the drawbacks of the domination strategy with a further aggravation: Covert maneuvers encourage power games and destroy organizational integrity. In a private conversation, a sales representative convinces his manager to allocate a new account to him rather than to the colleague who made the initial contact. The escalator lobbies the park ranger to shut down the route she doesn't want to take before her companions have a chance to argue for it.

Majority. This is another variance of domination, but instead of exercising direct authority, the dominator attempts to get his way by coaxing others to vote for what he wants. Instead of lobbying an authority figure, this "soft" dominator lobbies the members of the group to gain a majority. This fosters political games and abuse of minorities. Moreover, there is no reason to believe that quantity equals quality in decision making, especially when personal interests are at play. Many executive teams act like Congress where each member fights for the interests of her area rather than as a unit where everybody shares a vision and acts with solidarity. A majoritarian cajoles his fellow hikers to take the route he likes, promising that he'll buy them dinner if they do so.

(It is crucial to distinguish a simple democracy, which equals pure majority rule, from a republic, which is based on constitutional guarantees — for example, the U.S. Bill of Rights — that protect each individual's rights to life, liberty, and property.)

Majority rule is four wolves and a sheep voting on what's for dinner.

ANONYMOUS

In matters of conscience, the law of the majority has no place.

MAHATMA GANDHI

Compromise. In a compromise, each person ends up with more than what she had, but with less than what she wanted. Everybody loses a little. Meeting halfway may be better than not meeting at all, but it tends to breed mediocrity, not excellence. Furthermore, splitting the difference can be lethal, as the story of King Solomon and the baby with two mothers suggests. Everybody feels unhappy with a mediocre team decision, but everyone accepts it because it incorporates everybody's input. If one traveler wants to cross the cliff using the bridge to the east and her partner wants to cross on the bridge to the west, the worst possible thing is to go straight ahead where there is no bridge.

All these methods are problematic. Their common weakness is that they take the possible solutions as given: Either one party wins imposing his position over the other, or both parties agree to implement some middle-of-the-road alternative. In chapter 5, I called these negotiations "potluck," because everybody brings precooked ideas ready to serve (or cram down others' throats). It is much more effective to bring the ingredients and cook something new together.

This is precisely what happens in *constructive negotiation*. Constructive negotiation allows people to express and understand each other's needs and create new solutions. It addresses the issues through consensual decision-making, the relationships through mutual respect, and each individual's self-worth through the consideration of his needs and values.

Constructive negotiation creates new possibilities. People become more focused on winning *with* the other than *over* the other. They understand that in order to create the most value, they need a working relationship, and that such a relationship can only be founded on respect for every individual's interests. This approach reveals people's preferences and constraints, and engages everyone in constructing solutions that go way beyond the original alternatives. It maximizes efficiency through cooperation. Yet it is the most unusual. Why? Because it requires shifting from unilateral control to mutual learning; it requires going beyond our narcissism.

WHY DO CONFLICTS GO SOUR?

Conflicts generally appear as daunting challenges because people approach them thinking only about ego gratification; they adopt the perspective of the narcissist. The term comes from Greek mythology. A young man named Narcissus spurned many women (and even the nymph Echo) before he found his only true love staring back at him as he looked down into a pool of water. Narcissus fell in love with himself and spent the remainder of his days pining away at the side of the pool.

A narcissist is someone who displays excessive interest in himself, his importance, and his image. Narcissism is a psychological condition characterized by self-preoccupation, lack of empathy, and unconscious deficits in self-esteem. The narcissist craves the feeling of superiority. He constantly compares himself with others, looking for evidence that he is better than everyone else. He overvalues himself and his actions and devalues others and their contributions. For the narcissist, demeaning others is just as worthwhile as inflating his own image.

Consider a classic narcissist: the school bully. A bully demonstrates his self-absorption by tearing everyone else down. He will steal your lunch money or throw dirt on your shirt in an attempt to build his "tough" image. He doesn't care whether he's bragging or beating. His goal is simply to show that he is better than you.

Unfortunately, school bullies don't remain on the playground; they grow up and enter the workplace. You can spot them fairly easily. They are the ones shouting down the people who don't agree with them. They sit in meetings and make long lists of demands. They want more and more of everything; nothing ever seems to be enough. They constantly feel wronged. Like victims, narcissists are both defensive and aggressive. They interpret any message other than accord or flattery as an attack and respond with hot attack or cold withdrawal.

Narcissists have a perverse approach to conflicts. They are more interested in winning over the other than in actually getting what they really want. They would rather hurt their counterpart (who they see as their opponent) than improve their lot. Actually, a narcissist feels that hurting his opponent is *the best way* to improve his lot. It is a cannibalistic ritual: In his mind, diminishing his opponent's self-esteem enhances his own.

This is a consequence of a phenomenon called "identification." If you ask me to talk about myself, I'll probably speak about my work, my family, or my personal history. If you ask me to go deeper, I'll reveal my beliefs, needs, and wants. That is who I think I am. That is why when someone disagrees with my ideas I take it as a disagreement with *me*, rather than with my ideas. The disagreement becomes a personal affront since I am identified with my ideas. I am unable to distinguish the thinker from the thought.

It is necessary to go beyond this kind of identification in order to negotiate constructively. When you relax your identification, you can change your mind without having an identity crisis. In fact, you can develop an even more secure sense of identity by remaining open to change. What if, instead of identifying yourself as the one who has to fire people in order to trim the budget, you tell yourself, "I am the one who has to trim the budget, and I am open to learning and choosing the best course of action, given all the information available"? This shift sets the stage for a constructive negotiation where you may learn of better ways to cut expenses. The key is to loosen your attachment to your surface position and focus on your true interests. This is exactly what the narcissist cannot do.

CONFLICT 101

Conflicts may be hard to resolve, but that doesn't make them mysterious. In fact, conflicts are quite easy to understand. By examining them—looking under the proverbial hood—we can learn a lot about how to transform their power from a destructive force into a productive one.

Let's take a simple conflict and use it to identify its core elements. Two managers in a technology firm are locked in a fierce debate. The woman who manages the help desk wants to hire another phone operator, while the man who manages the sales force wants to hire another salesperson. There's only enough money to hire one person. Who gets hired? The two managers have been arguing with each other about it all week. There are three factors necessary for a conflict.

Disagreement. A disagreement is a difference of opinion. The disagreement here is obvious: The help desk manager and the sales manager disagree about which employee to hire. Notice that if either of them agreed with the other, the disagreement would disappear and so would the conflict.

Scarcity. Some limitation prevents each party from obtaining what each wants independently of the other's actions. Scarcity creates interdependence, which in turn creates conflict. In this case the scarcity involves money. There is only enough money to hire one candidate. If there were enough money to have each of the managers hire his or her preferred candidate, they might disagree about which candidate was better, but they would not have a conflict. Each could hire the employee he or she wanted.

How scarcity is invented in the Kofman home:

Sophie *(entering the kitchen and seeing a cookie on the counter)*: "I call that cookie."

Tomás *(entering beside her)*: "I saw it first."

Sophie: "No, it's mine."

Tomás: "No, it's mine."

Fred *(who wrote a book on conflict resolution and knows that without scarcity there is no possible conflict)*: "Relax, guys, here is a box full of cookies. You can each have one." *(Fred produces a box full of cookies* exactly *the same as the one on the counter.)*

Sophie *(pointing to the cookie on the counter)*: "It's not the same. I want *that* cookie."

Tomás *(equally adamant as he points to the cookie on the counter)*: "No, that is *my* cookie."

Disputed Property Rights. The parties disagree about who has the power to allocate resources, or about what decision-making mechanism will be used in the case of irresolvable differences. Neither manager in the hiring example owns the budget, so neither has the authority to make a decision. If both managers report to a single person who has final say over hiring decisions, then they could bring the issue (together) to their superior.

When property rights are clear, differences in opinions and scarcity need not lead to conflict; they may even lead to cooperation. In the case of my children, if one of them claims (truthfully), "That cookie was my dessert; I saved it for later," the other will accept the claim and promptly change his tone and plead, "Can I have a bite?"

On a larger scale, disagreements, scarcity, and clear property rights are the foundations of free markets. Let's say I have a thousand shares of a publicly traded company and you have a thousand dollars. There's no dispute about property rights here. We agree to an exchange where you will give me your thousand dollars and I will give you my shares. Each of us has a different opinion about the value of the shares. I think they are worth less than a dollar each; you think they are worth more than a dollar each. Both of us recognize the scarcity of the situation; we each would like to have both the money and the shares. In this case, the first two elements of conflict—disagreement and scarcity—simply create an opportunity for us to trade.

If any of the three elements disappears, so does the conflict. We will use this insight to develop a conflict resolution process.

PERSONAL CONFLICTS

Consider a typical tussle between my kids.

"Lemon is the best ice-cream flavor," argues Rebecca.

"No, chocolate is better," replies Paloma.

"You're wrong," insists Rebecca. "Lemon tastes better than chocolate."

"No, you're wrong," counters Paloma. "Chocolate tastes better than lemon."

Every parent knows that there's something wrong with this endless argument. Why are these kids fighting? Nothing material is at stake. This is just a matter of personal preferences. Why can't they just respect their different opinions? They can't because they have set up the situation so that one needs to win and the other needs to lose. The word "best" creates the illusion of scarcity. Only one of the flavors can be the best, so only one of the kids can be right. This is an example of what I call a *personal conflict*.

It is not just kids who fight about preferences. During my youth in Argentina, I saw many arguments between fans of opposing soccer teams end in violence.

"River Plate is the best!"

"No, Boca Juniors is better, River Plate sucks!"

"Don't talk like that about River Plate!"

"I'll talk about River Plate any way I want!"

"Over my dead body!"

Similarly, nothing material is at stake when someone burns an American flag, but that may not stop some people from attacking the flag-burner. Clearly, people take debates that lack material consequences quite seriously. But what is really at stake? Usually we are protecting some cherished belief with which we identify ourselves. The ultimate issue under discussion is one of identity and self-esteem: who's right and who's wrong, who's smart and who's stupid, who's righteous and who's not.

As we learned in chapter 4, we all experience the world through our own mental models. We have different tastes, different personal histories, different cultural backgrounds, and so on. Of course, we have different opinions. The problem is that we take our opinions to be more than simply our view of the world; we think of them as an accurate description of the world. Furthermore, we identify with our opinions and hold them as if they were essential parts of ourselves. We get very attached to our *thoughts*, rather than considering ourselves the free *thinkers* of such thoughts. A challenge to our opinions becomes a personal affront, an insult that calls into question our worth. Of course, we jump into the fray to defend ourselves.

It doesn't have to be that way. When opinions don't affect anything beyond personal preferences, the reasonable way to proceed is to acknowledge and respect each person's right to think what they think. We need to recognize that each individual enjoys property rights over his or her opinions. The only way to solve a personal conflict is to "dissolve" it, demonstrating that there is no scarcity of "rightness" and "self-worth." Your high self-esteem does not detract from mine, and vice versa. Each party is entitled to his opinion, and nobody has the right to claim ownership of the truth. Thus, we can agree to disagree and be at peace.

As soon as the question of "which ice cream flavor *is* best" turns into "which one *I like* best," the scarcity disappears and there is enough room for each person to have his or her preference without impinging on or being impinged on by the other. Thus, the conflict dissolves as soon as one says, "I like lemon better than chocolate," and the other replies, "and I like chocolate better than lemon."

Even if one of the parties wants to impose his view on the other, the second one can assert her right to have whatever preferences she has without engaging in a fight. If the first party attacks with, "I can't believe you're so stubborn! Don't you see that lemon is better than chocolate?" the second can respond, "I understand that you like lemon better, and I have a different taste. I like chocolate better than lemon."

Unfortunately, things don't work out so easily when the dispute concerns religious, moral, or political issues, especially when we are in relationship to each other and we need to adopt a common set of values. If we want to stay together, we cannot just agree to disagree and go our separate ways. Relationship means precisely that we *do not* go our separate ways. We need to find some common ground to resolve our interpersonal conflicts.

In 2001, the National Center for Health Statistics reported that 20 percent of all first marriages ended within five years, 33 percent within ten years, and 50 percent after twenty years. The era of once-in-a-lifetime, stable marriage appears to be over.

The outcome is even worse for second marriages. Two-thirds of all second marriages ultimately end in divorce and second marriages end faster than first marriages. In truth, long-term marital relationships are probably in even worse shape than these straightforward divorce statistics suggest, since many married couples separate but never legally divorce. There are also marriages that are "emotionally terminated." In these "dead" marriages, spouses continue to live together but are emotionally estranged. Some of these couples openly agree to stay together for the sake of the children, for economic reasons, or even for the sake of appearances, while maintaining their own separate lives. Other couples live this way without overt agreements but with similar unspoken provisions, often with one or the other partner having an extramarital affair.

JOHN W. JACOBS[2]

INTERPERSONAL CONFLICTS

Business relationships are as demanding as personal ones. The essential challenge of professional relationships is that while you are discovering and learning how to live with the differences between you and your boss, colleagues, employees, suppliers, customers, and others, you must simultaneously get your job done. You must cooperate and achieve concrete results in the face of environmental and interpersonal obstacles. You must collaborate with people who espouse radically different lifestyles. For most of us, this is very hard to do.

Today's global economy requires us to work with people of diverse genders, races, religions, cultures, generations, sexual orientations, and educational levels. The need to be in close relationship with such diversity creates fertile soil for interpersonal conflicts. It is not enough for people to tolerate differences and stay out of each other's way. Organizations demand that leaders foster an inclusive environment in which all employees feel respected, respect each other, and cooperate. The need to work with people who hold different values and attitudes can produce great stress. There are many dilemmas and paradoxes that demand profound sensitivity, wisdom, and skill. For example, consider my diversity and inclusion work with an oil company: How can you simultaneously include and respect the beliefs of fundamentalist Christians and homosexuals? How can you ask the former to respect the latter without disrespecting their own religious beliefs? At the same time, the corporation is clear in its commitment to include both groups in its workforce.

Relationship conflicts are murky because they challenge individuals' deeply held beliefs. As opposed to purely personal conflicts, there is no easy way out. If we want to stay together, we cannot just agree to disagree about fundamental values and behaviors. We need to establish shared standards that allow us to work together in harmony. This can be tremendously enriching, but it is also extremely difficult. Unfortunately, many of us settle for pseudo-harmony rather than face the hard work of creating the real thing. The desire to keep the (semblance of) peace often leads us to avoid conflict, sweeping our differences under the carpet. Unaddressed, these disagreements turn into contempt, resentment, and mistrust.

A relationship lives or dies based on the ability of the partners to negotiate significant differences. Peripheral disagreements such as me being vegetarian and my business partner eating meat have no consequence. But if essential disagreements abide, the relationship won't. If I expect my partner to give priority to the business but he takes off to attend his children's school plays, or if my partner expects me to be available but I disconnect for a silent meditation retreat, we have a problem. We had better talk about our mismatched expectations or we'll soon kill the relationship. This is not so much a matter of who is right, but of how to live with each other. School plays or meditation retreats are not objectively more or less important than business demands, but neither are they merely a matter of personal preference. To stay together we need to define mutually acceptable standards of behavior.

In the previous chapter I explained how to communicate authentically. Those principles are essential in addressing relationship issues. Let's take an example from one of my clients. Ian, a senior partner in a consulting company, found himself repeatedly butting heads with Esther, one of his colleagues. Whatever one said, the other would immediately counter, continuing a vicious cycle of resentment and grief. Marcus, the office head, asked me to help the two contenders improve their relationship. I knew that without Ian and Esther's commitment my help could not make a difference, so I checked with them. Both Ian and Esther told me that they really wanted to stop the antagonism. They knew they needed to work together, and that their feud was not only making them personally miserable—it was seriously hurting their firm.

I told them that we needed to start with an authentic conversation in which each one expressed what was bothering him or her, and then both negotiated some clear and mutually satisfying agreements. In a hopeless tone they told me that they had tried that already, but had gotten into a fight and couldn't resolve anything. In fact, they had only made things worse. I replied that their failure indicated to me that they didn't know how to handle "hot" topics safely. I offered myself as a "translator," so that each of them could talk only to me, and then I would refine the message before conveying it to the other. If either party thought that I had twisted the original meaning of the message, he or she could stop me and restate it. Here is an approximate account of the beginning of that conversation:

Esther (to Fred): "I can't work with you when you undermine me all the time."

Fred (translating Esther's message to Ian): "Ian, I would like to work with you more effectively, but some things you do make that difficult for me. I would like to explain to you why I find some of your behaviors undermining, and understand your perspective on the situation."

Ian (to Fred): "I don't mean to undermine you. You are too sensitive."

Fred (translating Ian's message to Esther): "I am sorry you find my behavior undermining. I appreciate how that would make it really hard for you to work with me. You are not the first person to tell me that I am not very supportive, so I can relate to what you say. Let me assure you that undermining you is the last thing I want to do. You are my partner and an essential member of our firm. I realize, however, that in stressful situations I tend to act unconsciously and can undermine others. Could you give me an example of my undermining behavior?"

Esther *(to Fred)*: "Lots! Take, for example, the meeting with our prospective client last Friday. When the client questioned the price of the project, I tried to hold the line on our fees, but before I had a chance to state our position you jumped in and offered a discount. What the hell were you thinking? You made me look unreasonably tough, while you looked like the flexible, friendly guy."

Fred *(to Ian)*: "I hear that you don't mean to undermine me, and perhaps I am too sensitive. It really affects me when I fear that my partners are not supporting me. If I understood the reasoning behind your behavior, I think I could get over some of my sensitivity. Would you help me with this? Take for example our meeting with the prospective client last Friday. My recollection is that when I was negotiating our fees, you jumped in and offered a discount. I found your interruption undermining—although I believe that that was not your intention. If you agree that that's what happened, could you tell me what led you to do it?"

Ian *(to Fred)*: "I wasn't tying to undermine you. You were about to lose the deal! The client was clearly frustrated with the price of the project, and you were only making it worse by being inflexible. Even with the discount we stand to make lots of money."

Fred *(to Esther)*: "I can see how my jumping in was problematic. I cut you off and took the role of the 'good cop,' leaving you as the bad one. Besides, I see that you were trying to uphold the fee structure that the partners agreed to. I guess I acted hastily, shaking the ground beneath your feet. I see that now. At the moment, I was blinded by my anxiety. I was terribly worried we'd lose the account. My intuition told me that the client was getting upset, and we would soon be invited to leave. I just wanted to ease the tension and make sure we got the project. Even with the discount I offered, this would be quite a profitable engagement. I am not justifying myself. As I said, I think I acted with haste. I am just trying to explain my reasoning so you understand where I was coming from."

After a long discussion, Ian and Esther found that they both had understandable reasons to act in the ways each of them did. With my help, they agreed to a set of ground rules. They also realized that the skills I had presented to them in a previous seminar were not as easy to apply as they thought. "This stuff is good, but we already do it," the partners of the firm kept saying. In the next partners' meeting, Esther and Ian both reported, "This stuff is simple, but really difficult to practice. Let's not delude ourselves. *We do not already do it.*"

OPERATIONAL CONFLICTS

Not all conflicts can be resolved in the emotional domain. If two managers can hire only one candidate and disagree on the best choice, this is no mere difference of opinion. The conflict cannot be addressed by improving the relationship. They cannot simply agree to disagree and feel connected to each other. The two managers need to reach an operational decision with real-world consequences: which candidate will get hired for the job. If each manager had his own budget, each could make his own decision, but here, that is not the case. They need to work together to make the hire—and yet they disagree. I call this an *operational conflict.*

An operational conflict involves a decision that will affect what resources get allocated to each party. The ultimate issue under discussion is who gets what. In operational conflicts, there is a concrete decision to be made which will have objective consequences.

The best way to address an operational conflict is through consensus. In order to work toward a consensus, each party must be granted veto power in the decision process at the outset; a decision is not reached until everybody—not a simple majority, or all but one person, but everybody—accepts it and commits to implement it.

Consensus doesn't mean that everyone believes that the decision is the best. Consensus means that everybody can live with the decision. Consider one of the most common methods of consensus decision-making in democracies: the election. Every four years voters choose a president. People disagree strongly about who the president should be. Quite often, roughly half the electors want one candidate while roughly half want the other. How can this be an example of consensus? The key is that all voters in the United States agree that whoever wins more Electoral College votes will become president. Everybody agrees that whoever wins the election should be the president of all citizens. Not just of the ones who voted for the winning candidate, but also all the others who voted for someone else or didn't vote. This is called *process consensus*.

We see a lot of process consensus in the business world. Imagine a manager and an employee who are trying to figure out how to ship product to customers. The employee wants to use a first-in-first-out process to queue customer orders, while the manager wants to ship to the largest customers first. The two talk out the issue for a while but cannot agree. Most of us would not be surprised to learn that the largest customers got their deliveries first. That's because both parties (like voters) may have a say in the argument, but they both agree that the manager makes the final call (just as the Electoral College elects the president).

Authority-based consensus—in which both of us agree that you have ultimate decision rights—is a delicate matter. Unless the senior person knows how to wield this power wisely, decisions will get made but the *process* will not encourage collaboration and creativity. How much is the employee really going to advocate his perspective when he knows his efforts are almost certainly in vain? What if the employee's suggestion was better than the boss's? Authority, as a primary form of decision-making, tends to weaken interpersonal relationships and erode effectiveness. To counter this, constructive negotiation creates an environment in which the employee can be encouraged to contribute his information, while the manager maintains the power to make decisions if consensus cannot be reached in a reasonable amount of time.

Not all conflicts occur between people; some occur within a single person. We call this type of conflict a *dilemma*. We normally express a dilemma by saying: "On the one hand, I'd like to do this. On the other hand, it seems better to do that." No one else is around, yet our own internal contradictions threaten to mire us in confusion and inaction.

These conflicts are *intra*-personal rather than *inter*-personal. Instead of being different people, the parties involved in this type of conflict are a single individual's concerns. Let's say you're offered a promotion that requires a move to Asia. One part of you—the part driven by professional success—is enthusiastic and wants to accept it; another part—the one that cherishes personal and familial stability—is worried and wants to reject it. You are only one person, but you are torn by opposing internal drives.

It's possible to work out dilemmas exactly as if they were interpersonal conflicts. It's necessary to give each part its own voice. The person experiencing a dilemma can adopt the voice of each part, present its arguments, inquire into the other part's argument, and engage in a dialogue. Once all the parts have had their say, it's possible to uncover deeper interests and search for a solution that serves every part. With this slight modification, all the material in this chapter becomes directly applicable to dilemmas.

START TAKING IT PERSONALLY

As the example of the bickering soccer fans reminds us, it is possible to have personal and interpersonal conflicts without having an operational conflict. But it is impossible to have an operational conflict without having personal and interpersonal conflicts. The debate between two managers about who to hire has obvious material consequences, but it also has personal and interpersonal aspects. Each manager is invested in his position; each feels his reputation and self-esteem are at stake. Each wants to be heard and respected by the other. If the managers address the operational aspect of the conflict but disregard the personal and interpersonal aspects, they run the risk of losing trust and resenting each other. Every operational conflict has personal and interpersonal aspects, which is precisely why these must be addressed at the outset.

What follows is a step-by-step guide to take you through a personal or interpersonal conflict. I have found that a structured methodology can do wonders to help people adopt new practices for conflict resolution. This methodology restrains the drive toward fight or flight and opens possibilities for cooperation. It helps people steer clear of denial, avoidance, surrender, domination, majority, escalation, or compromise, and adopt a constructive approach.

Imagine that you and your colleague are arguing over where to invest your capital budget. You want to buy new desktop computers and your colleague wants to upgrade the telecommunications hardware. You go back and forth on this issue for quite some time. Now, having read this book, you decide you want to approach this conflict using constructive negotiation. You first realize that you and your colleague have a material issue at stake: how to spend your budget. You know now that you can't address that issue constructively without addressing the personal and interpersonal components first. So you follow the steps below. As I describe them, assume that you are person "B."

- **Individual Preparation.** Before talking to your colleague, take some time to explore your position and clarify what your real needs and desires are. As you do this, reaffirm your commitment to consensus decision making and mutual learning. It is critical that you set up the conversation as an exchange where everybody has the right to speak and be heard. If you engage in a battle to overpower your colleague, the results will be poor. It is also critical to find a time and space that are conducive to the conversation. Engaging a conflict under the wrong circumstances can exacerbate emotions and conspire against resolution. As we saw in chapter 5, even the right conversation—or the right negotiation—in the wrong context is the wrong conversation.
- **Establish your Best Alternative To a Negotiated Agreement, your BATNA.** Your BATNA is your worst-case scenario for a negotiation. It is the independent outcome you can guarantee for yourself if no

interdependent solution works for all parties. For example, if you are negotiating with a potential customer, your BATNA is to keep your product. If you are negotiating with a potential employer, your BATNA is to not take the job. The BATNA is also called the walk-away point. If none of the solutions that are acceptable to the other party offer you a value above your BATNA, the best thing to do is to walk away from the deal.

If you and your colleague can't agree on how to allocate your budget, what will you do? Your negotiation will be very different if you lose your entire budget than if it is split in half and each of you can decide what to do with your part. By discovering your BATNA, you clarify the lower boundary of your negotiation space. It gives you confidence because it lets you know what value you can guarantee for yourself even in the no-agreement scenario. One of the most useful things you can do in preparing to negotiate is to take action to improve your BATNA. For example, negotiating the sale of my house when my alternative is to be foreclosed by the bank and lose my down payment is very different from when I have an offer from a potential buyer that guarantees that I will get a price above my original investment. Your BATNA is not a given. You can work to improve it. For example, before you apply for a job at a particular company, you can acquire skills that make you more appealing to other employers. If the market salary of an unskilled worker is twenty dollars an hour, and the one of a skilled worker is thirty, you can raise your "minimum wage" from the former to the latter through your educational investment. There is nothing more self-empowering than doing one's homework and entering a negotiation with a high BATNA.

A wise man lived poorly.

"You must not be so wise," a neighbor challenged him. "If you bowed to the king, you wouldn't need to live with so little."

"And if you lived with little," the wise man responded, "You wouldn't need to bow to the king."

In day-to-day negotiations, this preparation stage is usually overlooked by most people. We rush in and trample over others, discussing issues in public that would be better dealt with in private, making bold claims that only inflame the conversation, and accepting deals that yield outcomes below our BATNA. Professional negotiators take at least ten hours of preparation per hour of conversation. Even if you can only spend ten minutes preparing, it is always better to take a few breaths and find your center before jumping into the fray.

- **Process Clarification.** At the beginning of the conversation, present the situation from the perspective of "the third story" that honors both positions (described in the previous chapter). Explain to your colleague your intention to resolve the conflict constructively and ask her if she is willing to use the structured process presented here. (If she does not want to follow the process, you can still use the principles, but it will be more demanding.) Sketch the following steps, with the reasoning behind them, and invite your counterpart to follow them for the sake of the task, the relationship, and the well-being of both of you.

- **A expresses, B listens.** Person A presents her position while you (B) listen without interrupting. I described the best format for this in the last chapter's section on productive expression. Ideally, A will be familiar with the format; if not, you can assist her through productive inquiry. Let A present her point of view, reasoning, desires, and recommendations for action. Keep quiet during this time. It's very important to provide A with the space to express her views without interruptions. In most negotiations, participants continually interrupt each other. This kind of behavior prevents them from fully understanding each other, a fact that not only hinders the conversation but also demonstrates lack of respect.

- **B clarifies.** Ask clarifying questions. Inquire about A's position and fill in any information you may need to fully understand it. The key here is to not slip into narcissistic questions like, "Don't you think it's wrong to … ?" or, "Why would you want to do something so absurd?" The questions in this step should help A express her position in the clearest possible way. Remember that the goal is to understand, show respect, and satisfy A's legitimate desire to feel heard.

- **B summarizes A.** Once you believe you've understood A's position, summarize it. The summary has four goals: a) acknowledge A as a human being worthy of respect; b) verify that what you understood is what A wanted to convey; c) indicate to A that you've listened carefully; and d) show A that you're interested in ensuring that your understanding is correct.

- **A approves B's summary.** A evaluates whether your understanding is congruent with what she intended to communicate. It is not enough to summarize what you heard; it is necessary to give A the chance to accept or reject your summary. If A is not satisfied with it, she can correct it, changing or adding whatever she thinks is necessary. After A's comments, you present your new summary for her consideration. And so on, until A is satisfied with your understanding.

- **A and B reverse roles.** Repeat the preceding four steps with the roles reversed. If A doesn't follow the process, you can remind her (gently, without self-righteousness) of her initial agreement and commitment to listen without interruptions, ask only clarifying questions, and verify her understanding with a summary until you are satisfied that she "got" what you are trying to say.

- **Dialogue.** Once each party is satisfied with the other's summary and feels understood, open the conversation to a spontaneous exchange of questions and answers for an agreed-upon amount of time. The tone of this dialogue should be one of mutual learning, not unilateral control; the objective is to compare opinions and find the root of the differences. *This is not a time to resolve anything.* The focus is on reaching a deeper mutual understanding.

- **Do we need to agree?** Consider whether there are practical consequences that arise from the conversation. If the conflict has no material consequences, you have an exclusively personal conflict and you can end the conversation with an agreement to disagree. If the conflict has operational implications, you will need to continue with the steps I describe later under "Operational Consensus."

At this point, several important goals have been achieved. Everybody has had a chance to express his or her views. Everybody has had a chance to listen to and understand the other's views, and reflect this understanding as a sign of respect and as confirmation. Everyone feels respected and respectful, and recognized as a human being worthy of consideration. This is the right context in which to address operational issues.

Nothing in the world
is as soft and yielding as water.
Yet for dissolving the hard and inflexible,
nothing can surpass it.
The soft overcomes the hard;
the gentle overcomes the rigid.
Everyone knows this is true,
but few can put it into practice.

LAO TZU, *TAO TE CHING*

WHAT DO YOU REALLY WANT?

At this point, you have taken care of the personal and interpersonal aspects of the conflict. If you need to continue with the negotiation, it is because something material is at stake. Now comes the time to introduce perhaps the most crucial tool of this chapter. It is a question that holds the key to resolving most operational conflicts constructively, a question that you can ask again and again to create a chain from means to ends.

When we discover that we have significant differences, we often infer that we have very little in common. This misconception plays a big part in the conflict, leading us to view negotiations as confrontations. The truth is that behind every conflict is a large space of collaboration. If the parties did not have common interests they wouldn't even be talking to each other. No matter how much we might feel at odds, we need each other to take care of our concerns. For example, during trench warfare in World War I, enemy soldiers stationed across from each other for long periods of time developed protocols to minimize the damage they inflicted on each other. Discovering how we can offer the other what she really wants without giving up what we really want is the basis for resolving operational conflict.

To do this, it is necessary to distinguish between positions and interests. A *position* is an explicit demand that each speaker brings to the negotiation. An *interest* is the desire or need lying at the root of the position. We need to go beyond our incompatible positions (I want to buy new desktops, you want to buy telecommunications equipment) to discover our more compatible deeper interests (we both want to maximize the company's profits).

Think of something you want right now. Let's say it's a glass of water. If I ask you, "Why do you want a glass of water?" you might say, "To quench my thirst." So you don't *really* want a glass of water; what you really want is to quench your thirst. The water is a means towards quenching your thirst. In fact, quenching your thirst is probably a means to a further end, perhaps "feeling satisfied."

Again, a *position* is an explicit demand that each speaker brings to the negotiation. In our example, you want to buy new desktop computers and your colleague wants to buy new telecommunications hardware. An *interest* is the desire or need lying at the root of the position. You want the new computers in order to run new software at the workstations, whereas your colleague wants the telecommunications hardware in order to allow sales people to have wireless access to the company's databases.

To uncover the interest beneath a position, I recommend asking a key question: *"What would you get through X that is even more important to you than X itself?"* For example, you might ask your colleague, "What would you get through the new telecommunications hardware that is even more important to you than the hardware itself?" Or in a shorter form, *"Why is X important to you?"*

Your colleague's answer expresses the interest beneath her original position: to offer sales people wireless access. But that interest is a position, too. You can dig deeper. You might ask again, "What would you get by offering our sales people wireless access?" She might answer, "I could enable them to check our inventory and make firm delivery commitments to customers in real time." Offering wireless access to sales people is very different than offering broadband access to the web for local users, although new tele-communications hardware could be devoted to either objective. Once you understand your colleague's chain of reasoning, you may change your mind and agree that real-time inventory information for sales people is more impor-tant than improved capabilities for local workstations. Or perhaps there are other ways to provide this information that don't require spending the entire budget on telecommunications upgrades. By asking a simple question, you have created space and flexibility in a decision-making process where none previously existed. This is the key to win-win negotiations.

How deep can you go in analyzing interests? There are generally two stages. The first three or four times you ask, "Why is X important to you?" the answers will refer to external needs. If Joe wants a raise, he might tell you that he wants to save money to send his children to a good college. He wants his children to go to a good college so they can have the tools necessary to succeed. Joe wants that so that his children will thrive and be happy. If you keep asking the ques-tions, Joe's answers will increasingly reflect internal needs. If Joe's children are happy, he will feel happy and at peace, having fulfilled his responsibility to his children. As we discussed in chapter 3, human beings have a short list of essen-tial common interests: peace, happiness, truth, love, freedom, and fullness.

Joe may walk into a negotiation asking for a raise. His boss may start out believing that he wants more money, but through skillful inquiry he would real-ize that what he really wants is the peace of knowing that his children's college education is taken care of. Joe believes that a pay raise is a good means to achieve that end—and he may be right—but that is not the *only* means to that end. Perhaps his company can address his concern in another way, such as tuition support or scholarships—which may be worth much more than a raise to Joe.

OPERATIONAL CONSENSUS

Let's translate that same lesson into our step-by-step process. At this point, remember, we've explored our personal conflict and discovered that we have operational disagreements. What do we do then to achieve consensus?

- **Find the underlying interests.** Here's where we use the question to uncover the interests underlying the positions. Each party asks the other, "What would you attain through X that is even more important to you than X itself?"
- **Brainstorm.** Once you discover the underlying interests, you try to develop new options. The key to brainstorming is that every proposal is valid. No criticizing, evaluating, or debating is allowed. The goal is to make the longest possible list of alternatives. Even the "craziest" options can be useful. Sometimes, it's precisely those "out in left field" options that can be modified to achieve a consensus solution.

  Imagine a husband who wants to go on a ski vacation negotiating constructively with his wife who wants to go to the beach. "What do you like about the beach?" he asks. "Being able to relax, the warmth of the sun, and the water," she answers, and asks, "What do you like about skiing?" "Exercising in a natural environment, the feeling of adventure and speed," he answers. All sorts of ideas come up while they're brainstorming: windsurfing, water skiing, sailing, surfing, snorkeling, white water rafting, kayaking, scuba diving, hiking, tour biking, mountain biking, rock climbing, a ski resort with hot springs, skiing on sand dunes or grass, roller-skating, etc.
- **Negotiate and Select.** After creating a list of options, the parties can discuss the relative attractiveness of each. New options might appear during this dialogue. This process of selecting and negotiating leads to two possible conclusions: achieving outcome consensus (agreeing about what to do), or not.
- **Outcome Consensus.** After pursing the previous steps, many parties will find shared solutions. Having explored their underlying interests fully, perhaps the couple will decide to go to a mountain lake for windsurfing. This provides the husband with the chance to exercise in nature while she gets to relax by the water in the sun. If the parties can reach an outcome consensus, the conversation proceeds to "commitment to implement," described later in this chapter.
- **Process Consensus.** If the previous step yields no material consensus,

then the parties can implement an agreed-upon decision-making process. The goal of the conversation is to not have to use this mechanism, but if outcome consensus seems beyond reach, this strategy will bring about a resolution. Examples of such mechanisms are authority, majority vote, arbitration, etc. In hierarchical organizations, the regular mechanism for resolving conflict is authority. The "owner" of the decision space can choose what to do. This is a reasonable option as long as the manager in authority remembers that the goal is to use this mechanism only in extreme cases, and *after going through all the previous steps.*

Before exercising his authority the manager could say, "We have explained to each other how we see the situation and what we think would be the best way to address it, and we have checked that we all understand each other. We have explored our needs and concerns and tried to reach a solution that we can all agree on. Unfortunately, this issue is difficult and ambiguous enough that intelligent, well-intended people like us cannot resolve it unanimously. Does everybody agree?" And if people agree, the manager would continue, "In that case, I'd like to ask for your support in allowing me to make a decision. I'm ultimately accountable for this decision, and although I cannot be sure that I'm right—people have made excellent arguments for different solutions—I believe that this is the best course of action under the circumstances. Can I have your commitment to implement it? I promise you that after we try this strategy for a while we will reconvene and evaluate how it is working. If we have misgivings, we will re-open the discussion."

One hears a great deal today about "the end of hierarchy." This is blatant nonsense. In any institution there has to be a final authority, that is, a "boss"—someone who can make the final decisions and who can expect them to be obeyed. In a situation of common peril—and every institution is likely to encounter it sooner or later—survival of all depends on clear command. If the ship goes down, the captain does not call a meeting, the captain gives

CONSCIOUS BUSINESS

an order. And if the ship is to be saved, everyone must obey the order, must know exactly where to go and what to do, and do it without "participation" or argument. "Hierarchy," and the unquestioning acceptance of it by everyone in the organization, is the only hope in a crisis ... It is a sound principle that one person in an organization should have only one "master."

PETER DRUCKER[3]

- **Avoiding the End Run.** Just as courts don't accept testimonies from undisclosed accusers or evidence obtained without a warrant, managers shouldn't accept unilateral attempts to escalate conflicts. To avoid these spurious attempts, it's necessary to establish certain principles and behaviors. The ground rules I suggest are the following:

  Information is free; everybody can speak to anybody about any issue they find relevant.

  If two people have an operational conflict they must first try to solve it themselves using the process described in this chapter.

  If they can't reach an agreement, they must bring the problem to the attention of their manager (or managers) *together.*

  If one of the parties refuses to take the problem jointly to their manager, the other must inform the first that he'll do it alone and invite the reluctant party, once again, to escalate the matter together.

  If the former continues to refuse, the latter can then unilaterally take the problem to a superior.

In order for this mechanism to work, the manager must refuse to listen to any argument brought to her by a subordinate unilaterally unless she obtains an affirmative answer to the following questions:

1 "Have you and your colleague tried to resolve this problem using constructive negotiation?" (If the answer is no, say "Go and try that first." If it is yes, ask the next question.)

2 "Have you invited your colleague to be here to jointly escalate the problem with you?" (If the answer is no, say "Go invite him first." If yes, ask the next question.)

3 "Have you told your colleague that if he didn't come with you, you would bring the problem to me alone?" (If the answer is no, say "Then go and tell him first." If it's yes, listen to the employee's situation, or call the colleague to attend the discussion.)

Some managers go to the opposite extreme, considering that any escalation attempt is the consequence of a failure of their subordinates to do their jobs. "Upward delegation" is a scornful term they apply to any requests for help in mediating and arbitrating an issue that lower-level managers cannot resolve. Although it is possible for lower-level managers to shirk their responsibility and attempt to transfer it to their bosses, it is an incorrect generalization to think that all escalations are examples of incompetence. And if the topic under discussion has global implications, it is essential that the counterparts involve a senior manager in the discussion.

- **Pursue BATNAs.** If disagreements remain intractable, every person should pursue his or her BATNA independently. Some people think that not reaching a consensus is a bad outcome. This is wrong. Often the best possible outcome, the one that adds more value to all parties while respecting everybody's property rights, is to not agree. Suppose that I am selling computers that cost me $1,000 to produce. And suppose that you place a value of $900 on a computer like the ones I sell. It wouldn't make sense for you to pay any more than $900 for my computer. It wouldn't make sense for me to sell you my computer for any less than $1,000. The best possible outcome is to not make the transaction, for you to respectfully walk away with your $900, and for me to respectfully keep my computer. It is very important to understand that it is possible to say "no" to the transaction while saying "yes" to the other person and the relationship.
- **Commit to implement.** Whatever decision participants have reached,

they now make the necessary commitments to implement it. The next chapter is devoted to investigating how to develop impeccable commitments and coordination.

- **Evaluate and learn.** Once the negotiation is over, it is useful to evaluate together the reasons for the conflict, the level of satisfaction with the process, and whether everybody feels at peace with the outcome. This assessment can clear up any emotional residue and improve both the relationships and the prospects for future collaboration. Some useful questions are:

  What can we learn from this conflict?

  How could we minimize the chances of having a similar conflict again?

  How did we behave during the negotiation?

  What could we have done (and what could we do in the future) to improve?

  How are our emotions? Is there something we need to clear?

  How is our relationship? Is there something we need to clear?

- **Celebrate.** Take a minute to celebrate. You have done a great job of working together, solving the problem, strengthening the relationship, and improving everybody's sense of well-being. That deserves acknowledgment!

◆

To tell whether constructive negotiations are working, look for these signs:

- **Flexibility.** One of the most visible results of implementing constructive negotiation is more relaxed and fluid interaction. When people get a chance to share their perspectives and are taken seriously, they become less emotionally attached to "being right" and holding on to their original positions; parties are able to talk more reasonably and productively about their real needs.

- **New solutions.** This method promotes digging beneath entrenched positions to discover deeper interests. When the method is applied, people discover new information that reshapes their positions. Through the process of inquiry and expression, new solutions to problems emerge that no individual could have foreseen. People truly cook new dishes together, bringing their ingredients into the kitchen, instead of eating "potluck" style where all the dishes are precooked!

- **Competitive advantage.** When people show respect for each other and produce better solutions, they also develop more confidence in their ability to work together. In a business world ruled by power struggles and dominating personalities, organizations capable of resolving conflicts constructively have a significant and sustainable source of competitive advantage.

BRUCE AND LARRY RELOADED

Suppose that Bruce and Larry, the managers from the automobile company in the example at the beginning of this chapter, had mastered the practice of constructive negotiation. How would they dialogue about the conflict between safety and pollution control?

Bruce: "Larry, let me hear your thoughts about the new vehicle."

Larry: "Sure. According to the simulation models, the vehicle's fuel economy does not comply with governmental regulations. In order to improve its gas mileage and reduce its emissions, I propose we make it lighter."

Bruce: "Let me make sure I understand your position. You want to improve its mileage because as it is, it doesn't comply with government standards. You think that one good way of doing this is to reduce the weight of the car so it will require less gas. Is that correct?"

Larry: "That's a good summary. I'm ready to hear your perspective."

Bruce: "Okay. I understand that we can't disregard the regulations on pollution control, so we need to do something about the fuel economy of this vehicle. I am concerned, however, that if we reduce its mass we are going to pay a heavy price in safety. In the event of a crash, the less mass, the more likely it is that the occupants will be seriously injured or die. I don't want to make a vehicle that is so dangerous. My suggestion is that we get our average ratio within government standards by finding some other way to improve the performance of the powertrain."

Larry: "Let me summarize. You agree that we need to comply with government regulations, but you think that it's too dangerous to do so by reducing the vehicle's mass. You would like to achieve compliance by improving the efficiency of the powertrain. Did I get it right?"

Bruce: "You did. So what do we do now?"

Larry: "Let's make sure that we understand the concerns behind our positions. What would you get if you kept the vehicle mass as is?"

Bruce: "Safety. I want people to be as safe as we can make them in the event of an accident. What about you, Larry, what would you get if we improved the vehicle's fuel economy?"

Larry: "Compliance, which means the ability to continue our business without astronomical fines and court injunctions."

Bruce: "Sounds good to me. I want that too."

Larry: "Well, safety sounds good to me as well. I want it as much as you do."

Bruce: "Good, we seem to agree that both safety and compliance are desirable. The million-dollar question is whether there is a way that we can make the vehicle compliant without making it less safe. Tell me, Larry, what would it take for us to be compliant? How much do we need to reduce fuel consumption?"

Larry: "Well, it's not that easy. Compliance is assessed not at the level of the individual vehicle, but at the level of the fleet. We get an average mileage for the fleet, and that number needs to be within government standards."

Bruce: "So if some other vehicle became more efficient then we'd be okay leaving this one as it is?"

Larry: "That's theoretically correct, but no vehicle chiefs are banging at my door saying they're ready to improve their fuel economy."

Bruce: "I understand, but at least that would be an option."

Larry: "Yes. Speaking of options, Bruce, are there ways in which we can reduce the fuel consumption that would keep the vehicle equally crashworthy?"

Bruce: "We'd need to improve the engine's efficiency."

Larry: "Any other ways?"

Bruce: "Well, advanced engineering has been testing a new alloy and a 'crumpling' technology that can maintain the toughness of the chassis while reducing the weight by a third. It's very promising, but at this stage it is quite expensive."

Larry: "How expensive?"

Bruce: "My guess is that it would add at least five hundred dollars to the cost of the vehicle."

Larry: "That's a lot less than it would cost to be non-compliant. It's also less than what it would cost us to have a bad safety rating in government tests and *Consumer Reports*—without even considering the human costs in extra injuries and deaths."

Bruce: "Probably, but I don't have the authority to make that call."

Larry: "Who does?"

Bruce: "We'd have to talk to Frank. He might have to check with the leadership board for North American Operations."

Larry: "When could we talk to Frank?"

Bruce: "Let me call his secretary and ask for an hour. He's been breathing down my neck for weeks, so I'm pretty sure he'll see us tomorrow."

Larry: "Great, call me as soon as Frank gives you a time."

Bruce: "I sure will. Thanks a lot. I think we have some good ideas to bring to Frank."

RESOLVING CONFLICTS WITH THE BULLY

It's wonderful to work with colleagues who will engage in the process outlined above, but that will not always be the case. We often have to hash out our problems with the ex-school bullies. In a personal conflict you can always walk away and take the initiative to agree to disagree. In an operational conflict, however, a destructive counterpart can present a serious challenge. The good news is that it only takes one person to prevent a conflict from escalating. The bad news is that it takes two people to create a win-win solution.

The key is demonstrating respect for the other person through active listening. If one party wants to impose her view, the other speaker can respectfully assert his position. If one party insists on attacking the other, he doesn't need to respond in kind. Now we'll look at how to respond to an aggressive comment without either becoming aggressive or ceding ground. Let's see how a skillful Larry would manage a tough Bruce.

Bruce: "People are going to die. I don't give a damn about your fuel economy numbers. This vehicle is already too light. If we take out any more mass, we might as well call them rolling coffins."

Larry: "You're worried that if we lower the mass of the vehicle, its occupants will be more likely to die in a crash …"

Bruce: "Some may not die, but they'll be horribly injured. We've already shaved as much weight as we safely can. This is Powertrain's problem; their damned engine burns too much gas for the power."

Larry: "I see. You also worry that those who survive would suffer severe injuries. The car's safety is very important to you, and I assure you, it's also important to me. You think it would be possible to improve its fuel economy if the engine were more efficient, so why isn't it?"

Bruce: "Don't ask me! Why don't you talk to Harvey, who runs Powertrain? He's the one who needs to get his act together."

Larry: "I *am* talking to Harvey, I'm also talking to you right now, and I'm talking to anybody who can help get the vehicle into production."

Bruce: "Well, don't bother me. I've done as much as I can with this mass-fuel trade-off."

Larry: "You believe that you can't do any more to improve this situation?"

Bruce: "Not without compromising safety."

Larry: "Let me ask you a technical question, Bruce. Are there ways that we could improve safety without increasing mass?"

Bruce: "Of course, there are hundreds, perhaps thousands of variables we could tweak to improve safety."

Larry: "Could we implement some of those safety-enhancing changes and reduce the weight of the vehicle without decreasing its crashworthiness?"

Bruce: "Yes, but they'd make us go over budget. These things cost money. Now if you give me more budget we could do lots of things. In fact, there are other ways to improve the fuel efficiency without even touching the weight. If we make the body more aerodynamic we should get a significant improvement in miles per gallon."

Larry: "Okay, so why can't we try some of these things?"

Bruce: "I've got my budget, and I've used it. With respect to the streamlined body, Chuck, who's in charge of Manufacturing, says that our stamping plants can't shape the metal to our specifications without a major retooling investment. Powertrain is a world of its own. I have no idea what Harvey's doing over there. Why are you bothering me with this issue? People will pay a little more for gas, what's the big deal?"

Larry: "The big deal is not the cost of gas. The big deal is that this vehicle makes us non-compliant with government emission standards. We can't produce it as it is unless we want to bring the wrath of the regulators upon us. I want to see this vehicle out on the streets as much as you do. I also want it to be as safe as we can make it. And if we don't improve its fuel efficiency it will never go into production. The leadership board has been crystal-clear about this: Any new programs need to be compliant."

Bruce: "Well, I don't know what you want from me."

Larry: "I don't want you to reduce the vehicle mass without any offsetting safety improvements. Given the complexity of the trade-offs, what I want is for you to help me organize a meeting with the key managers who can influence the vehicle design. I want us to prepare a set of viable options to make the vehicle compliant and then check with the leadership board to see what they think would be best to do in the situation."

Bruce: "Another meeting! I spend my life in meetings!"

Larry: "Do you have a better idea?"

Bruce: "No."

Larry: "Will you help me then?"

Bruce: "When do you want to meet … ?"

Working constructively in the midst of conflict requires perspective and discipline. My immediate impulse is often to advocate for my position and try to win by getting what I am asking for. Then I remember that what I am asking for is rarely what I really want or need. There is always a deeper interest beneath my position. So if I can maintain discipline and engage in a constructive conversation, I can always discover ways to add value to all parties. This approach not only fosters creative solutions, but also establishes a firm foundation for cooperation in the future. On an even more basic level, constructive negotiation shows people that when they pierce the apparent scarcity of material resources, there is an infinite abundance of possibilities. As individuals trust their resourcefulness, they become less defensive, more creative, and more collaborative.

An old children's riddle asks, "Five frogs are sitting on a log. Four decide to jump down. How many are left on the log?"

If you said, "Five," you are right. Deciding something does not mean doing it. The benefits of constructive negotiation will only accrue to those who carry through with the agreements reached. Unless people apply their energy to fulfilling their commitments, the agreement will fall through. The task will be unfulfilled, the relationships will become strained as people lose trust, and everybody will fall into a reproachful mood. In the next chapter, we will see how impeccable commitments bring constructive negotiation into fruition. We will learn how to build a bridge of integrity to cross the chasm between decision and action.

CHAPTER 7

Impeccable Coordination

◆

Trust is the lubrication that makes it possible for organizations to work.
It's hard to imagine an organization without some semblance of trust
operating somehow, somewhere. An organization without trust is more
than an anomaly, it's a misnomer, a dim creature of Kafka's imagination.
Trust implies accountability, predictability, reliability.
It's what sells products and keeps organizations humming.
Trust is the glue that maintains organizational integrity.

WARREN BENNIS AND BURT NANUS[1]

Economic life ... depends on moral bonds of social trust.
This is the unspoken, unwritten bond between fellow citizens
that facilitates transactions, empowers individual creativity,
and justifies collective action ...
The social capital represented by trust is as important as physical capital.

JOHN G. BRUHN[2]

◆

Brazilian pink granite, in slabs two feet square, sliced to face onto twenty-four-foot precast concrete columns. The granite should be half flamed and half polished. The joints have to be perfect so the columns look like solid granite. We need thirty columns, by the end of April at the latest. Can you do it?"

Henry, Municipal's sales manager, pumps his fist. The voice at the other end of the line belongs to Felix, a vice-president of Roush and Co., one of the region's largest construction management firms. Felix has invited Municipal to become a supplier for one of its biggest projects, an office development in the heart of the city. Henry knows that this job could lead to more work with Roush and Co. and with other construction companies as well.

Offers like this don't come around very often, he thinks to himself. "End of April," he says to Felix, "No problem."

"Excellent!" says Felix. "I'll draft the contract today and fax it tomorrow."

Henry hangs up and walks into the plant. He finds Elena, the operations manager, who is supervising a complicated job. "Elena, got a minute?"

"A minute?" she asks. "I can give you fifty seconds. We're seriously behind. What's the matter?"

Henry explains the situation with Roush and Co.'s order.

"End of April? I don't think so. It's too close. We'd have to work around the clock to make it on time."

"Elena, this is the big break we've been waiting for. If we come through for Roush, we'll get to play with the big boys. We need to take this one on! Quit thinking like a factory rat and put on your Municipal hat!"

"All right," says Elena sheepishly, "We'll do our best."

"Great. I knew I could count on you!" He leaves as Elena mutters under her breath, "I'll try, but I'm not making any promises ..."

The problems start right away. Quarrying and shipping pink granite from Brazil turns out to be no simple affair. First one delivery date is missed, then another. By the time the granite arrives at Municipal, it's just two weeks away from Roush and Co.'s deadline. Feeling under the gun, Henry makes a fateful decision: He orders Elena to postpone a job for Municipal's oldest customer, the Martin Group, to make room for Roush's.

Two weeks come and go. Despite heroic efforts, the job remains unfinished. Under pressure from Henry, Elena orders more overtime. Now the project is over budget and still unfinished. Another week passes, then another. Tensions grow. Henry feels compelled to supervise the production personally, while Elena finds Henry's presence at the plant disruptive. Henry grows gloomy and waits for the fateful call. Finally, it arrives.

"What the hell is going on?" yells Felix. "We've got the construction stopped because of your damned slabs! Where's the granite you promised for the end of April?"

Henry stumbles through an explanation. He complains about the Brazilians and the delayed shipments, but Felix interrupts. "I don't give a damn about your problems with the Brazilians. You promised the job would be done four weeks ago. I'm coming over right now. Wait for me at the plant."

Felix arrives and looks shocked when he inspects the nearly two hundred slabs that have been completed. "These are wrong!" he screams. "Half of each slab is flamed and the other half is polished! That's not what we specified!"

"Yes it is," Henry counters. "We did exactly what you told us to do—each slab is half polished, half flamed."

"I wanted half of the slabs entirely polished and the other half entirely flamed, not each slab half and half. Don't you understand simple instructions? Now what are you going to do?" Felix continues, his red face just inches away from Henry's. "'End of April, no problem,' you said. Well, you're five weeks behind, and you've ruined over three-quarters of the slabs. Now you'll have to call the Brazilians and have them quarry and ship almost two hundred new slabs! Do you know what my client is going to say? Do you know what that does to our whole schedule? Do you?"

Before Henry can respond, an assistant walks up and whispers in his ear, "Mr. Martin is waiting in your office. He's furious. He wants to know why his job got bumped from the schedule."

◆

Two fateful words, "No problem," triggered a chain reaction of ineffectiveness and stress. What was the final result? Damaged relationships and potentially catastrophic problems for all involved. Businesses can—and do—fall apart as a result of conversations like Henry and Felix's first phone call. Unfortunately, few of us are strangers to this kind of mess. Most of us have experienced the dangers and frustrations of requests and promises gone awry.

Henry's accepting of Felix's order affected many people: Felix and Henry, of course, but also Elena, Municipal's workers, Roush and Co.'s staff and customers, the Martin Group and people affiliated with them, and many, many others. One simple exchange—"Can you do this?" "Yes."—gave birth to an intricate sequence of actions and reactions affecting thousands.

The evolution of humankind owes more to the division of labor than to the invention of the wheel. There were civilizations without the wheel, but no societies without specialization. In today's world each of us needs the cooperation of an unimaginable number of people simply to survive. Take the coffee you drank this morning. Consider how many people helped deliver it to you. The growers, shippers, sellers, buyers, packagers, retailers, and all those who provide services to them are part of an amazing network of coordinated action.[3] Whether we are working together as employers and employees, fellow team members, or husband and wife, we are constantly exchanging requests and promises that allow us to coordinate our actions.

These conversations carry huge consequences for our lives and our relationships. Are you impeccable about your commitments, or do you take them lightly? Is your word your bond, or wishful fluff? How you answer these questions, not just in language but also through your actions in daily life, says a great deal about you. Some people always make their deadlines and turn in top-notch work. Other people consistently miss their deadlines and turn in subpar material. You can notice the same dynamic playing itself out in groups. Some organizations grow permissive of tardiness and inefficiency. Others take commitments seriously. In my years of consulting, I have noticed a remarkable correlation between the impeccability of commitments and the effectiveness of individuals and groups. In a culture in which people hold each other accountable for their impeccability, where commitments are taken seriously, there is trust, coordination, and efficiency. Perhaps most important, a culture of impeccability in commitments fosters a sense of achievement, dignity, and self-worth in its members.

We all intuitively understand what commitments are. Everybody asks for things. Everybody promises things. Most of us end up doing what we said we'd do—unless we don't. Of course, we always have a good reason. So are we a little sloppy with our commitments, and is that really such a big deal?

For Felix it clearly is, and he's not alone. Breakdowns around commitments are ubiquitous in corporate as well as personal life. Too frequently, people make promises without much thought about how they will honor them. In this chapter, I will show what it means to commit impeccably and how to create and maintain reliable networks of commitments. We will seek to establish integrity, trust, and effectiveness through impeccable commitments. We will see that part of honoring commitments is recognizing when circumstances change, calling for changes to agreements, and learning how to honor commitments impeccably even when it is impossible to fulfill their original terms.

HUMAN INTERACTION

Two parents and their four-year-old son sit at a table, ready to order lunch. The waiter comes out and takes orders from the mother and the father before turning to the child. "And you, sir? What would you like to order for lunch?" The boy's face lights up. "Dad," he exclaims, "he thinks I'm a real person!"

When the waiter asked the child for his order, he took him seriously. To put it another way, the waiter acknowledged the child as a valid requester, someone who could hold him accountable for his commitment. That felt good to the child—it is the life-affirming recognition that every person, young or old, craves. Commitments remind us that we are social animals. We crave feeling part of something larger than we are.

Sometimes we forget this simple truth. It is easy to view a request as a tool for manipulation, a way to compel others to do what we want. This is not the main goal, however. A commitment seeks to foster cooperation, develop trust, and demonstrate impeccability. The essential ingredient is clarity. A successful commitment maintains clarity among its participants about the most concrete of matters: who commits (is accountable) to deliver what by when (to whom). When this information is clear and recognized by all concerned, a solid commitment has been established. When this commitment is honored with impeccability, people feel secure, relationships of trust develop, and actions unfold in coordination. Impeccable commitments make life more productive and enjoyable. When commitments go awry, however, productivity plummets, trust turns into resentment, and people suffer.

Most commitment conversations begin with a request. "Can you come to my office?" "Please ship the order to my new address." These requests appear to be so straightforward that we don't think much about them. However, they are worthy of attention; many commitment conversations go off track at this early point.

THE COURAGE TO ASK

A production manager struggles to meet a tight deadline. After evaluating the situation, he concludes that he needs to add a shift to finish his project on time. Since the overtime will cost the company money, he needs to get approval from the plant manager, but he feels uncomfortable about asking openly. He has heard his boss complain repeatedly that budgets are tight and Corporate is breathing down his neck to control costs. He decides to use a soft approach. During a staff meeting he mentions that his project could really use a second shift. People nod; everybody feels stretched. The production manager walks out feeling relieved. He believes that his boss knows he needs help. He waits for his boss to call him after the meeting to implement the second shift, but he never does. Disappointed, the production manager assumes that the plant manager would prefer to have a delay than spend the extra money. He finishes the job late. Imagine his surprise when he gets chewed out for not finishing it on time!

Like many of us, the production manager tried to ask without asking. His indirect approach avoided an open admission of need, but it also prevented a frank discussion of the trade-off between the costs of additional labor and the delay. In addition, it opened the door for misinterpretation: While the plant manager heard an expression of desire—which he fully understood but didn't think required an answer— the production manager heard the plant manager's silence as a decline of his request and an acceptance of the deadline slippage. In fact, the plant manager would have authorized the additional expense if he had understood that it was a requirement for an on-time shipment.

Every time we make a request, we expose ourselves. We acknowledge that we need someone's help to achieve a desired result. In the same way that asking a question shows that I don't know an answer, making a request implies that I cannot accomplish something alone. If I have a fragile ego, admitting that I'm lost might strike a blow to my self-esteem. I might decide, like the stereotypical male, to avoid this problem by never asking for directions. This choice seems shortsighted, yet many people fall into it, unconsciously, in both their personal and professional lives.

Many professionals derive their self-esteem from "making it alone" or "knowing it all"—or at least from looking like they can or do. That is why many refrain from asking for help, often at the expense of not getting the job done. A culture of "lone rangers"—where the most competent is the one who asks for the least help—wreaks havoc in organizations. People hide problems until it's too late to solve them, and then try to affix the blame to external circumstances.

Beyond exposing one's need, asking someone to do something entails the risk of rejection. The person you are asking can say no. The possibility of being declined is too much for individuals who take things personally. They feel hurt and shamed when someone does not accept their requests. To avoid this frustration, they would rather not ask, even though not asking guarantees that they will not get what they want. Can you think of times in your life when you chose to hold your request back, hoping that the other person would read your mind and offer you what you wanted?

The story of the production manager illustrates a common tactic to avoid making a clear request—make a muddled one. The production manager might protest that he did request additional resources. He could argue that he asked for a second shift at the staff meeting. He's got a point. He did raise the issue, but he didn't make a clear request. A clear request requires a number of basic elements and the manager was missing almost all of them. He didn't direct his request to a particular person (his boss), and he certainly never asked for a response. "But my boss nodded!" he might claim. That doesn't constitute an agreement, just as saying "okay" may mean "I understand," not "I agree." The manager chose to make a muddled request because he was reluctant to make a clear one. As a result, his conversation about additional resources never got off the ground.

This kind of fuzziness plays out in many different contexts. If I ask a colleague to send me some information "as soon as possible," she may accept doing the assignment as soon as it is convenient for her, while I expect her to start working on the project immediately. That is why it is not unusual for some of these "polite" commitment conversations to end up in the courts. People who recognize how dangerous it is to ask without really asking are more prone to take the risk of rejection and state their requests clearly. To do so, the following elements must be included.

Expression. A request must be expressed in a way that can be received and understood by the receiver.

Requester. When the identity of the person who makes the request is uncertain, it is impossible for those receiving the request to know with whom they are dealing. Imagine you receive a voicemail from someone who asks you to call back. But the person doesn't leave a name and you can't recognize the voice. You aren't going to return the call.

Receiver. A request without an intended receiver is like an e-mail without an addressee. When the receiver is unidentified, there is no one designated to respond to the request or responsible for fulfilling it. If you declare at a meeting that "Someone should let the sales force know about the changes" and "everybody" agrees, my guess is it won't happen. Why? Because in commitment conversations "everybody" means "nobody" and "someone" means "no one."

Standards. The goal of the requester is to obtain some service from the receiver by a specific time. To maintain clarity, these conditions for satisfaction—what, by when—must have defined observable standards. If these conditions are ill-specified, there is little chance that the conversation will stay on track. For instance, a manager who asks his employees to be "more proactive" is asking for trouble. What does he mean by "proactive"? What are his criteria? When does he expect to see these changes? The main difference between an *expression of desire* and a *request* is the existence of measurable standards for assessment of fulfillment.

Need. At the root of each request there is a need or desire that the requester is trying to satisfy. Letting the receiver of the request know what the underlying need is can open many opportunities for counteroffers that satisfy the need without necessarily satisfying the request.

Agreement. Just stating the request is akin to sending the text of a contract to the other party; until they sign it, there is no contract. The question "can you commit to that?" finishes the request by placing the ball squarely in the other's court. It also emphasizes that the request is not "to try" to do something, but "to commit" to do it.

We can express a well-formed request using the following formula:

In order to accomplish W (the satisfaction of a need), I ask you to do X (a specific action) by Y (a specific time). Can you commit to that?

Requests breed another type of problem. Some people assume that the act of making a request is tantamount to a commitment from the receiver. You might receive an e-mail informing you that there's a meeting next Monday. Unless you have a previous agreement with the person calling the meeting, you can fairly consider this notice a request—which you may accept or decline. A request is *not* a commitment.

On the other hand, if you are the requester, I suggest you always ask for a response. You can't claim to have a commitment until you hear back from the receiver—or from someone authorized by him. Nobody can make a commitment for anyone else. The person making the promise needs to sign on the dotted line. (Of course, people make global commitments for recurrent situations. You may have a standing commitment to your boss that you will always attend a meeting that he requests by e-mail twenty-four hours in advance. If you have that agreement, then a proper invitation could be considered a commitment.)

Even if you find these practices reasonable, not everyone will accept them. To avoid breakdowns with people who tend to assume that their requests imply your commitment, it is in everyone's best interest to bring the matter to their attention immediately. An ill-formed request can be corrected with a clear response.

RESPONSE

Requests are not the only part of commitment conversations that get murky. People bungle responses all the time for similar reasons. We don't want to be constrained by a commitment or we don't want to turn another person down. So we choose to give a muddled response. This often produces short-term gain. Elena gave Henry a muddled response, and for a few weeks the two co-workers were able to act as if everything was fine. But when the production delays began, Henry wanted to hold Elena to a commitment that she had never made. If Elena had been clear that she could not commit to satisfying Felix's request, she could have saved Henry from his own murky commitment. Instead, her murky response only made things worse.

If the challenge of a request is summoning courage to initiate a conversation, the challenge of a response is finding the strength to continue the conversation honestly. In order to respond with sincerity, I suggest that before you make a commitment, you take a breath and consider four questions.

1 Do I understand what the other is asking of me?
2 Do I have the skills and resources to do it?
3 Am I convinced that those on whom I depend will deliver for me?
4 Am I willing to be held accountable for anticipating potential breakdowns?

If you can't say "yes" to these four questions, you cannot commit in good conscience — at least not without further clarification.

I believe there are six, and only six, clear answers to a request. These answers let all participants in a conversation know who is committing to do what by when and who has the right to hold whom accountable for what. These clear responses can be used as a checklist by accepting statements included in it and challenging any others. The six answers are:

1 "Yes, I promise."
2 "No, I do not commit." (Although I can try …)
3 "I need clarification."
4 "I commit to respond by (a definite date)."
5 "I accept conditionally. I can commit to do what you ask if R (a mutually observable condition) happens. Would that work for you?"
6 "Let me make a counteroffer. I can't commit to doing X by Y, but I could do S by T. Would that work for you?"

Perhaps you know another response that is not on this list. I claim that it is either a derivation of one of these six or it is not clear. Any other response, and there are thousands of possible unclear responses, will likely derail the conversation.

The first answer is, "Yes, I promise." A promise is a commitment to produce something in the future, or to have it produced by others who have empowered us to make commitments on their behalf—a statement such as "I'll go to the meeting," "I'll deliver the package before six-thirty," or "Our technician will check your computer tomorrow afternoon." When you say "I promise," you accept the unconditional responsibility to honor the commitment. Excuses such as "I *couldn't* say no" or "He insisted so much that I finally *had* to accept" are not valid. Impeccability in commitments entails owning your promise and taking care of your creditor (the person to whom you have made the promise) under any circumstance.

The second possible answer is, "No, I do not commit." As a receiver, you can always decline a request—that's the difference between asking and coercing. There could be many excellent reasons: You may not understand what the other is asking; you may not have the resources; you may not have the skills; you may not trust that others on whom you depend will deliver; you may think that what the other is asking is counterproductive or incompatible with a previous commitment of yours; you may anticipate problems that you don't know how to resolve; or you may just not want to do it. When you say "I decline," you might still try to do what you were asked, but you don't make a commitment. You do not give the other the right to hold you accountable. It is much better for all parties to have a clear "no" than to get bogged down in a wishy-washy "Let me see what I can do."

The third possibility is a request for clarification. When the request is unclear, you can ask for more information. For example, if I ask you to help me with a project, you might ask, "What kind of help do you need?" Then you can make an informed choice. If you fear that asking clarifying questions will make you look ignorant or unwilling, you will often accept requests without really understanding what you have committed to do.

The fourth possible answer is to commit to respond by a certain date. This is the appropriate response when you need to find out whether you can answer yes to the four above questions in good conscience. You may need to check for resources, obtain clear commitments from others (and validate their reliability), or anticipate possible breakdowns and convince yourself that you have the means to resolve them. For example, when I ask you to have a certain project ready by Friday, you may think that you'll need the help of two of your colleagues. Then your answer might be, "Let me check with my colleagues, because I need their help and I'm not sure if they're available. I'll get back to you in an hour." It is very important that when you say, "I'll get back to you," you define a time. If you just say "Let me see what I can do," nobody knows where the conversation stands.

The fifth legitimate answer is a conditional acceptance. In this contingent contract, the commitment depends on a condition that will be observed to happen—or be made to happen—in the future. For example, when I ask you to prepare some information on our product line and send it to one of our clients this afternoon, you can commit to do it only if I send you the latest version of our electronic catalog within one hour. This is the appropriate response when the fulfillment of the promise requires that circumstances beyond the promisor's control take place.

The sixth and last clarity-preserving response is a counteroffer, or a proposal to negotiate. Suppose that a client calls me and says, "Fred, I need you to fly to Atlanta *today* to make a presentation to our leadership team tomorrow." Suppose that I am already committed to another engagement. I can reply, "I'm sorry but I am not available tomorrow. What if my colleague Patrick goes instead? I can check with him within the hour to see if he's available. Or perhaps you can wait an extra day and I can be there on Thursday." My offers are an attempt to fulfill the requester's need although not in the way that he requested.

This sixth response is extraordinarily useful. Employing the tools we've learned in previous chapters—effective expression and inquiry for constructive negotiation—we can use it to navigate the conversation to reach a clear, mutually beneficial arrangement.

IMPECCABLE COMMITMENTS IN ACTION

Now that we have learned tools to create impeccable commitments, let's look at how Henry might have better managed his conversations with both Felix and Elena.

"Brazilian pink granite, in slabs two feet square, sliced to face onto twenty-four-foot precast concrete columns. The granite should be half flamed and half polished. The joints have to be perfect so the columns look like solid granite. We need thirty columns, by the end of April at the latest. Can you do it?"

"Felix, I'm delighted that you've thought of Municipal as a possible vendor," Henry says. "With respect to the granite, I don't know yet. I'll have to get back to you tomorrow, after I get some more information."

"You don't know if you want our business?" asks Felix.

"Of course Municipal wants your business," Henry replies, "but only if we can serve you well and maintain our service to our other customers at the same time. We take commitments very seriously here, and I don't want to make a promise I can't keep. April isn't very far away, and I need to find out if I can get the quarry to ship the granite from Brazil in time. And then, when we get it, I have to make sure that I can turn it around in time. I believe that we can deliver what you are asking, but I need to do some homework before I commit with impeccability. I can call you within twenty-four hours with a definite answer."

"All right, twenty-four hours. Talk to you then."

Henry explains the situation to Elena. "What do you think?" he asks.

"End of April?" Elena replies. "I don't think so. It's too rushed. We'd have to work around the clock to make it on time. Oh well, we'll do our best."

Henry laughs. "That means, 'I don't think so, but I don't want to say no to Henry.' Okay, let me put it this way: Once all of the granite is here, how long will you need to cut the slabs and flame and polish them?"

"Without overtime, we'll need six weeks at a minimum. With overtime, maybe we can do it in four."

"Maybe? I need more than a 'maybe' to commit to Felix."

"Okay. If you authorize the overtime I can finish the job in four weeks."

"Thanks, Elena." Next Henry talks to the Brazilian quarry that has the biggest supply of pink granite. He learns that quarrying and shipping will take three to four weeks longer than he had imagined. But he also learns that the quarry has a smaller quantity of unused pink granite already in the United States.

After consulting with shippers and estimators, and confirming the drop-dead delivery dates for other customers whose jobs are already in progress, Henry calls Felix—twenty-two hours after the first conversation.

"Felix, I can't get you the whole job by the end of April. If I have the quarry cut all the stone at once and then factor in shipping and the amount of cutting and finishing on our end, the best I could do is May twenty-fifth. Frankly, I don't know how any other company could do any better, given your requirements. But I have a proposal—how about half of the job by May fifth and half by May twenty-fifth? I can get half of the granite from the same quarry a few weeks earlier."

"Well, that's not ideal, but it might be workable," Felix replies. "I'll have to rearrange some other schedules." He thinks for a moment, "Okay, let's do it."

"Hold on, Felix, before we launch this major project I want to confirm the flaming and polishing requirements," Henry says. "I wrote down yesterday that each slab should be half flamed, half polished. Do I have that right?"

"No, you have it wrong," Felix corrects. "We'll be alternating the slabs on each column—one flamed slab, one polished, one flamed, and so on. So that's a hundred twenty slabs flamed, a hundred twenty polished."

"Thanks for the clarification," Henry says. "That would have been an expensive mistake. Can you fax the specs as soon as possible? Then I'd like to go over them with you to make sure we order everything correctly. Can we meet, say, on Friday afternoon?"

Felix and Henry meet on Friday, make slight adjustments to the production schedule, and shake hands as they sign the contract. "Felix, I'll call you every Monday morning to give you an update on our progress," Henry says. "If I run into any problems, you'll be the first to know. You'll see a sample in about three weeks. I want to keep you involved and informed every step of the way, so there are no unpleasant surprises in May. That's my commitment to you."

There are two important things to notice about this situation. First, Henry was able to make *everyone* work more effectively together, *without* Felix and Elena needing to know anything about commitment conversations. Second, *any one* of the three key participants in the conversation could have altered the disastrous course of events described at the beginning of this chapter if they had known how to manage commitments effectively. For example, let's revisit the conversation between Henry and Elena and assume that only Elena has mastered the concepts of commitment conversations. As we'll see, she could have altered the dynamic of the situation on her own:

Henry: "Elena, got a minute?"
Elena: "Sure, what's up?"
Henry: "I just took this order from Roush and Co. We need to deliver it by the end of April."
Elena: "End of April? How do you plan on doing that?"
Henry (laughing): "Me do it? I'm counting on you. You're the factory rat."
Elena: "So count on me when I tell you that we can't do it. We won't finish

that job by the end of April. We're already working around the clock to deliver on our regular orders."

Henry: "Elena, this is the big break we've been waiting for. We need to take this one on. Quit thinking like an engineer and put on your Municipal hat!"

Elena: "I understand that this is a big opportunity, and I am thinking with my Municipal hat. That's why I don't want to make a promise I don't believe I can fulfill. It would be better to negotiate a different schedule with Roush now than disappoint them by failing to deliver on our promise."

Henry: "Felix won't like it when I call him and go back on my word."

Elena: "You wouldn't have to do that if you'd told him you needed to check with your production manager before you committed."

Henry: "That would have made us look indecisive; I wanted to show our resolve."

Elena: "You'll look even less decisive now."

Henry: "Elena, you're letting us all down. He won't like this at all. And neither will I."

Elena: "I understand that this is a problem, but I am sure Felix will like it even less if we let him down later. And so will you."

Henry: "You're not being a team player. Can't you just try harder?"

Elena: "Of course I can try, and I'll do my best to speed things up. But I will not promise to do something that I don't believe we can do. That would be worse than not being a team player."

Henry: "I respect your high morals, but if you can't do it, maybe we should find someone else who can."

Elena: "If you know somebody who can do it, give them the job. But be careful whom you trust. A lot of people are willing to make promises they know they can't keep. They'll tell you that they'll do 'the best they can.'"

Henry: "Oh, come on. Is there nothing you can do?"

Elena: "I'm sure there is, but in order to find out what that is, I'll need to talk directly with Felix. If he gives me the details of his schedule, I bet we can come up with some creative ideas."

Henry: "What if Felix draws a line in the sand? What if he says that it's either by the end of April or he'll give the job to our competition?"

Elena: "We've still got some options. If Mike [the CEO] believes it's worth it, we can always off-load some of our current work to subcontractors. It will be expensive, and risky in terms of quality control, but feasible. If we decide that's not the way to go, we can always tell Felix that we are not a good supplier for him on this job. It's not the ideal response, but if he gets burned by one of our less scrupulous competitors, maybe he'll reevaluate and become more appreciative of our impeccability on commitments."

Henry: "Okay, let me set up a conference call as soon as possible."

Elena: "Let me know when and I'll make myself available."

◆

Now imagine that Felix is the one who understands the meaning of impeccability in commitments. Henry is agreeing with everything Felix wants but Felix is wary. At the same time, Felix doesn't want to offend a potential supplier by challenging his integrity. How can he guide Henry into an impeccable commitment conversation without offending him?

Felix: "Brazilian pink granite, in slabs two feet square, sliced to face onto twenty-four-foot precast concrete columns. The granite should be half flamed and half polished. The joints have to be perfect so the columns look like solid granite. We need thirty columns, by the end of April at the latest. Can you do it?"

Henry: "End of April. No problem."

Felix: "No problem? I'm impressed. What makes you so sure you can make that deadline?"

Henry (reassuringly): "Well, I'm sure we can beat that April date."

Felix: "I hear you, Henry, and I am delighted. I just wonder how you can be so sure so fast. From past experience, I expected just getting the granite would take until sometime in April. Let me impress upon you that delays are unacceptably expensive for us. If we plan our construction schedule counting on this delivery and you let us down, we'll all be in serious trouble. That's why I want to be extra careful with the delivery date. Are you sure you don't want to check with your operations department first?"

Henry: "Now that you mention it, it seems like I might be jumping the gun here. Let me check and I'll call you back."

Felix: "Thanks, Henry. When can I expect your call?"

Henry: "How about tomorrow?"

Felix: "Tomorrow it is. Please let me know what you can guarantee in terms of delivery dates. Emphasize 'guarantee.' I don't want to know when you *think* you can do it, or by when you will *try* to do it. I want a guaranteed date, with reliable commitments from your suppliers and a planned production schedule that we can check together weekly. I also want to make contingency plans with you in order to mitigate the impact of any breakdowns. Since this is our first deal, I'd like to keep a close eye on it. Let's start our relationship off on the right foot."

◆

Once a clear request has received a clear affirmative response, a great deal of work has been done. By that point, all participants should be in agreement about the fundamental issues involved in the discussion. Everybody is ready to move forward in a spirit of collaboration and mutual understanding.

Of course that doesn't mean that everything will work out. Even the most impeccable commitments can break down. Life is unpredictable, situations change, and people find themselves unable or unwilling to follow through. Under these circumstances, it is all the more important to maintain effectiveness in the task, trust in the relationship, and integrity in the self.

Once again this is simple, but not easy. It sounds good in theory, but it is very challenging in practice. A few years ago I taught a series of seminars for an information technology corporation. During our first meeting, we worked intensely on impeccable commitments. The attendees all said they found the material useful and agreed to implement the methodology at work. In the interval between conferences, I received e-mails with excellent reports about the new system, but when the second conference rolled around I saw something different. Managers had identified a date that everyone agreed was acceptable, and all of the attendees entered into a commitment with me and each other to make that date. Yet when I showed up that first day, less than half of the participants were present. Where was everyone else?

I asked the person in charge of logistics. His answer shocked me. Over the previous two days, almost everyone had contacted him and said that "scheduling conflicts" prevented them from making the opening of the conference. These same people claimed that they understood how to hold commitment conversations impeccably. Well, they were wrong. Beside the fact that "scheduling conflicts" is the ultimate victim explanation (it is never a matter of time, only of priorities), impeccability demands far more than a last minute self-excusatory phone call.

They didn't understand the serious implication of giving their word. They lacked an appreciation of maintaining impeccability. Just think of how many times you've participated in a conversation when someone asked for help and you promised to be there in five minutes. How often did you really show up in five minutes? You may be reluctant to admit that you've broken a commitment, as were the participants in my program—and quite adamantly. I raised a complaint with the people who didn't show up the first day. One objected. "But I called to cancel!" he said. By the time he called, it was too late. His apology didn't help the task (a well-attended seminar) or relationships (the people who showed up also had other work to do and resented the absences); it only assuaged his guilt about the whole situation. Each time something like this happens, we break our word, decrease trust, and slacken coordination. Over time, we create a culture lacking accountability, reliability, and dignity.

In order to make impeccable commitments work, it is essential to understand how to revisit them. Sometimes commitments conflict with other responsibilities. Things change. We know this. The question is how to deal with it. How do we balance honoring our commitments and fulfilling our other responsibilities? The first lesson is that honoring a commitment doesn't require that you fulfill it.

THE PRODUCTIVE COMPLAINT

"When is he going to call?" wonders Felix. "Henry promised to call, but he hasn't!" Many of us have been in Felix's shoes, waiting for the call or the report, knowing that things aren't going well but feeling powerless to change them. They've already made an agreement, so what else can Felix do until Henry falls flat on his face? One option is to get bent out of shape. "Henry is unreliable!" Felix complains to a coworker. "I'm getting screwed by that guy!" That may earn Felix sympathetic nods around the office, but not much else. This type of behavior is indicative of what I call an *unproductive complaint*. An unproductive complaint seeks to soothe one's hurt. Unproductive complaints look for sympathy and support from third parties; they are repetitive and conclude with negative personal judgments; they discharge emotions and seek revenge. Predictably, they do little to improve matters.

Felix is not as powerless as he imagines. As long as he is a party to a commitment, he has plenty of tools at his disposal for holding the other party accountable and reviewing the terms of the agreement. One of these tools is the *productive complaint*. A productive complaint has four immediate goals: Repair or minimize the damage to the task; mend and strengthen the relationship; restore impeccability; and learn from the mistake in order to design more effective ways of cooperating in the future. In the long term, a productive complaint seeks to establish an organizational culture of achievement, trust, and mutual accountability.

Productive complaints are addressed directly to the person who made the commitment; they are made as soon as possible and only once; they end with requests and promises that take care of people's concerns; they help reestablish the impeccability of all parties; and they encourage learning.

Let's give Felix a break and look at how to approach a similar situation and transform it into a positive, productive opportunity. The following steps provide an easy way to structure a productive complaint.

- **Check your intention.** Review your purpose for complaining and ensure that it is virtuous. If you are looking to blame the other, you're off track. A productive complaint is a mutual learning conversation as described in chapters 4 and 5.

- **Establish the appropriate context.** Remember that context is as important as content, so make sure you set an appropriate one (time, place, confidentiality, emotional tone, etc.). It's useful to express your intentions openly to the recipient. You don't want to fight; you want to improve your working relationship. You don't intend to start an argument, but rather hope to solve a problem that is affecting your work, your relationship, and your well-being. You don't want to accuse the other person; you want to give him a chance to explain what happened and maintain his impeccability.

- **Verify the previous commitment.** Many problems result from miscommunication of the original request and promise: You tried to request X, but the other heard (and promised) Y. It is crucial to revisit the original commitment and ensure that both parties had the same understanding. If you do, you have established the foundation from which you will communicate your complaint. If you don't agree, explain to each other what happened, and figure out how to avoid similar misunderstandings in the future.

  Many managers challenge this step. They worry that it provides an opportunity for the other to claim confusion ("I never said I'd do that!") and get off scot-free. This is a real risk, but the cost pales in comparison to the damage caused by holding someone to a commitment they haven't made. In my experience, it is advantageous to let someone squirm out of a commitment one time rather than running the risk of prosecuting them mistakenly. The next time you enter into a commitment conversation with this person, you should practice extra diligence. At the end of a conversation, verbally summarize all the established agreements and verify that the other party concurs. Then, e-mail him the summary and ask him to correct any mistakes you might have made.

- **Verify the failure to honor the commitment.** Both parties need to agree that the promisor did not keep his promise. This is necessary, as the other party might argue that he did fulfill it. It's also possible that the commitment has been honored and you just don't know it. If you both agree that the promisor broke his commitment, then once again you have a strong shared foundation for moving ahead with the complaint. If you don't agree, discuss how the misunderstanding arose and create a mechanism to ensure that it won't happen again. Make sure to distinguish the lack of fulfillment from its justification. At this point, you're only trying to define whether the commitment was broken, not whether the breakdown was justified.

- **Inquire into what happened.** Both parties now agree that there was a problem with the commitment, but you still don't know why the promisor didn't keep his promise. By inquiring, you hear the other's story of what happened from his point of view. Besides helping you understand this perspective, the inquiry shows that you respect the other person and are curious; it suggests that you're not limited by preconceptions and negative judgments.
- **Evaluate the damage and express the complaint.** A broken commitment creates difficulties on three levels: operational, relational, and personal. The task suffers from a lack of coordination, the relationship suffers from a loss of trust, and the individual suffers from the stress and grief of having been let down. The first step in repairing these damages is to recognize and validate them. By clearly communicating the damages, the person who broke the promise can better understand the ramifications and you can express your pain. The purpose here isn't to whine or assign blame, but to reveal the impact the broken commitment has had on you, your work, and your relationship with that person.

Always discuss hurts before anger ... If we initiate important conversations by attacking or angrily criticizing [the other], we immediately set off in our partner the need for defense. If the listener feels attacked, she will immediately shut down emotionally and begin to focus on how to protect herself or withdraw from the fray. This can be avoided by beginning any conversation over an issue that has angered you by first explaining how the situation has hurt you ... [This] arouses less need for self-defense or counterattack. Much more often than not it will open the door to real dialogue ... Beginning dialogue with an angry critical attack usually precipitates a fight, shuts off real discussion of the issues, breeds resentment and frequently stifles any real change.

JOHN W. JACOBS[4]

Just as there are three levels of damage, there are three levels of complaint. The superficial level concerns the task. The promisor can have an excellent explanation for not keeping his promise. In Henry's case, the granite was late arriving from Brazil. The second level concerns the trust in the relationship. Felix can complain to Henry that he never got a warning that the job was delayed. It's much harder to justify the lack of an early warning than a task breakdown. The deepest level is that of personal impeccability. If Henry insisted that he didn't have to call because the Brazilian delay was not his fault, Felix might complain about the value of Henry's word. The promise came from Henry; therefore, he's obligated *by his own word* to honor his commitment.

A person who breaks a commitment jeopardizes the task, the relationship, and his honor. The complaint gives the receiver an opportunity to compensate for his failure on all three levels. Therefore, the productive complaint doesn't create conflicts; rather, it resolves them.

- **Request reparations and negotiate a recommitment.** Every productive complaint will include your request for reparations. This can be as simple as asking the receiver to recommit to keeping his original promise, or it can include additional compensation. The key is that you, as the person with the complaint, are the one who defines the conditions for satisfying your request; if these are met, you can declare the problems of the past addressed, resolved, and closed.

A danger here is that in seeking to be "nice," you might ask for something that doesn't really close the issue for you. Often, this misguided kindness generates resentment in the long term. Your request must be made in such a way that, once the recipient accepts and fulfills it, you won't use this situation as justification for future rancor.

Your request is also an offer of forgiveness: "If you do what I ask, I promise to close the issue and not hold a grudge." This request initiates a conversation for negotiating new commitments.

There are situations in which the damage or hurt experienced by the person who suffered the breakdown is so great that no reparation can resolve it. In these extreme cases, the relationship will suffer the consequences, perhaps even come to an end.

- **Learn and prepare for the future.** The last step in this process is to look for opportunities to improve. A broken commitment represents the proverbial "defect" the Japanese regard as a "treasure" for learning. By understanding which part of the process is weak under which conditions, both parties can plan strategies or design mechanisms to strengthen it. Thus, not only will you both avoid repeating the same mistake, but you'll also preclude making many others. The complaint doesn't only repair; it can also enhance efficiency, deepen trust, and create peace.

PRODUCTIVE APOLOGIES

A few years ago, Motorola commissioned a survey asking microchip customers to name the most reliable supplier.[5] The customers favored Hewlett-Packard (HP). The survey was accompanied by a statistical analysis that revealed something shocking: HP's delivery record wasn't significantly better than its competitors, yet its customers viewed it as much more reliable than its competitors. For Motorola managers, this was a crucial riddle to solve.

The answer was found in HP's business practices. Every time an HP account manager discovered that the company couldn't deliver a product by a promised date, she immediately called the client to apologize and make alternative arrangements. Employees never hid a delay from their customers; instead, they were proactive. In the process, they transformed the problem into an opportunity by stepping up to the accountability plate. They assumed responsibility and did what they could to correct the situation. This policy reaped enormous rewards in terms of client loyalty.

When we realize that there is a serious risk that we will not fulfill a promise, we can still honor our word by apologizing. An effective apology requires much more than simply muttering "I'm sorry" and asking for forgiveness. Expressing regret is a crucial step, but it is only the beginning.

It is also essential to accept accountability and do what's necessary to recover impeccability: Address the incomplete task, restore trust to the relationship, and help minimize the damage caused to your counterpart. If your supplier promises to deliver a part that never arrives, a mere "I'm sorry" won't go very far with you. You want the part. When the participants of the seminar I mentioned earlier failed to attend the first day of the conference, even though they left messages announcing they would not be there, I did not consider their behavior to be up to the standards we had established. They called at the last minute, they did not offer to take care of the breakdown, and they did not apologize to others when they showed up the following day.

The following steps outline a structure for apologizing productively. Since they are mirror images of the steps of the productive complaint, I will not repeat the explanations.

1 Establish the appropriate purpose (individual context) for the apology. The goal is to repair the breakdowns in coordination, trust, and impeccability, and the hurt feelings.
2 Establish the appropriate context (prepare the conversation). Choose an appropriate time and place and express to your counterpart your desire to repair the breakdown.
3 Acknowledge the previous commitment. Own your promise.

4 Acknowledge your failure to honor the commitment. Take responsibility for the non-fulfillment. Offer an explanation. Explain what happened. Distinguishing this explanation from an excuse that invalidates the commitment is paramount. You aren't trying to justify yourself or evade your responsibility; instead, you're trying to share your experience and situation as part of the problem's context.

5 Inquire about the damages and apologize. Before offering to repair any damages, you must first know what they are. By inquiring into them, you more clearly understand the ramifications of the problem; this also helps the other to express his pain. Your goal isn't to argue but to listen to and acknowledge the other's perspective.

6 Offer reparations and negotiate a recommitment. Although you can offer reparations, it's important that you ask the other what he needs to feel appropriately indemnified and allow him to declare the issue resolved.

7 Learn and prepare for the future. As with a complaint, the last step of the apology is transforming the mistake into an opportunity to learn.

RECOMMITMENT COSTS

From the very moment we make a promise, the costs of apologizing and renegotiating begin to grow. The creditor expects fulfillment in due time and form; thus, any changes in schedule may result in damages. The closer we get to the due date, the less room there is for mitigating action. There-fore, it is best to give notice of the risk of default as soon as we assess that it is "significant." In addition, when we give the warning or amend our promise, we should be sure to render an apology and address any inconveniences. We owe our best effort to minimize the negative consequences to those who will suffer for our failure.

If a promisor does not announce the risk of breakdown as soon as she becomes aware of it, there are only two possibilities: She may still fulfill the promise on time without causing any loss to the receiver, or she may end up breaking the promise and informing those involved at a later date. In the first case, it may seem as though there is no problem. In fact, many people do not notify their creditors of risks that may prevent them from meeting a deadline, instead counting on the possibility that somehow they will be able to overcome them. "If I can fix things on my own," they think, "there is no need to make trouble." Unfortunately, these hopes do not always become realities. The work falls further and further behind, while the creditor is in the dark, unable to hedge against a risk he knows nothing about.

When should you announce the possibility of missing a deadline? The easiest way to answer that question is by applying the Golden Rule: Treat others as you would like to be treated yourself. If you are the creditor, would you like to know that there is a chance you won't receive what you expect on time? Or is the probability small enough that you would prefer not to be bothered and let the debtor who made the promise deal with it? In answering this question, you need to consider this possible demand of the creditor: "If you knew you had problems that were going to prevent you from getting this to me on time, why didn't you tell me earlier? If you'd warned me at that time, I could have taken measures to diminish the costs of the delay."

You might justify not giving an early warning if there is a high chance of correcting the problem, but there is no justification for silence at the due date. By then the clock has run out. Any hope of solving the problem on time has vanished. Of course, you may still think that the job will get done "very soon," and continue working without calling the creditor to apologize. This is self-serving rationalization. There are no excuses for not apologizing and leaving the creditor hanging out to dry.

Let's go back to the situation with the executives who didn't show up for the first day of the seminar. The next day, with 90 percent of the participants present, we had a long conversation about apologies. I reminded them that an effective apology entails much more than just leaving a message. I challenged them that to honor their word they would have had to: 1) inform the appropriate people about their decision not to attend the meeting as early as they knew about it; 2) explain why they *decided* not to come (claiming that they *couldn't* come due to "unavoidable commitments" is irresponsible); 3) apologize; and 4) ask if there was anything they could do to minimize the inconveniences they caused. Had all of the late participants done this, we would likely have postponed the conference for a day. We would have easily resolved a situation that instead created friction between those who decided to come the first day and those who chose not to attend.

As I said earlier, there's a big gap between understanding these principles conceptually and putting them into practice. During the seminar, everybody agreed that his or her explanations had been insufficient, and pledged to be more impeccable with commitments in the future. Nonetheless, the following week, a manager told me that five participants had scheduled a meeting with an instructor who was coming from overseas to teach them a new programming tool. Only one of them showed up. The other four "apologized" by e-mail … the night before! Old habits die hard.

The power of apology isn't limited to the organizational realm. When I started going to school at age six in Argentina, I discovered *dinenti,* a game similar to jacks in which you have to toss a few pebbles into the air, collect others on the ground, and catch the ones you tossed. It was the most popular game at school. Each child had his own set of pebbles; the pebbles were a kind of status symbol. At the top of the social hierarchy were those who owned perfect marble cubes the size of dice. Those of us who had street pebbles were in a lower class.

One day, as I practiced with my pebbles on the floor of my grandfather's store, one of his suppliers came in. Seeing me play, he asked a question that made my heart race: "Hey kid, would you like to have marble pebbles that look like dice?" An offer of a million dollars couldn't have made me happier. "Yes sir!" I replied, full of hope. "Can you get them for me?" "No problem," said the man, "I'll bring them the next time I come." I was beside myself with happiness; I was already gloating, picturing myself with my beautiful marble cubes.

Each afternoon after school I'd run to see my grandfather and ask him if the man had brought me the pebbles. My grandfather's answer was always "No." After a week, he must have gotten tired of my persistent questions: "No, he didn't bring them, and I don't think he ever will. He has been here twice to take orders from me and he never mentioned the stones. He's probably forgotten."

Forgotten?! How could he forget? I thought, absolutely stunned. *You can forget to eat, or even to breathe, but how can you forget the marble pebbles? They are the most important thing in the world!* Those pebbles were certainly the most important thing in my world at that time.

Not having them broke my heart. Nonetheless, I eventually got over it. However, I was left with a bitter aftertaste unrelated to the pebbles. I had learned that the promises grown-ups made to children didn't count. As a child I wasn't a "person" capable of receiving commitments or with the right to hold grown-ups accountable for their fulfillment. The vendor was probably a good man, and my grandfather loved me dearly. I don't think either of them had the slightest intention of hurting me. But by never mentioning his promise again (with my grandfather acting as an accomplice, since he never demanded the pebbles from him), the vendor gave me the following implicit message: *"My commitments to you don't count because you don't count."*

Impeccability in commitments is an unconditional discipline; it doesn't depend on others. You don't behave impeccably only toward people who behave impeccably toward you. You behave impeccably because that is the way you want to live. To think that you need to behave with integrity toward adults but that you can be excused when dealing with children is a dangerous trap (for the children, and for you). Yet, how many times do we break our promises to our children (whom we love dearly) without apologizing? The same dynamic applies in hierarchies. Many of us think that we need to behave with impeccability toward our peers and managers, but that we can be excused when we deal with employees at lower levels. Many of us can find situations in which we compromise our impeccability by not honoring a promise to a subordinate or to our children. To restore impeccability and trust, we must apologize.

A CULTURE OF ACCOUNTABILITY

Through their behavior, leaders communicate that "this is the way we do things around here." Their actions tell people, "If you want to fit in this organization, you must act in alignment with these standards. If you don't, you will be ostracized, you will be shunned, you will be expelled." Many leaders pepper their talk with big words such as "impeccability," "accountability," and "dignity." But talk is cheap. The expensive proposition is to live these values day in and day out—and to challenge those who don't, even if they seem to be delivering business results, to change or to leave the organization. Actual behavior is where the rubber meets the road. When leaders don't act in alignment with their espoused values, their words mean nothing. As Emerson remarked, "What you do speaks so loudly, that I cannot hear what you say."

In terms of cultural change, the impact of a leader apologizing to his direct reports trumps any "mission statement." Similarly, a leader inviting his colleagues to call him when he misses a commitment trumps any training session. And a CEO firing a senior executive who lacks impeccability trumps any written communication. Mission statements, training sessions, or communication campaigns are important, but insufficient. In fact, if leadership behaviors do not validate them, they are less than worthless—they are counterproductive. When people observe inconsistencies between the organization's espoused values and the values-in-action demonstrated by its leaders, they will become cynical.

At the end of the seminar I have been referring to throughout the chapter, I had a serious conversation with the leader. I explained to him that in order to kill the old unproductive habits and substitute them with new and more effective ones, he would have to make a stronger commitment.

"What are you talking about?" he said defensively, "I have been following your instructions to the letter!" I acknowledged that he had been acting as a role model of impeccability but, I added, "You have not been acting as a *leader* of impeccability."

"What is the difference?" he challenged me.

"As a leader," I answered, "you are not just responsible for doing it, but for holding others accountable for doing it as well. I see that you behave with integrity, but I do not see you holding people accountable when they behave without integrity. When they betray the company's values and you don't do anything, you become their accomplice."

"But I've told them that their behavior is unacceptable!"

"Yes, you've told them. Has it made any difference?"

"Not really," he confessed.

"Then perhaps you need to take some action and establish real consequences."

Cultural change is a double-or-nothing deal. When leaders don't hold themselves and others accountable for living up to stated values, they make a bad situation worse. They create a schizophrenic organization ruled by duplicitousness, contempt, and cynicism.

IMPECCABLE PRAISE

Holding people accountable for broken commitments is not enough. To create a culture of impeccability you also need to acknowledge and praise their contributions. A leader who does not confront broken commitments encourages polite complacency. He fosters a culture of niceness where nothing gets done and everything is excused. A leader who does not recognize integrity, on the other hand, discourages passionate dedication. He fosters a culture of callousness where things get done, but only out of compliance. When people aren't recognized for their accomplishments they feel a sense of unfairness, a lack of justice that saps their enthusiasm. When the only message they get from their leadership is "What have you done for me lately?" they begin to wonder, "And why should I do anything for you beyond my job?"

For most companies, recognition equals material reward, so they provide incentives through compensation. There are very few companies that encourage excellence through appreciation. Yet all employees want more than monetary incentives; they desire meaningful challenges, dignified treatment, and heartfelt words of praise. As Peter Drucker points out, "We have known for fifty years that money alone does not motivate to perform. Dissatisfaction with money grossly demotivates. Satisfaction with money is, however, mainly a 'hygiene factor.'"[6] The same point has been verified by The Gallup Organization. Based on more than two million surveys and eighty thousand interviews, its researchers found that the fourth most important indicator of a high-performance organization is whether people say "yes" strongly when asked: "In the last seven days, have I received recognition or praise for doing good work?"[7] In the frenzied rhythm of today's organizations, however, hardly anyone takes the time to express appreciation or admiration consistently.

True appreciation can be very moving. It supports excellence. A high-praise environment is a high-performance environment. Why is praise so important? Because we want to know that we are significant. We want to be respected and appreciated. We long to feel that we matter, that our presence and our actions are relevant. When someone affirms our importance, we feel worthy. Knowing that another, particularly an authority figure, cares about us and what we do focuses our attention and increases our commitment. In fact, according to the Gallup research cited above, the fifth most important indicator of a high-performance organization is whether people say "yes" strongly when asked, "Does my supervisor, or someone at work, seem to care about me as a person?"[8]

Indeed, appreciation yields large benefits, but even when people appreciate each other, they can do it poorly. Compare the impact of telling an employee, "Good job!" as you cross him in the hallway, versus addressing him in front of the team and saying, "Matthew, when I got that extraordinary feedback from our customer on your performance, I felt really proud. I am delighted to have you on my team. I admire your dedication and commitment to excellence. Thanks for your great effort!" If you were Matthew, which one would make you shine the most? Powerful praise is public, direct, concrete, and respectful. Just as a laser is more powerful than diffused light, focused praise goes much deeper than abstract remarks.

There are three fundamental mistakes people make when appreciating others. People say things such as:

1 "I wish to appreciate Elena's efforts. Without her, we wouldn't have finished the Municipal job on time. Let us thank Elena for her contribution."
2 "You did great at the meeting with Felix! Thank God you were there."
3 "You are wonderful! You are such a hard worker. And a real team player. You are helpful, reliable, and intelligent. You're a real asset to the team!"

Mistakes? you might wonder. *What's wrong with these expressions of appreciation? I wish we treated each other that way at my company!* These statements are not wrong, but they are much less powerful than they could be. These statements are:

1 *Indirect.* Effective recognition is direct. Rather than speaking *about* the other in the third person (as if they weren't present), recognize *them* in second person. When you communicate in the third person, you address everybody *except* the acknowledged. Your recognition will reach far deeper if you address the other directly. Compare the original statement with, "Elena, I want to tell you how much I appreciate your efforts. Without you, we wouldn't have finished Municipal's job on time. Thank you so much."
2 *Abstract.* Effective recognition is specific. Rather than using generalities, identify the specific consequences of the other's tangible actions. When you speak abstractly, the other does not learn what he did and how it benefited you; your words may even sound shallow. Your recognition will be much more powerful if you highlight concrete behaviors and results. Compare the original statement with, "Henry, I'm very grateful for the stance you took at the meeting with Felix. The way you negotiated his demand for a rush job will allow us to deliver impeccably."

3 *Imposing.* Effective recognition is respectful. Rather than telling the person who they are, let them know how their actions affected you positively. When you label the other, you impose your perspective on them. Your recognition will be more freeing if you own your opinions. Compare the original statement with, "Elena, I am delighted to have you on our team. Your impeccable fulfillment of Municipal's order has earned us tremendous good will with them. I have already received a call from Felix asking us to bid for a job twice as large as the one we just finished. Your reliability makes my work much less stressful and much more fun. Thank you!"

Acknowledgments that are direct, specific, openhearted, and respectful require a high level of disclosure. You may feel more exposed making them, but they are fresh, intimate, genuine, and sincere. If you want to create a culture of impeccability, you need to care for people both by demanding accountability and praising contributions.

◆

In the last three chapters I have presented practices that help people understand each other, resolve conflicts, and coordinate their actions. These practices both rely on and express the core values of the three previous chapters: unconditional responsibility, essential integrity, and ontological humility. Most of us fall short of these standards. Awareness seems to be the missing piece of the puzzle, a piece added by a serious reading of the last six chapters. When trained in this material, most of us can demonstrate our strong commitment to the values and can put the tools into practice rather quickly in normal everyday situations. There are instances, however, when our good intentions fall apart and we behave in completely unskillful ways.

What trips us is the flaring up of our emotions. Some circumstances trigger emotional states in which we find it impossible to remain congruent with our values and apply conversational tools. In the next chapter, we will look at the seventh and last discipline of success beyond success, emotional mastery.

CHAPTER 8

Emotional Mastery

◆

The heart has reasons that reason knows nothing about.
PASCAL

... the higher the rank, the more interpersonal and human
the undertaking. Our top executives spent roughly 90
percent of their time concerned with ... people problems.
Our study of effective leaders strongly suggested that a key
factor was the creative deployment of self.
WARREN BENNIS AND BURT NANUS[1]

◆

"That conscious business stuff of yours doesn't work!" Barry barked. I was not surprised, even though the seminar with Barry's executive team had finished on a high note. Intellectual knowledge is quite different from practical skill.

"What happened?" I asked.

"I tried to have a conversation with George," he said. "It started out all right until he pulled one of his 'yes buts' on me, and I totally lost it. The guy is a jerk! I can't stand him."

"Were you upset that he disagreed with you?"

"Not just disagreed. He used that sickly sweet patronizing tone of his. He talked down to me as though I was a five-year-old who needed to learn how to calculate an ROI. He's such a know-it-all! He got on my nerves, and I blew up. All that left-hand-column toxic waste you talk about? Well, it came out perfectly raw. Of course, that just started a pissing contest. George lost it, too, and matched me blow by blow. What a mess!"

"Barry, I've got good news and bad news. The good news is that this conscious business stuff works—"

"What's the bad news?"

"*You* don't work!"

◆

Barry knew that blowing up was the worst possible thing to do. He knew that his outburst would start a downward spiral. He knew that George and he wouldn't be able to work together after a fight. He knew that this would hurt the relationship. He knew that, in the end, both George and he would sulk and feel sour. He knew all of this and in the moment, he didn't care. He did it anyway.

If you pay attention, you'll see that in emotionally charged situations you don't want to use the techniques you know will make things better. Good intentions go out the window—and so do the concepts and tools of the last seven chapters. Intellectual understanding is worth nothing if you can't use it in a difficult situation. Just as an automobile needs its wheels balanced and aligned to move quickly and smoothly, an individual needs his emotions balanced and aligned to act skillfully. Whether a car or a person, the faster the periphery rotates, the more still the center must be; otherwise the vibration will destroy the structure.

Emotional intelligence is missing from our school curricula. Formal education eschews the development of emotional competencies to focus exclusively on intellectual matters. This, despite evidence that workplaces badly need people who are more emotionally astute (see below). This becomes even more of an issue when people move into managerial roles because the focus of their work shifts from technical to social. Emotional incompetence becomes a significant leadership handicap.

> What you learned in school distinguishes superior performers in only a handful of the five or six hundred jobs for which we've done competency studies. It's just a threshold competence; you need it to get in the field, but it does not make you a star. It's the emotional intelligence abilities that matter more for superior performance.
>
> LYLE SPENCER JR., THE HAY GROUP[2]

> [After analyzing 181 competence models from 121 organizations worldwide,] I found that *67 percent*—two out of three—of the abilities deemed essential for effective performance were emotional competencies. Compared to IQ and expertise, emotional competence mattered *twice* as much.
>
> DANIEL GOLEMAN[3]

How can we develop emotional mastery? First, we need to understand what emotions are and how they operate. Second, we need to consider the emotional double-edged sword: On the one hand, emotions can derail our thought processes; on the other hand, without them there is no reason to think. Emotions are absolutely necessary for rationality. Third, we need to find ways in which we can use the powerful information contained in emotions without letting them take over. Finally, we need to develop equanimity to stay centered in the midst of challenging circumstances. At the end of this process, we will be able to keep ourselves together where others, less aware, would fall apart.

WHO'S AFRAID OF THE BIG BAD CAT?

Imagine yourself on top of a mountain on a beautiful day. What do you notice? The deep blue sky, the crisp air, the vast horizon, the silence. What do you do? Sit, rest, drink, eat, shoot some photos. Now, without changing the scene, imagine that you hear a growl. You recognize the sound. It's a cougar!

In an instant, everything changes. You don't care about the crisp air; all you want is an escape route. You don't notice the vast horizon; all you notice is that you are alone. You can't imagine sitting silently. You want to flee.

The growl doesn't change the external world, but it does change your internal world. It changes your emotional state, shifting your perceptions and acts. When you were calm, you paid attention to the landscape; when you got scared, you focused on possible escape routes. The landscape didn't disappear with the growl; you just stopped paying attention to it. As I explained in chapter 4, our mind directs our attention automatically. Emotions play a key role in this process.

Emotions condition not only our experience, but also our actions. They define the range of possible behaviors. Just as a calm mind is well suited for relaxing or taking photos, an alarmed mind is efficient at self-defense or flight. It is as natural to defend yourself when you feel threatened as it is to rest when you are calm.

Emotions also affect physiology. Different emotional states correlate with the secretion of different hormones and with metabolic changes. When you are afraid, the amygdala secretes corticotrophin, which mobilizes your fight-or-flight reaction. It also releases noradrenaline and dopamine, which heighten your senses. These hormones divert your energy from nonessential functions like memory and logic, redirecting it to the senses and various perception centers. The same hormones also influence your cardiovascular system: Your heart rate accelerates and your blood is diverted from your brain toward your muscles and extremities, preparing your body to respond to the emergency. Your blood-sugar level rises, providing necessary fuel for action; nonessential activities like digestion slow down. The overall effect is to heighten your senses, cloud your reasoning, and switch on your "automatic pilot" for survival. In this state, you tend to fall into conditioned behaviors such as fight or flight.

The growl is not a stimulus that conditions your reaction. You are a human being with free will and response-ability, so the growl is data, a challenge that demands a response (see chapter 2). If you were a hunter, you might be excited by the growl instead of afraid. Instead of looking for escape routes, you would search for a place to stalk the animal. Even your physiology would be affected differently. You would secrete adrenaline, which would enable you to hunt much more effectively than corticotrophin. By activating your sympathetic nervous system, adrenaline elevates your energy, supporting maximum mental and physical effort. This is "good stress," as opposed to distress.

Now imagine that the growl is not coming from a cougar, but from a boom box in the bushes. As long as you believe there's a cougar, you will feel fear. It doesn't matter if it is really there or not. If you find the boom box, however, your fear disappears. Your beliefs generate the fear regardless of whether they are true or false. If you heard the same growl coming from your family room, you would not be scared. You would assume it was the TV—even if a real cougar had somehow gotten into your house. Strictly speaking, you are not afraid because of the cougar; you are afraid because you believe that you are at risk.

Recall the discussion of mental models in chapter 4. Your emotions arise from your perceptions and interpretations, and those perceptions and interpretations are shaped by your mental models. You don't experience reality as it is, but as your individual mental model filters it. What you feel depends on what happens "out there" only insofar as it triggers what you experience "in here."

THE HEART OF REASON

Many people believe that emotions stand in opposition to rational thought, but scientific evidence suggests the opposite. While emotions can overwhelm your rationality, you cannot be rational without being emotional. Emotions predate thoughts in the evolution of the human species and our personal development. The neurobiologist Antonio Damasio points out that rationality depends upon a deeper system of regulation that consists largely of emotions and feelings. Emotion can disrupt reasoning in certain circumstances, but without it there is no reasoning at all. Traditional cognitive models don't understand that "reduction in emotion may constitute an equally important source of irrational behavior."[4]

Damasio had a patient named Elliot who was a successful businessman. Elliot was diagnosed with a small brain tumor. During the operation to remove the tumor, the neurosurgeon accidentally cut the connection between the frontal lobe (center for thought) and the cerebral amygdala (center for emotions). When he recovered, Elliot had changed. When he recalled tragedies of his life, he spoke with a coldness and detachment incompatible with the severity of the events. He spoke as if he were a spectator instead of a participant. Damasio concluded that the operation had separated Elliot from his emotions. He could think, but he couldn't feel.

Elliot retained his intelligence, but he had become completely inept at his work. Without his emotions, he couldn't make any decisions. Damasio asked Elliot to pick a time for the next interview. Elliot responded with a long explanation about the pros and cons of various times, but couldn't choose one. He simply didn't have a preference.[5] The rational center of your mind can generate a series of alternatives and arguments, but in order to make decisions you require an emotional faculty. Your mind needs to evaluate the emotional weight of each option and choose by way of feeling.

Unconscious feeling, on the other hand, can overwhelm your decision process. Appropriate decisions require a state of relaxed awareness, a state that is difficult to attain when you face trying circumstances.

THE RELAXATION RESPONSE

At daybreak, two monks walked along the bank of a river looking for a place to ford it. The water was high due to the spring thaw and the only crossing for many miles was two feet deep. They came across a young lady dressed in silk, frozen in front of the raging water. The monks observed vows that prohibited touching women, yet without uttering a word, the first monk lifted the woman in his arms and carried her across the river. The monks continued on, walking in silence, until evening when their vows allowed them to speak.

"How did you dare carry that lady across the river this morning?" the second monk said. "You've blemished your honor and that of all your brothers. You're a disgrace to our order!"

"My dear brother, I unloaded that lady at daybreak," the first monk replied. "You have been carrying her all day."

The mind is sometimes called the "organ of misery" because of its capacity to ruin life with its incessant rambling. Your mind may be yours, but it doesn't always do what you want. If you have tossed and turned through a sleepless night or gnashed your teeth over the tiniest slight, you know exactly what I'm talking about. Who hasn't carried the lady in his mind long after having physically put her down?

You may understand that your thoughts can be deceptive, but your body doesn't. Your body doesn't know whether your mind is accurately perceiving the external world or just freaking out. It responds to all mental messages as though they were accurate. There is a way you can turn this apparent handicap into an advantage.

Let's try an exercise. Close your eyes. Take a deep breath and relax your body. Take another deep breath and let even more stress go. Now imagine that you're in a kitchen. Go to the refrigerator, open it, and take out a juicy yellow lemon. Feel its weight and notice its shape. Rub your finger on its surface and scratch its rind with your fingernail. Notice its sweet-sour smell and its moisture on your fingers. Now place the lemon on the table, take a knife, and slice it in half. Raise one of the halves to your mouth and slowly pass your tongue over the juicy surface.

I bet you have puckered your lips or begun to salivate. The lemon doesn't exist, obviously, but we can manufacture our physiological response by imagining the stimuli. If we can salivate over non-existent lemons, we can create other scenarios in our minds. We can imagine frightening situations that trigger stress, or we can imagine peaceful situations that trigger relaxation. Dr. Herbert Benson, the founder of Harvard University's Mind/Body Medical Institute, calls this *the relaxation response.*[6]

Dr. Benson proved that any form of mental concentration that distracts the individual from his or her usual concerns and anxieties can produce relaxation. The relaxation response is an innate mechanism of the hypothalamus and works independently of the individual's will. The capacity to relax is a natural gift of all human beings. Once our mind is clear of its usual sources of worry, serenity seems to be its natural state. An apocryphal story tells of someone once asking Michelangelo how he could carve such magnificent sculptures. He replied that he simply removed the excess marble. It seems that the secret to a relaxed body, heart, and mind is to let go of excess preoccupations.

As you relax, your pulse slows and your blood pressure decreases. Your breath deepens. Your brain waves shift from beta—those that correspond to being alert and aroused—to alpha, indicative of a relaxed state. The blood flow to your muscles decreases and is redirected to your brain and skin, producing a sensation of warmth and mental serenity. Your muscle tension decreases and you feel tranquil.

Stress in itself isn't harmful. The fight-or-flight response has served humans well. We couldn't have made it out of the caves without it. But this response only works for short periods of time. When your body operates in a state of emergency, it depletes all its available reserves without considering replenishment. This is unsustainable. That's why you normally shift into a state of relaxation after an activity that demands physical exertion. For cavemen this happened naturally. We have a harder time. Today's challenges are more subtle and require less extreme action than ever before, but at the same time, they don't have a clear ending. Because of the human capacity to imagine and fantasize, we can become permanently anxious. As opposed to normal stress, this is *distress*. Today, distress is one of the principal causes of mental and physical illness.

A powerful tool for ending distress is conscious breathing. This is a meditative technique intended to interrupt the vicious cycle of stress. The mind and body operate as a psychophysical unit, both to generate stress and to relax. It's easy to use this knowledge to create stress; if you stop breathing, you'll soon feel anxious. Likewise, when you harbor anxious thoughts, your breath becomes shallow and agitated. This negative cycle of fretful thoughts and poor oxygenation can escalate into a panic attack.

You can use your breath as a circuit breaker. You can relieve stress and stop anxiety with a deep breath. Breathing consciously simply entails paying attention and using your will to bring air to your belly. Concentrating on the breathing process immediately brings your attention to the here and now and soothes your mind. This is a simple yet very effective way to control stress.

A meditation master stood by the bank of a river speaking to a group of new students. "To meditate," he said, "you need to concentrate on your breathing. When you inhale, focus completely on inhaling. When you exhale, focus completely on exhaling."

"Can't we do something more interesting, some visualization or concentration exercise?" asked one student. "Breathing is so … boring."

The master grabbed the student by the neck and thrust his head under the water. The student struggled but the master held him. After a minute, the master relented and the student emerged, gasping for air. The master smiled at his soggy charge. "Do you still think breathing is boring?" he asked.

ZEN PARABLE

TOWARD EMOTIONAL MASTERY

There are five basic competencies for working with your emotions: *self-awareness, self-acceptance, self-regulation, self-inquiry,* and *self-expression.* These competencies correlate with five skills for working with other people's emotions: *recognition, acknowledgment, influence, inquiry,* and *listening.*

Self-awareness

Self-awareness is the capacity to know what is happening within yourself. The capacity to feel one's inner state is a basic survival skill of every organism, but human beings can develop it to a very high level. You not only experience your inner states; you can reflect on them and make them an object of your awareness. When you say "I feel fear," a part of you is afraid, but not all of you. There is a part that notices that the other part is afraid.

You can increase the intensity of your awareness at will. Like a theater set that is illuminated with more or less intensity, awareness occurs along a continuum. You can be more or less aware, more or less observant, and more or less mindful. The less attention you pay, the less alert you will be, and the greater will be your probability of living a mechanical life governed by unconscious impulses and automatic routines. The less aware you are, the less able you will be to develop the objective witnessing part of yourself, the part that can perceive and respond impartially. Awareness is at the foundation of freedom and responsibility; it is the basic tool for managing emotions and actions.

In order to notice feelings, you need to separate from them and adopt an objective viewpoint. Instead of looking at the world *through* your emotions, you need to look *at* them in order to gain perspective. When you get hijacked by an emotion, you are totally taken over by it. You can't be aware of the emotion, because there is no objective rational part of you that can be aware. The aspect of your mind that is capable of observing your emotion has disappeared and has been engulfed by the emotion. There's no space left for objective self-awareness. Instead of you having an emotion itself, the emotion has you.

That is what happened to Barry at the beginning of the chapter. He became overwhelmed by his anger. The part of him that could witness his anger had disappeared, taking with it any possibility that he could separate from his anger and choose to respond consciously to George. Barry wasn't in charge; his anger called the shots.

Anger can trigger destructive actions, so you may try to repress it. The problem with repressing emotions is that it creates stress and a dangerous imbalance in your body. It also prevents you from addressing problems and ends up damaging your relationships. As we saw in chapter 5, keeping toxic thoughts and feelings to yourself does not work. On the other hand, dumping your toxic waste does not work either. Barry recognized that he "lost it" and spilled the toxic content of his mind. The unfettered expression of emotions is generally harmful toward others and yourself. If it is problematic to succumb to the emotion, and it is problematic to repress the emotion, what to do?

> Since intense negative emotionality expressed as angry, rage-
> ful, vicious, or hurtful attacks can ruin effective communication
> and harm relationships, it is necessary to calm down and control
> excessive negative feelings to be able to communicate success-
> fully ... *As with tuning forks, individuals have the power to mute*
> *the emotional reactions of each other by simply containing and*
> *dampening their own emotional responses.*
>
> JOHN W. JACOBS[7]

You can manage your emotions by expanding your inner space to hold them without repressing them. You can stretch your awareness through "witnessing": that is, adopting a perspective from which you can observe the emotion with little attachment, capture the information that it provides you, and respond in alignment with your values. A useful metaphor is that of controlling a wild horse. You can tie the horse down or confine him in a tight corral, but this infuriates him. It is dangerous for both the horse and those around him. If you can put the horse in a vast field, he can run at will and burn his excess energy without hurting himself or others. Instead of tying down your emotions, it is better to give them lots of space.

From the witness perspective, you can observe with equanimity the part of yourself that is taken over by the emotion. If Barry had done this, he could have observed in the moment (as opposed to later on, when the damage had been done) that he was angry and that he wanted to lash out at George, even though he knew that nothing good would come of it. Taking a breath, he could have reengaged his thinking faculties, undoing the short circuit that left his rational mind offline.

Self-acceptance

The second step to managing your emotions is to accept them without judgment. You need to realize that your emotion is an automatic impulse that arises beyond your control. Thus, there can be no moral prescription about what you ought or ought not to feel at any moment. There can be no moral judgment regarding involuntary feelings. Judging yourself for feeling some emotion is like judging yourself for feeling tired, hungry, or cold. You just feel the way you feel, and the best thing to do is to accept it. It would only make things worse if Barry started berating himself for feeling angry. He would simply add guilt to anger. On the other hand, accepting his anger does not mean that Barry should refrain from analyzing the reasons he feels angry or question how to express his anger in congruence with his values. Compassionate acceptance and critical analysis are equally necessary for emotional mastery.

It is impossible to prevent an emotion. What is possible, and vitally important, is to abstain from acting impulsively. As Nathaniel Branden says, "Emotions need not be acted on when we see that to do so is counterproductive, but if they are treated with respect they can become invaluable pathways to important information … It is a mark of wisdom and maturity to understand that we have the power to be a nonjudgmental witness to our emotions, thoughts, and memories without being controlled by them or driven to act in self-destructive ways."[8]

It is helpful to remember that an emotion *always* has a valid foundation of thoughts. There's no such thing as a bad or unreasonable emotion. It is possible that the thoughts at the root of an emotion are inaccurate, unfounded, or destructive. Before you can analyze these thoughts, however, you need to pierce the emotional layer that surrounds them. The only thing that will drill through this layer is compassionate acceptance, and the one thing that will most harden it is harsh judgment. To master your emotions, you need to treat yourself with the same kindness with which you would treat a child. When judgment presides, understanding hides. If you criticize your emotions, you will never understand them. Without understanding, you can't discharge them appropriately. In order to understand your emotions, you need to treat them with respect and curiosity. You need to understand that you are not guilty or bad for having them.

As Nathaniel Branden explains:

CONSCIOUS BUSINESS

Desires and emotions as such are involuntary; they are not subject to direct volitional control. The result of subconscious evaluations, they cannot be commanded in and out of existence, any more than beliefs can. But it is impossible to compute the amount of guilt and suffering produced by the notion that certain desires and emotions are proof of moral culpability. "Because I feel such-and-such, I am a rotten person." "Because I *don't* feel such-and-such, I will burn in hell." Self-[acceptance] requires the freedom to approach the content of one's inner experience as a non-critical observer, an observer interested in noting facts, not in pronouncing moral judgments ... To approach self-examination with the question "What does it imply about my character if I have such-and-such thoughts or such-and-such emotions?" is to make perceptual self-censorship a foregone conclusion.[9]

Self-regulation

The third step in working with your emotions is regulating your impulses. You need to maintain awareness in the face of instinctual pressures. To regulate means to have control and give direction to the emotional energy. According to Daniel Goleman, the capacity to subordinate immediate gratification to transcendent objectives and values is a key psychological skill: "There is perhaps no psychological skill more fundamental than resisting impulse. It is the root of all emotional self-control, since all emotions, by their very nature, lead to one or another impulse to act."[10]

Widespread ignorance about emotional regulation has created two common myths: that both explosion and implosion are healthy. The first myth is the idea that the "free expression" of our impulses is productive. The second is the notion that the way to handle emotions is to repress them.

Impulsive indulgence is not emotional intelligence. You can unload without examining the foundations of your emotions and their effects. These actions usually perpetuate the cycle of suffering, plunging you into a state of increasing frustration. Shouting at others never solves the problem—on the contrary, it usually makes it worse—so you may have learned to stuff your anger. When you experience the downside of your emotional outbursts, you may want to tighten the reins of your heart and become stoic.

But stoicism is not equanimity. You can remain impassive on the outside while boiling over on the inside. Pressure accumulates until you reach your limit and explode—or implode. In Western cultures, people tend to explode; in Eastern cultures, to implode. One is as bad as the other. As Goleman says, "Imploders often fail to take any action to better their situation. They may not show outward signs of an emotional hijack, but they suffer the internal fallout anyway: headaches, edginess, smoking and drinking too much, sleeplessness, endless self-criticism. And they have the same health risks as those who explode, and so need to learn to manage their own reactions to distress."[11]

Regulating your emotions involves conscious expression. To channel emotional energy you need to recognize it, embrace it, and understand its origins. You also need to acknowledge its impulses, but without surrendering to them. When you develop this discipline, you can fully accept what you feel without acting against your values. In regard to integrity, you are only accountable for your actions, not for your emotions. Emotions are good advisors, but terrible masters. You need to listen to them, but without abdicating your responsibility to behave with integrity.

Those who enter the gates of heaven are not beings that have no passions or who have curbed the passions, but those who have cultivated an understanding of them.

WILLIAM BLAKE, FROM *THE MARRIAGE OF HEAVEN AND HELL*

Self-inquiry

In order to master emotions, you need to find their root stories. You need to analyze your thoughts in order to separate useful information from neurosis.

Every emotion grows out of an interpretation and blossoms into an impulse. If you honor that impulse with integrity, you achieve success beyond success. Conscious action guarantees a feeling of dignity and inner peace regardless of the final outcome. It provides the serenity of knowing that you did everything you needed to do. Here are some common emotions with their corresponding root stories, calls to action, and emotional rewards.

Happiness: We feel happy when we believe that something good has happened. Think of a time when you felt happy; notice that your happiness grew from your assessment that you had gained something you valued. Happiness calls for celebration. When we celebrate, we recognize what we have achieved and face the future with equanimity. Question: Are there significant achievements that you (or your team) need to celebrate?

Sadness: We feel sad when we believe that something bad has happened. Sadness is the expression of care in the face of a loss. Think of a time when you felt sad; notice that your sadness grew from your assessment that you had lost something you valued. Sadness calls for grieving. When we grieve, we acknowledge the importance of the loss and recover a sense of inner peace. Grieving closes the past, honoring our love for what we lost, and lets us refocus on the future. Question: Are there significant losses that you (or your team) need to grieve?

Enthusiasm: We feel enthusiastic when we believe that something good may happen. Think of a time when you felt enthusiastic; notice that your enthusiasm grew from your assessment that you could attain something you valued. Enthusiasm calls for effort to achieve the desired objective. When we channel enthusiasm into concrete actions, we increase the probability of achieving our objectives. Question: Are there significant opportunities on which you (or your team) need to focus?

Fear: We feel afraid when we believe that something bad may happen. Think of a time when you felt scared; notice that your fear grew from your assessment that you could lose something you valued. Fear calls for risk mitigation, preparation, and protection. When we channel fear into concrete actions, we decrease the probability (or the impact) of the loss. Question: Are there significant risks that you (or your team) need to mitigate?

Gratitude: We feel grateful when we believe that someone went out of his or her way to do something good for us. Think of a time when you felt grateful; notice that your gratitude grew from your assessment that someone, without being obligated, helped you attain something you valued. Gratitude calls for appreciation. When we thank the person who helped us, we recognize his deed and acknowledge its impact on our well-being. Question: Are there significant gifts that you (or your team) need to appreciate?

Anger: We feel angry when we believe that someone has hurt us inappropriately. Think of a time when you felt angry; notice that your anger grew from your judgment that someone had harmed you by doing something they shouldn't have. When you are angry you believe that, through some transgression, someone damaged something you value. Anger calls for a complaint, an effort to reestablish the violated boundaries. It also calls for repairing what was damaged and protecting it for the future. When we express our anger productively (recall that productive expression of anger always starts with describing your hurt), we reaffirm our values and begin the process of forgiveness. Question: Are there significant angers that you need to express and forgive?

Guilt: Guilt is anger directed toward oneself. We feel guilty when we believe we have done something inconsistent with our values. Think of a time when you felt guilty; notice that your guilt grew from your judgment that you committed a transgression that hurt someone. According to your own values, you did something you shouldn't have. Guilt calls for an apology, an effort to make amends. When we express our remorse productively, we do our best to repair the damage and recover our integrity. Question: Are there significant apologies or reparations that you need to make?

Self-expression

To move from self-inquiry to self-expression you need to articulate the story behind the emotion. Here are a few questions you might use to do it.

Sadness. What are you sad about? What do you think you've lost? What leads you to believe that you lost it? What value did it have for you? How could you lessen or recover from the impact of its loss? How could you mourn what you lost in order to work through it and honor how important it was for you? Is there something else that you might need to do to feel at peace?

Fear. What are you worried about (or afraid of)? What do you imagine might happen? What would you lose if that happened? What makes you think that this might happen, and that if it does it will harm you? How could you reduce the chances of it happening? How could you minimize the damage you would suffer in case it did happen? What else might you need to do to be at peace?

Anger. What are you angry about? What hurt have you experienced? Who do you think caused it? What did he or she do? What boundaries did he or she transgress? What would reduce the damage or feel like reparation to you? How can you express your complaint? What else might you need to do to be at peace? Would you be willing to forgive?

Guilt. What do you feel guilty about? What damage have you inflicted? Who have you hurt? What boundary did you transgress? Could you ask the damaged person about their loss? How could you minimize the damage and offer reparations? How could you express your apology? What else might you need to do to be at peace? Would you be willing to forgive yourself?

❖

The Latin root of "emotion" means "move out;" the French, "stir up." The natural emotional cycle is to get stirred up (feeling) and then move out (action). When feelings are acknowledged and expressed appropriately, they foster personal, interpersonal, and operational health. According to Dr. David Viscott, author of *Emotional Resilience,* "If you lived honestly, your life would heal itself ... If you acted with total honesty, expressing your true feelings to the person who most needed to hear them, you would be doing your part [in the process of natural healing]. The benefits you would receive would be peace of mind, enduring health, and comfort with yourself just as you are."[12]

When the emotional cycle gets blocked, emotions turn stale. Those who dam the flow of feelings fall into negative moods such as resignation, resentment, and depression. These moods are frozen and pervasive emotional states that take on a life of their own. One is sad *about* something, but one is just depressed. While sorrow can be addressed through grieving, depression lingers like a heavy fog. It is much more difficult to lift it because clearing it requires first unfreezing the stuck emotional energy. It often requires the assistance of a mental health professional. Every time we block an emotion we incur an emotional debt, which sooner or later we have to pay—with high interest.

Most people don't express their emotions because they don't know how to do it. Many of us have had painful experiences of hurting others or being hurt in emotional exchanges. We tend to identify the hurt with the expression of emotion, but it is truly a consequence of our ineffective mode of expression. Here's a formula that can help you express emotions consciously and turn them into effective action:

I feel "A" when "B," because I think "C." Does this make sense to you? (Listen in silence and acknowledge.) What I'd like is "D," so I want to ask you "E." Is that acceptable to you?

"A" is an emotion (such as sorrow, fear, anger, or guilt); "B" is a factual report or observation; "C" is an assessment or interpretation; "D" is a need or interest; and "E" is a request. This formula helps you take responsibility, avoiding the "you make me feel" mistake. It also reports the facts while acknowledging the thoughts and desires that underlie your emotion. It gives the listener a chance to respond and share his or her feelings and interpretations. Finally, it concludes with a well-formed request and an invitation to commit with clarity. This formula is like a set of training wheels. When you become competent it is no longer necessary, but it can be an excellent aid in the learning process.

For example, Barry could tell George, "I feel frustrated when you oppose my proposal because I believe I've put out a convincing argument, but you have rejected it without giving me an explanation. Does this make sense to you?" George would respond, "Well, it's not my intention to frustrate you, but I don't think that this project is going to work." Barry would acknowledge, "I hear that you don't have much faith in the project," and continue with, "What I want to understand is *why* you think that it won't work. I want to hear your reasoning with as much detail as you can give me." After this, either George would provide some solid argument, which Barry would then consider, or George wouldn't have much to offer, which would put him in a difficult position. Either way, the conversation would move forward. Of course, this behavior demands that Barry "love the truth more than he loves saving face." Emotional mastery requires that you be more interested in being effective than in saving face. In Barry's case he'd have to stop pushing to get the proposal approved, so he could check whether his ideas are as sound as he believes they are.

◆

Healthy emotional expressions are adequate responses to life's circumstances. After suffering a misfortune, for example, it is reasonable to feel sad, try to resolve the problem, and avoid similar situations in the future. If someone defaults on a commitment to us, it is reasonable to feel angry and complain. It is perfectly healthy to feel fear at the chance that someone we love may be hurt; that fear is the impulse to protect what we value. It is useful to feel guilt if we think we have done something wrong, since our guilt impels us to apologize and try to repair the damage. Problems arise when our distorted thoughts exacerbate our emotions to the point that they become harmful, preventing all productive expression.

COGNITIVE DISTORTIONS

If you examine the particular story of an emotion, you will find a series of assessments and beliefs. Whenever you are sad, you believe that you've lost something valuable; whenever you are angry, you believe somebody wronged you, and so on. These beliefs may be false. You may have inaccurate information about the facts, or you may be using defective logic. Many beliefs are a product of cognitive distortions. The three most relevant cognitive distortions around emotions are victimhood, confusion, and judgment ("should-ing").

Victimhood: When Barry says that George "made him angry," he is displaying a lack of responsibility. Barry sees himself as a victim of an external factor—George—that "caused" his emotions. As we saw in chapter 2, unless you see yourself as a contributor to your experience, which includes your emotions, you cannot see yourself as able to influence your experience. Another example of victimhood is Barry saying, "I was so upset I couldn't help myself" or "My anger made me do it." Barry presents himself as unable to choose, controlled by his impulses. Although emotional drives exert influence, ultimately your behavior is an act of will. It is possible to feel intensely without acting unconsciously. In fact it is only possible to feel intensely when you trust yourself *not* to act impulsively.

Confusion: Statements like "I feel betrayed by my boss" or "I feel that this project is not worthwhile" confuse emotions and interpretations. "Betrayal" is an interpretation, not an emotion. "Feel that," "feel like," or "feel (verb in passive voice)" are phrases that precede an interpretation, not an emotion. Emotions are "hot;" they require acceptance and regulation. On the other hand, thoughts are "cool" and call for analysis. Instead of saying that he felt patronized by George, Barry would be better served by realizing he felt angry because he *interpreted* George's behavior as patronizing. George did what he did, and it was Barry who experienced what happened as patronizing. Furthermore, Barry made the angering inference that George's intention was to patronize him. As we saw in chapter 5, this is a dangerous mistake. "Patronizing," like any other assessment, is in the eye of the beholder.

When people are clear about the difference between thoughts and emotions, their speech patterns change. If Barry were more skilled, instead of claiming, "I feel patronized," he would reflect, "I feel angry because I interpret George's behavior as patronizing." Similarly, instead of "I feel that you won't support me," one would say, "I am worried because I don't know whether you will support me." Instead of "I feel like you don't pay any attention to me," "I feel sad because I think that you are not interested in my ideas." Instead of "I feel rejected," "I feel angry because I did not receive any response to my suggestions."

When people fall prey to confusion and assume that their thoughts are emotions, they close off rational inquiry. Imagine that a colleague complains, "I feel left out by the team." You inquire, "What leads you to feel left out?" And your colleague replies, "That's just how I feel." Unless your colleague realizes that "left out" is an assessment, it will be very difficult to ask him to explain why he holds the assessment and to offer suggestions about what the team can do to improve the situation.

Confusion gets magnified when people consider their emotions to be supporting evidence for their opinions. In the example at the beginning of this chapter, Barry might argue, "I'm angry with George, therefore he must have patronized me," or, "I feel resigned and hopeless about my relationship with George, therefore our problems must be unsolvable." It's impossible to address difficulties when people operate on the basis of emotional reasoning. Imagine a domestic dispute.

"You treat me poorly," she says.

"What did I do now?" he asks.

"You made me feel bad."

"But I didn't do anything to you," he protests.

"If you hadn't done anything to me, I wouldn't feel bad."

Should-ing: This is the tendency to think in terms of obligations as opposed to possibilities. When people impose expectations on others, on the world, and on themselves, they spend most of their time feeling angry and guilty. For example, someone who thinks "I should be more successful" or "I shouldn't have said that in the meeting" is likely to feel stress and remorse; paradoxically, one who rebels against these oppressive self-commands is likely to feel apathetic and unmotivated. When the person turns these "should" thoughts on others, he sets himself up for disillusionment and frustration. For example, Barry's beliefs that "George should agree with me" and that "he shouldn't have expressed his disagreement to others before talking to me directly" promote a permanent state of indignation. There is no problem in holding standards or preferences such as "I would prefer having George agree with me" or "I would like George to talk to me directly before he talks to others." "Would" opens a conversation, while "should" closes it.

Checking an emotion's underlying story for cognitive distortions enables us to validate its grounding and find positive ways to express it. It's crucial to distinguish rational reflection from repression. To analyze doesn't mean to invalidate or censure; it means to consider the validity of thoughts and the relative convenience of different possible actions. Given its underlying story, every emotion can be investigated through a corresponding series of questions. These questions can be part of an internal dialogue (asking oneself) or an external dialogue (asking another).

This being human is a guest house.
Every morning a new arrival.

A joy, a depression, a meanness,
some momentary awareness comes
as an unexpected visitor.

Welcome and entertain them all!
Even if they're a crowd of sorrows,
who violently sweep your house
empty of its furniture,
still, treat each guest honorably.
He may be clearing you out
for some new delight.

The dark thought, the shame, the malice,
meet them at the door laughing,
and invite them in.

Be grateful for whoever comes,
because each has been sent
as a guide from beyond.

RUMI, "THE GUEST HOUSE"[13]

Anger and guilt are two particularly challenging emotions to master. Besides skillful expression, these two emotions call for an additional step: forgiveness.

FORGIVENESS

Forgiveness is an essential practice for emotional mastery, but it arouses strong reactions. "How can I forgive him after what he did?" "Forgive her? Are you crazy? She doesn't deserve it!" Without forgiveness, anger turns into resentment and guilt into shame. If you want to be free of resentment and shame, you need to forgive others and yourself. To learn to forgive we must first correct erroneous interpretations of forgiveness.

Forgiveness is *not* absolving bad behavior. Forgiveness doesn't mean approving or condoning actions that fail to meet your standards. It doesn't exclude demanding compensation or taking corrective action. You may even sever the relationship. You can forgive an employee who isn't doing his job to your satisfaction and still fire him. Forgiveness allows you to do what you need to do without resentment.

Forgiveness is *not* pretending that everything is all right when you feel it isn't. At times, it is difficult to distinguish between forgiving and denying anger and sorrow. Genuine forgiveness can only be achieved if you pay attention to your emotions. A false smile and a "don't worry, everything's fine" are the opposite of forgiveness.

Forgiveness is *not* adopting a holier-than-thou attitude or doing others a favor. If you forgive out of a sense of superiority or pity, you are confusing forgiveness with arrogance. You don't forgive out of generosity or charity; you do it as an act of integrity, as a way to close a painful past so that it won't continue to negatively affect your future.

So what *is* forgiveness?

Forgiveness is the choice to let go of resentment. It's a commitment to live in the present, free of anger's inertia. To resent is to cling to the past, to keep alive the original suffering. Resentment is self-righteous rumination. It calls for revenge rather than reparation. It promises relief, but it yields only suffering. As Robin Casarjian says, "Resentment has been compared to holding onto a burning ember with the intention of throwing it at another, all the while burning yourself. In fact, the word *resentment* comes from the French *ressentir*—to feel strongly and to feel again. When we feel resentful, we feel strongly the pain of the past again and again."[14] On the other hand, forgiveness releases the painful past through an act of will. When you let go of resentment, resentment lets go of you. Forgiveness allows you to grow beyond painful circumstances, to carry on without unfinished business.

When you forgive, you accept what has happened without denying your grief. You establish your inner peace and freedom—not freedom from loss, but freedom to respond openheartedly to any loss. This lets you feel secure and powerful in a world full of risks. As D. Patrick Miller says, "Forgiveness replaces the need to anticipate fearfully with the capacity to accept gracefully and improvise brilliantly. It does not argue with fate, but recognizes the opportunities latent within it. If necessity is the mother of invention, forgiveness is the midwife of genius."[15]

Forgiveness is not just for others. Emotional mastery requires that you forgive yourself. It's critical, however, that you distinguish self-forgiveness from self-indulgence. Just as forgiveness doesn't absolve wrong behavior, self-forgiveness doesn't erase justified guilt. On the contrary, self-forgiveness takes guilt as the trigger for atonement. Self-forgiveness is the ultimate source of resilience. It allows you to bounce back after a setback and grow from the failure. It turns errors into steps along the learning path. When you master forgiveness you can identify mistakes (yours and others') compassionately, without excuses.

MASTERING OTHERS' EMOTIONS

For most people, to master implies to dominate. That is *not* the connotation I intend to convey. Just as I argued in chapter 5 that productive inquiry is geared to help the other express his or her truth effectively, I argue here that mastering others' emotions aims to help them achieve emotional mastery, improve the relationship, and complete the task at hand. Before you can help others, however, it is absolutely essential that you attain emotional mastery yourself. The most important tool for helping another master his or her emotions is "resonance."

Put two tuning forks of the same pitch side by side. As you strike the first, you will notice that the second starts vibrating in resonance. In a relationship, each individual acts like a tuning fork that receives and transmits emotional waves. When one person has an emotional reaction, the "vibrations" affect the other—who starts vibrating in response. This response cycles back and either intensifies or dampens the first person's emotion.

If the two people are emotionally reactive, they will escalate their negative interactions into a frenzy. If one of them stays centered, she can start a dampening cycle even when the other person stays reactive. When you master your emotions, you can bring equanimity to any relationship. If you can stay grounded in the midst of an emotionally charged situation, you can help others stay conscious. On the other hand, unless you master the emotional skills I described above, you cannot hope to help others.

Each of the five competencies of self-mastery correlates to mastering other people's emotions: *recognition, acceptance, defusing, inquiry,* and *listening.*

Recognition

Although you can't observe the internal states of others, you can observe external signs. Emotions have a physical component (flushing cheeks) and a behavioral component (tightening fists). You can make valid inferences about the other's feelings based upon these observable emotional clues (physical and behavioral), an understanding of the other's situation, your attribution of values and objectives to the other, and your projection onto the other of the internal emotional dynamics you would experience in a similar situation (empathy).

It is important to realize that what you infer the other thinks and feels is *not* what the other actually thinks and feels. It is a cognitive distortion to believe that you can read another's mind and know what he or she is thinking and feeling. On the other hand, refusing to consider emotional signs is a great mistake. The skillful way to work with attributions (inferences about another person's emotional and mental state) is to base them upon the best evidence available, state them tentatively (acknowledging that they are just your interpretation), and ask the other to verify them.

For example, upon noticing that a team member is sitting with crossed arms, completely quiet, and a little distant from the meeting table, an alert leader could say, "Tim, I see that you're quiet, your arms are crossed, and you're seated far from the table. I'm wondering how you're feeling about our conversation."

Notice how different that is than attacking Tim with "You're upset! What's wrong with you?" Or, seeing that a client has glanced at her watch repeatedly, a sensitive salesperson could say: "You've looked at your watch several times. Perhaps this isn't the best time to talk. Would you like to postpone the meeting?" This would be much more productive than thinking (and even worse, saying), "I see that you aren't interested. Why did you ask me to come if you didn't want to listen to me?"

Acceptance

To work with others' emotions it is necessary to accept them without judgment. It's not only useless to chastise somebody for what he or she feels, it's also counterproductive. You might feel the urge to tell a troubled coworker to cheer up, or tell your child that things are not really so bad, but such admonitions never work. The receiver not only continues to feel troubled, but now he feels alienated as well. A manager who notices that employees are scared about an upcoming organizational change might feel inclined to assure them, "There's nothing to be concerned about." He may mean well, but his statement will most likely scare the employees even more. Challenging others' emotions makes them feel judged, misunderstood, and disrespected. In extreme cases, it can make them doubt their sanity.

Often, the hardest emotion to accept in others is anger. Most of us are inclined to protect ourselves against angry attacks. If someone calls you rude, your first response might be to point out that it is rude to call someone rude. That brings a moment of relief, but it only escalates the conflict. When someone gets mad at you, don't get mad, get curious. In the spirit of inquiry, you could say, "I see that you're angry with me. That troubles me because I'd like for us to have a good relationship. Can you tell me what I did to anger you?" This initiates a dialogue in which one can inquire about and analyze the other's interpretations without invalidating his emotions.

In chapter 5, I focused on the informational content of communications. Now I want to focus on the emotional context. In a real-world situation, it is impossible to separate content from context, but for learning purposes it makes sense to distinguish the two dimensions. Consider the following dialogue with a colleague whom I've asked for suggestions about this text.

Bill: "Fred, I'm upset with you."

Fred: "I'm sorry to hear that you're upset with me, Peter. What's up?"

Bill: "You made me work for nothing."

Fred: "Oh! I can see how believing that would anger you. Tell me, what did I ask you to do that you believe was for nothing?"

Bill: "You asked me to give you suggestions about your book."

Fred: "That's true, and I'm really grateful for your effort. What makes you think that your commentaries weren't significant for me?"

Bill: "You disregarded many of them."

Fred: "Disregarded? I don't remember having disregarded any. They all seemed relevant. I considered each of them carefully."

Bill: "I saw the edited version of your book and many of my suggestions weren't there."

Fred: "Ah! Now I understand the problem. Let me explain. When I asked for your help, I wanted ideas for improving the book. Many of your ideas seemed excellent and led me to modify the text. Other ideas didn't seem as appealing to me. But the ideas that I considered ineffective were in their own way as valuable to me as those that I considered excellent. Each of your suggestions made me think about what I wanted to say and how I wanted to say it."

Bill: "Then you admit that you disregarded many of my ideas."

Fred: "If by 'disregard' you mean, 'not to change the text according to them,' then yes, I admit I did that."

Bill: "That's exactly what I call working for nothing!"

Fred: "I'm sorry you think that way. I understand your point of view.

I want to express my appreciation for your work, but I also want to reserve editorial control over my book. I took your suggestions—and those of other friends who are helping me—as an offer. If I don't feel comfortable with a particular recommendation, don't you think that I have the right and the responsibility to choose according to my own criterion?"

Bill: "Well, after all, it is *your* book ..."

Fred: "True, but much of what makes it good comes from the help of friends like you. I really appreciate the effort and care with which you've read the material and given recommendations for improving it. How can I show my appreciation for your suggestions, even for those that I decided not to incorporate?"

Bill: "Hmmm. That's a good question. Perhaps if you had explained to me why you didn't accept them, I would've felt more recognized for my efforts."

Fred: "That's a great idea! I can show my appreciation for your efforts by telling you what I think about them. I commit to do so from now on. I'm sorry for not having been more considerate, and thank you for your work—and this conversation."

Bill: "You're welcome."

Defusing

Nothing defuses emotions like your own relaxed and centered stance. Simply not reacting exerts a tremendous dampening effect on intense emotions. Accepting the other's emotion without judgment helps him recover his equanimity. Even in extreme circumstances, when you can't imagine how to continue a relationship, it is possible to defuse the other's emotions. Someone may be very upset with you, but you don't have to escalate the conflict. You can take responsibility for the perception you triggered in the other and do your best to maintain serenity. Through open inquiry, you can allow the other person to express his feelings and thoughts fully. When you understand the story behind the emotion you can take appropriate action to address it. And if the situation proves intractable, you can always separate in peace and with integrity.

Charles: "You're inconsiderate!"

Fred: "I've heard that from others before. Maybe I'm acting inconsiderately without realizing it. What makes you think that I'm inconsiderate?"

Charles: "Everything you do. You never pay attention to me."

Fred: "Surely I could be more kind. When haven't I paid attention to you?"

Charles: "Don't you start with your trick questions. You're a know-it-all and I don't matter to you whatsoever."

Fred: "I admit that sometimes I think I know more than I really do. I'm working to be more open to learning."

Charles: "That isn't true. You're just trying to look like you are more open. The truth is that you don't care."

Fred: "I'm sorry that you think that. I'd like to show you that I really care. Is there something I can do that would change your opinion about me?"

Charles: "I don't think so. You're hopeless."

Fred: "If you're convinced and unwilling to change your mind, I guess there's not much I can do."

Charles: "That's right. This is over. I don't want to work with you anymore."

Fred: "I'm sorry you feel hurt because you think I don't pay attention to you. I also understand that you find me inconsiderate to the point that nothing I can do would affect your assessment. So you don't want to work with me anymore. I guess that under the circumstances, that's the best way to proceed. Thank you for your honesty."

Without a reaction, an attack can't last long. Like a fire that runs out of fuel, the emotional heat will consume itself. That's why the best way to receive another's emotion is with empathy, without judgment or argument. In order to defuse aggressive energy, look for ways to agree with the critic; don't concern yourself with how incorrect you may believe his opinions are. Look for the slightest grain of truth with which you can agree, so you can blend with the critical energy without sarcasm or defensiveness.

Remember that people who criticize you are speaking their truth. According to their experiences and their interpretations, they are perfectly right in feeling what they feel. If you can acknowledge that their emotions are valid, you will help them to express their truth not just as content (opinions) but also as context (emotions). This is the inter-subjective equivalent of the witness position. You are expanding the communication space so that there's enough room for the other's emotion in its full intensity. As the emotion is expressed without encountering any defense that intensifies it, it loses its charge. Once the emotion has lost its intensity, it's possible to move onto the next step: inquiry and listening.

Inquiry and listening

Inquiry aims to help others understand and express their emotions skillfully. The key is to help them present their needs and interests in a way that helps us see how to genuinely satisfy those needs and interests while also taking care of our own. Inquiry and listening are about influencing others, not manipulating them. The difference is respect for their autonomy, focus on valid information, and free choice. Manipulation is an underhanded attempt that, were it made public, would embarrass the manipulator and infuriate the manipulated. For example, distorting information in order to lead the other to act the way we want, while believing that if he knew what we know he would not want to act that way, is manipulation. Asking someone to do something, on the other hand, is not manipulation; it is an open request. Our influence is overt, not covert. One way to make sure you are not manipulating the other is to use the golden rule: Would you like the other to inquire and listen to you in the way you are inquiring and listening to him?

Let's see how to inquire into another person's anger.

Helen: "You undermined me at the meeting!"
Fred: "Oh, I'm sorry you feel that way. I didn't notice I was undermining you. It was not my intention."
Helen: "Well, intention or not, you did it!"
Fred: "Although I don't like it, I must admit that I've heard that from others

before. I guess I may have acted unconsciously. Can you tell me what I did that upset you?"

Helen: "Are you *that* dumb? You made me look like a fool in front of the boss!"

Fred: "I'm afraid I may be that dumb. I am not sure what you are referring to. I need your help here. How was it that I made you look like a fool?"

Helen: "Come on, don't you remember? When I was presenting the budget you opened your big fat mouth and said that the estimate for revenues that I had used was inconsistent with the one that the sales team had presented. It was so embarrassing."

Fred: "Oh yeah, now I remember. I feel bad that it hurt you. I see how you would experience it as an attack."

Helen: "Well, your bad feelings don't change a thing. You embarrassed me."

Fred: "I understand, and I hope you hear my regret about the way things went. If you're open, I'd like to ask you a couple of questions to try to improve the situation."

Helen: "Whatever."

Fred: "I understand that what I said was problematic for you. I'd like to get some advice on how to proceed more considerately if this happens again. Let's go back to the meeting in question. You'd just put your numbers up on the screen and I realized that your revenue projections were inconsistent. What would you have liked me to do?"

Helen: "You could have kept your mouth shut and told me privately at the end of the meeting."

Fred: "Yes, I could have. In fact, I thought of it. But then it struck me that I would have been willfully misleading the team. You made an honest error, but I would have been letting all of us go down the wrong path. That wouldn't work for me. Would you have waited if you had been in my shoes?"

Helen: "I don't know, probably not. But I wouldn't have humiliated you."

Fred: "Well, that's exactly what I'd like to learn: how to say what I said without coming across as humiliating. What could I have said that would not feel humiliating?"

Helen: "Instead of being so smug and bursting out with 'You got the wrong number!' you could have used a more humble tone and said 'I'm not sure, but the revenue number seems different than the one the sales team used for their estimation. Is that so?' That would have been a lot less aggressive."

Fred: "You're right. I could have said that without any problem. Indeed, it would have been a lot better! I feel sheepish. I guess I was a bit too full of myself."

Helen: "I guess you were."

Fred: "Would you accept my apologies? I did not mean to embarrass you."

Helen: "Okay. I guess I overreacted too. In the big scheme of things, it's not such a big deal."

◆

Emotional mastery preserves the ability to put into practice the principles and tools of past chapters in challenging situations. When your emotional circuits are strong, they can withstand high charges. When they are weak, intense emotions will blow your fuses and disable your conscious mind. Your behavior will then fall under the control of unconscious defense mechanisms. Regardless of how many books you have read or seminars you have attended, you will forget them all and turn into a fight-or-flight machine. Taking a conscious breath is the simplest way to reengage your awareness and choice. In breathing, as in any other skill, practice makes perfect. In order to take a breath when it counts—that is, under highly charged conditions—it is necessary to take about ten thousand breaths in training.

If a man is crossing a river
And an empty boat collides with his own skiff,
Even though he be a bad-tempered man
He will not become very angry.
But if he [thinks he] sees a man in the boat,
He will shout at him to steer clear.

If the shout is not heard, he will shout again,

And yet again, and begin cursing.

And all because [he thinks] there is somebody in the boat.

Yet if the boat were empty,

He would not be shouting, and not angry.

CHUANG TZU, FROM "THE EMPTY BOAT" [16]

CHAPTER 9

Entering the Market
with Helping Hands

◆

*The market system brings prosperity to those who satisfy
the desires of others in the best and least expensive way.
Wealth can only be attained by serving the consumer.*

LUDWIG VON MISES

*Some day after we have mastered the winds,
the waves, the tides, and gravity,
we shall harness the energies of love.
And then for the second time in the history of the world,
man will have discovered fire.*

PIERRE TEILHARD DE CHARDIN

◆

W ork is love made visible," said Kahlil Gibran. Service, rather
than greed, is what drives a market economy. Business is a
crucial arena for the expression of the human spirit. But love,
service, and spirituality are not terms usually associated with the marketplace. Many of us believe that it is necessary to sell out in order to succeed in
business, or to drop out in order to pursue a spiritual life. This is a false polar-
ity. When business is conducted with a high level of consciousness, there is
no tension between material and spiritual wealth. Conscious leadership can
create a conscious business, one that integrates wisdom and compassion in

support of human development. In a conscious business, ancient wisdom and modern economics come together.

One of the best-known maps of the spiritual path is a series of carvings called the Ten Ox-Herding Pictures. It comes from the Zen teachings of twelfth century China. These images depict the journey of a shepherd and his ox. At the beginning, the wild ox is lost; it doesn't even appear in the first picture. We only see the shepherd looking for it. As the journey progresses, the shepherd finds the ox, tames it, rides it home, and eventually becomes one with it. In the ninth picture, both the ox and the shepherd disappear, but in the tenth and final image the shepherd, transformed into a Buddha, shows up smiling. The last carving represents the shepherd's final awakening. Surprising those who think that business and spirituality don't mix, it is called "Entering the Marketplace with Helping Hands."

The shepherd represents the seeker; the ox, the seeker's mind. The journey begins when the human being realizes that his mind is out of control, that it has gone wild and trapped him in a world of illusion. He becomes conscious of his unconsciousness. Realizing the problem, he begins his search for truth. Near the end of his journey, in the ninth picture, the seeker reaches Enlightenment. He realizes the infinite spaciousness in which both he and his mind arise. He recognizes the empty nature of phenomena (from the Greek, "appearances") and actualizes the no-thing-ness of his true nature. Thus, he "disappears."

Commentator Lex Hixon says this about this next-to-last stage: "The process of enlightenment has come so far, through so many simplifications, that there is difficulty in recognizing and accepting the constructions of human personality and society: 'It is as though he (the shepherd) were now blind and deaf. Seated in his hut, he hankers not for things outside.' There is a subtle separation here between the Source flowing as pine or cherry trees and its manifestation as the chronic delusion and suffering of human civilization."[1]

When Hixon describes the spiritual seeker as "blind and deaf" and averse to engagement with human society, he touches on the main argument many business people make against the spiritual quest. The preoccupation with the sacred, they claim, ends in disregard for the mundane; if you are a mystic, you can't handle logistics. Many spiritual seekers, indeed, lose interest in daily affairs; some of them never return to the human world. For them, ordinary reality is simply an illusion that must be left behind; transcending means disappearing. However, as the Ox-Herding Pictures suggest, the spiritual path does not end in the void. On the contrary, it ends with a return to the world.

In the tenth picture, "Entering the Marketplace with Helping Hands," the shepherd, finally awakened to the Truth of Being, appears as "a jolly rustic that wanders from village to village, from mundane situation to mundane situation. His body is overflowing with life-energy. His being is full of compassionate love. His open hands express perfect emptiness."[2] A perfect emptiness that is ready to manifest as creative and helpful work.

If you follow the lessons presented in this book, you too will embark on an ox-herding quest. This journey will help you regain control of your mind, taking you away from ingrained habits into a higher level of consciousness. It will challenge you to take a stand for your values and interact with others authentically, constructively, and impeccably. It will help you reconnect with who you are and what you are meant to do in this world. It is an extraordinary journey that can rightly be called "spiritual."

The word "spirit" derives from the same root as breath, and it was once used to mean the principle animating a living organism. Over time, the focus shifted from life to consciousness as the central concept of spirituality. Thus, we can define "spirit" as the life principle manifest in consciousness, and "spiritual activity" as an effort to develop consciousness in oneself and others.[3]

Business is not typically seen as a spiritual activity. It is supposed to pursue only money-oriented goals devoid of any deeper significance. The only worthwhile businesses, however, are conscious businesses: those that tackle their work as a spiritual activity.

It is easy to dismiss the whole spiritual venture as pie-in-the-sky or removed from the cares of the world, but, as the Ox-Herding Pictures suggest, this is not the case. The story does not end with you holed up in a Himalayan cave. It ends with a more enlightened you returning to the marketplace with helping hands.

Contrary to business school doctrine, "maximizing shareholder wealth" or "profit maximization" has not been the dominant driving force ... of [exceptional] companies ... Yes, they seek profits, but they're equally guided by ... core values and sense of purpose beyond just making money. Yet, paradoxically, the visionary companies make more money than the more purely profit-driven comparison companies.

JIM COLLINS AND JERRY I. PORRAS[4]

THE REAL PURPOSE OF BUSINESS

I remember the first time my son, Tomás, beat me at a game of Scrabble. He was ten years old. His face was beaming. Mine was beaming even more! I was satisfied when I won, but I was elated when *he* won. I was so proud of him. Playing Scrabble with Tomás, I realized I couldn't lose. If I won, it was good; if he won, it was better. Although I continue to strive to win, I know that as I play with him, whatever happens will bring me joy. The reason is obvious: I love my son. I want him to grow and reach his full potential. I take delight in his intelligence, skill, and cunning, even when the little rascal gets a triple-point word and steals the game from under my nose!

I was stunned by the realization that it is impossible to suffer a loss when you love your opponent. There is loss, but no suffering. It is possible to compete with a loved one, but it is not possible to regret his success—even if it is at the expense of yours. The sense of separation is what creates fear and sorrow. "When there are two, fear arises," says the sage. In the oneness of love, there is only joy. The oneness of love seems easy to feel with a child, but is it possible to feel something like it with a business competitor?

It is possible, but rare. The inclusion of another in our circle of care and concern requires the development of consciousness. Only at the higher stages of maturity can we embrace our competitors as "neighbors" to love.

One of the markers of human evolution is the extension of our "circle of care and concern." At the lowest levels, the individual is concerned only with himself. Every one of us starts at the egocentric stage, where the only thing that matters is "me" and whatever makes "me" happy. A good example is a two-year-old throwing a fit because he does not get the full cookie he wants right now. He is enraged about his brother getting half. There is no concern for his brother's feelings. It's me first, me second, and me third; me all the way. Another example is Paloma, one of my daughters, who when she was five declared, "Daddy, I love you as much as the TV." In her love there is no room for me as a subject; I'm an object that she enjoys, just like the TV. She meant, "You make *me* as happy as the TV, and *I* would be as sad without you as *I* would be without the TV." This is fine at five, but quite problematic at twenty-five.

As the individual matures, he becomes ethnocentric. At this stage, he sees himself as a member of a community, one of "us." Instead of focusing on himself and what he wants, the individual begins to care for his fellow community members. The circle of care and concern extends to the family, the clan, the tribe, the nation, the race, or whatever group the person feels he belongs to. As opposed to the egocentric character, the ethnocentric one cares about others—as long as these others are "one of us." If they are not, then they are not worthy of consideration. As philosopher Ken Wilber is fond of saying, "Nazis loved their children."

For those who grow into it, the next stage is the world-centric. (Researchers assess that less than 15 percent of today's adult human population operates at this stage or above.) Here, the individual lives according to universal values; it is not about "us" anymore, but about "all of us." His circle of care and concern becomes impersonal and encompasses all humanity. This is a very general and somewhat abstract kind of care, illustrated in the Declaration of Independence of the United States of America: "We hold these truths to be self-evident, that all men are created equal, that they are endowed by their Creator with certain unalienable Rights, that among these are Life, Liberty and the pursuit of Happiness."

At the highest level is the spirit-centric stage. Spirit-centric development is quite rare; research suggests that less that half a percent of the world's population operates from this level of consciousness.[5] The spirit-centric individual extends his circle of care and concern to encompass each and every sentient being. At this level the individual experiences a sense of connection with others that transcends the appearance of separation. Objects and people in the world continue to appear separate, just as they did at the previous levels, but the individual now experiences a deeper truth. Waves appear to be individual entities, but they are really motion of the same sea—there's only one mass of water moving. The colors of the rainbow appear to be discrete, but they are really refractions of the same luminosity—there's only one light shining. Everything is seen as the expression of Consciousness. The spirit-centric individual loves his neighbor as himself effortlessly, because he realizes that his neighbor *is*, indeed, a radiant expression of his True Self.

I have been thinking of the difference between water
and the waves on it.
Rising, water is still water,
falling back, it is water,
will you give me a hint how to tell them apart?
Because someone has made up the word "wave,"
do I have to distinguish it from water?

KABIR[6]

At the highest level of human development, every entity is experienced as a unique and precious facet of Consciousness. As Plato described, the entire manifest world—*this world*— appears as a "visible, sensible God."[7] Just as there are different pieces of jewelry but all are made of the same gold, there are different entities but all are manifestations of the same energy; as Einstein postulated, $E=mc^2$. At this level, competition becomes cooperation. Opposition is merely a play that encourages everybody to excel. What appears as rivalry is really collaboration that transcends and includes competition.

At the lower levels of development, contests appear as opportunities to "prove" one's worth by beating opponents. People seek happiness through victories in sports and business. When they vanquish their opponents they achieve a feeling of superiority, the pleasure of "being someone." On the other hand, defeat is a serious risk. Losing can shatter these characters' self-esteem.

In chapter 3, I distinguished acting based on a sense of fullness versus lack. I explained that when you feel empty it is tempting to try to fill yourself up with accomplishments. Competition becomes a materialistic ego-boosting pursuit. When you feel full, there is no need to find your worth in external success. Competition becomes a spiritual practice, an opportunity to test your mettle and express your values. There is no need to prove that you are who you already know you are.

So if you are already full, why strive for success? Because the game is a fabulous arena for expressing your richness; because competition is a fabulous spur toward excellence. And there is no game without players who strive to succeed. *In fullness, you don't play the game in order to succeed; you strive to succeed in order to sustain the game.*

The larger purpose of business — or sports, or any competitive activity, for that matter — is not to succeed, but to serve as a theater for self-knowledge, self-actualization, and self-transcendence. We discover who we are and what we really stand for when we respond to (business) situations. We establish our values through our behavior and our dealings with other people and the world. We transcend ourselves as we expand our circle of care and concern to include colleagues, customers, and others. Of course, in order to keep the business game alive, players must strive to make money and accomplish their mission, but the game is about much more than winning. Material success is not the end anymore; it becomes a means to developing and expressing our highest nature.

What kind of work is aligned with the larger purpose of business? The work that enacts these principles is not just a material task but a spiritual practice as well. Psychologists have described such work as "self-actualizing" because it supports the worker's realization and well-being.

> A human being is a part of the whole called by us "the universe," a part limited in time and space. He experiences himself, his thoughts and feelings, as something separate from the rest—a kind of optical delusion of his consciousness. This delusion is a kind of prison for us, restricting us to our personal desires and affection for a few persons nearest to us. Our task is to free ourselves from this prison by widening our circle of understanding and compassion to embrace all living creatures and the whole of nature in its beauty.
>
> ALBERT EINSTEIN

SELF-ACTUALIZING WORK

Some people limit their spiritual activities to the private sphere, but our professional activities define our personal and social identities; they provide us with community, purpose, and meaning. Work gives us challenges, opportunities for achievement and integrity, and a sense of power and skill. If so much of our material, emotional, intellectual, and spiritual fulfillment depends on our work, why would we consider work merely an economic activity?

We spend more than half of our adult life at work. During our working years, work occupies more time than all other wakeful activities combined. If work time is "wasted time," "dead time," or "unconscious time," the majority of our life ends up "wasted," "dead," and "unconscious." If we conduct our professional activities pusillanimously (from the Latin, "small soul"), life itself becomes petty. That is why it is crucial to go beyond business as usual and recognize work as an essential component of a spiritual life, a gesture of human magnanimity (from the Latin, "great soul").

What kind of work environment supports fulfillment? An environment in which people feel respected, listened to, valued, supported, and entrusted with meaningful and challenging work, one that allows them to operate in alignment with their values as they contribute to the mission of the organization with autonomy, power, and integrity. This is what the psychologist Abraham Maslow called "self-actualizing work."

Self-actualizing work transcends the ego, freeing people from an exclusive preoccupation with themselves. Those who work for the sake of a transcendent vision, honoring their values through virtuous conduct, achieve a personal transcendence similar to what is called "enlightenment" in the East—but through a path much more in line with Western culture. As Maslow notes:

> ... Self-actualization work transcends the self without try-
> ing to, and achieves the kind of loss of self-awareness and of
> self-consciousness that the easterners ... keep on trying to
> attain. [Self-actualizing] work is simultaneously a seeking
> and fulfilling of the self *and* also an achieving of the self-
> lessness which is the ultimate expression of *real* self. [This
> work] resolves the dichotomy between selfish and unself-
> ish. Also between inner and outer—because the cause for
> which one works in [self-actualizing] work is introjected
> and becomes part of the self so that the world and the self
> are no longer different. The inner and the outer world fuse
> and become one and the same. The same is true for the
> subject-object dichotomy.[8]

What kind of work supports self-actualization? Any work, really. What matters is the attitude that accompanies it. Self-actualization is best supported through expressions of responsibility, autonomy, and essential integrity: a commitment to a meaningful purpose that goes beyond the immediate gratification of selfish desires and embraces others in service. This attitude not only maximizes the chances of success; it guarantees "success beyond success."

"Life, Liberty and the pursuit of Happiness," says the Declaration of Independence. Life and liberty are straightforward, but the pursuit of happiness is paradoxical. The only way to achieve happiness is *not* to pursue it directly. Happiness arises as a consequence of pursuing integrity and meaning, not happiness. As Viktor Frankl remarked, "happiness cannot be attained by wanting to be happy—it must come as the unintended consequence of working for a goal greater than oneself."[9]

The same happens with profits. The worst way to be profitable is to focus on profits. Profits are a consequence of customer care, employee engagement, enlightened leadership, and service orientation: of successful business strategies and efficient business processes running on capable business infrastructures. The most powerful of these infrastructures is a healthy organizational culture—a culture based on integrity, meaning, wisdom, and love. Such a culture not only produces extraordinary long-term business results, but extraordinary happiness and fulfillment as well.

Maximizing shareholder wealth has always been way down the list. Yes, profit is a cornerstone of what we do—it is a measure of our contribution and a means of self-financed growth—but it has never been the point in and of itself. The point, in fact, is to *win* ... in the eyes of the consumer by doing something you can be proud of.

JOHN YOUNG,

HEWLETT PACKARD CHIEF EXECUTIVE FROM 1976 TO 1992[10]

THE SOUL OF BUSINESS

In *Good Business*, Mihaly Csikszentmihalyi found that what distinguished extraordinary leaders, and what enabled them to build extraordinary organizations, was "soul." I find his clear words worthy of quoting in full.

> Perhaps the best way to explain what the word "soul" connotes is that, no matter how complex a system is, we judge it as having no soul if all its energies are devoted merely to keeping itself alive and growing. We attribute soul to those entities that use some portion of their energy not only for their own sake, but to make contact with other beings and

CONSCIOUS BUSINESS

care for them. In this framework, the soulless banker has no attention left for anything but his own goals, while we believe the cocker spaniel is loyal and selfless ...

Thus we infer the existence of soul when a system uses some of its surplus energy to reach outside itself and invest it in another system, becoming in the process a stakeholder in an entity larger than itself. At the human level curiosity, empathy, generosity, responsibility, and charity are some of its noteworthy manifestations. The most familiar example of soul in action is when a person devotes attention not just to selfish interests, or even to material goals in general, but to the needs of others, or to the cosmic forces that we assume must rule the universe ...

In many ways, the search for a life that has "relevance or meaning" beyond one's material existence is the primary concern of soul. This is precisely the need that a person who is aware of his or her own finitude feels, the need that motivates us to become part of something greater and more permanent. If a leader can make a convincing case that working for the organization will provide relevance, that it will take the workers out of the shell of their mortal frame and connect them with something more meaningful, then his vision will generate power, and people will naturally be attracted to become part of such a company.[11]

ALL YOU NEED IS LOVE

Many businesspeople consider "love" to be a personal matter, certainly nothing that belongs in the corporation, yet love forms the foundation of all human interactions. Without love, there is no teamwork; without love, there is no leadership; without love, there is no real commitment to customer service. I am not referring to the romantic love we hear so much about; I am talking about a different kind of love, *agape*.

The ancient Greeks had several words representing different aspects of love. *Eros* described sexual love. (This is where we get the English term "erotic.") *Storge* described familial affection and *philia*, heart-love. The noblest form of love was agape, a commitment to the other's well-being.

The Christian thinker William Barclay noted that "*Agape* has to do with the mind: it is not simply an emotion which rises unbidden in our hearts; it is a principle by which we deliberately live."[12] Agape is the love that Jesus advocated a person must have for all people—even his enemies. Jesus maintained that a mature human being always acted out of love. He did not instruct his disciples to fall in love with their enemies or feel for them as they felt for their families and friends. He asked them to nurture a gracious, determined, and active interest in their true welfare. He maintained that this affection could not be deterred by hatred, cursing, and abuse, nor limited by calculation of desserts or results. He invited his followers simply to act in the best interest of their fellow human beings: to love their neighbors.

Agape is not a feeling. Feelings arrive passively; we cultivate agape. We are not responsible for our feelings—we can't help how we feel—but we are responsible for our agape because agape is an act of will. Feelings are triggered by external events, such as people's actions or the weather, or internal processes such as digestion or thought. Agape comes from the soul. Liking is a feeling. Agape is a commitment, independent of our likes and dislikes. We can have all sorts of different feelings toward different people, but we can love them (in the agape sense) all equally and fully. As a Christian teacher said, "We fall in (erotic) love, but we rise in agape."

This notion of care and concern is not limited to the Christian tradition. In the Buddhist scriptures, one whose love extends equally and fully to all sentient beings is called a *bodhisattva*. This is a Sanskrit term derived from *bodhi* (enlightenment) and *sattva* (being). The bodhisattva is willing to undergo personal hardship to help another sentient being. One becomes an aspiring bodhisattva by vowing to cherish others' welfare as one's own. The vow-taker agrees to foster *bodhichitta* ("enlightened heart-mind"), a Sanskrit version of agape, in order to be of most benefit to the world. This is more than altruism. Buddhist teachers maintain that this vow not only serves other people, but liberates the vow-taker. The aspiring bodhisattva is released from the selfish attachments and preoccupations that are the root of all suffering.

The commitment to develop agape or bodhichitta may seem esoteric, but it is at the core of conscious business. It is the secret ingredient that allows the bodhisattva, the ox-herder, or the business leader to return to the marketplace with helping hands.

Be true to your own self, love your self absolutely. Do not pretend that you love others as yourself. Unless you have realized them as one with yourself, you cannot love them. Your love of others is the result of self-knowledge, not its cause. Without self-realization, no virtue is genuine. When you know beyond all doubt that the same life flows through all that is, and you are that life, you will love all naturally and spontaneously. When you realize the depth and fullness of your love for yourself, you know that every living being and the entire universe are included in your affection. But when you look at any thing as separate from you, you cannot love it for you are afraid of it.

NISARGADATTA MAHARAJ[13]

TURNING GREED INTO SERVICE

The argument for a spiritual view of business finds support from the great advocate of laissez-faire economics, Adam Smith. The eighteenth century ethics professor argued that businesspeople must concern themselves with other people's welfare. It is not about enlightenment, but simply good business practice. "The most apt to prevail [in the marketplace] are those who can draw others' self-interest in their favor," Smith wrote in *The Wealth of Nations*. "'Give me what I want, and you will have what you want,' is the meaning of every offer." In other words, every act of commerce is an act of mutual service. You may enter the business world out of self-interest, but in order to succeed you must serve others. For those who aspire to succeed beyond success, the market is an alchemical process that transforms self-interest into service, pettiness into greatness, and greed into the desire to satisfy others' needs.

For those committed to succeeding at any cost, the alchemy of the market corrupts. In the game of business, there are many temptations to take unethical detours that promise a competitive advantage. As we said in chapter 3, the sirens' songs of money, power, and fame shipwreck those who don't tie themselves to the mast of essential values. This doesn't mean that it's impossible to achieve success, money, power, and fame by breaking basic ethical rules—in fact, many do. Or that in the long term these mighty characters fail or get exposed—in fact, many don't. What it means is that those who betray fundamental human values for self-gratification end up in psychological hell. Those who indulge their greed by lying, cheating, and stealing become the "hungry ghosts" of Buddhism that we met in chapter 1: beings with huge mouths and thin necks that devour everything in sight but cannot get any nourishment or satisfaction.

This is how a human being can change:

there's a worm addicted to eating
grape leaves.

Suddenly, he wakes up,
Call it grace, whatever, something
wakes him, and he's no longer
a worm.

He's the entire vineyard,
and the orchard too, the fruit, the trunks,
a growing wisdom and joy
that doesn't need
to devour.

RUMI, "THE WORM'S WAKING" [14]

CONSCIOUS BUSINESS

The marketplace is the realm of voluntary transactions. When a voluntary transaction takes place, each party involved must receive more satisfaction from what he gets than he foregoes from what he gives up. For example, if I desire to trade my orange for your apple, I must want your apple more than my orange. Similarly, if you accept the trade, you must want my orange more than your apple. Thus, the transaction is based on two inequalities. This disparity generates a surplus in satisfaction: both you and I expect to be better off after the transaction. (Of course, you or I might be wrong. We all make mistakes, but who has more right than we ourselves to make our mistaken choices?)

This concern for and commitment to the other's well-being provide the foundation of a good business; they are also the essence of agape. I have found this transcendent love in many of the business leaders I've met in my fifteen years of teaching and consulting. Perhaps, just by coincidence, I've worked mostly with enlightened organizations, but I don't think so. Most people would not consider General Motors, Chrysler, Microsoft, Yahoo!, Google, EDS, Royal Dutch Shell, Citibank, or Unilever to be particularly "spiritual" organizations. Yet these companies are staffed by people seeking to do good work in the world, just like any true spiritual seeker. They are responding to the calling of their soul to make this world a better place.

Business is a field of possibilities. The market is a stage on which every human being manifests his values. When this manifestation is guided by selfishness and unconsciousness, work turns into hell, a swamp of suffering and bondage. When this manifestation is guided by success beyond success, business becomes a work of art, a work of love and freedom.

A WONDERFUL CAREER, A WONDERFUL LIFE

I was once flying to Buenos Aires with my children Sophie and Tomás, then four and three years old. We boarded the plane at midnight, an hour after the scheduled departure. It taxied for a few moments but soon stopped. The captain announced that maintenance was on the way. Since we were on an active runway, we had to keep our seat belts fastened.

Fat chance! Sophie and Tomás unbuckled themselves and started running up and down the aisle. I got very annoyed. As I was about to lambaste my children, Death whispered in my ear, "If the plane crashes, you will have wasted the last moments of your life yelling at your kids." I was struck cold. Death's advice changed my perspective. The delay became an opportunity to love my children; their mischief became an expression of their vitality. My anger dissolved and, surprisingly, I got my children to sit without much struggle.

I have found that Death's counsel helps me regain consciousness in moments of trial. When I start losing perspective, I hear Death's whisper, "If this were the last five minutes of your life, is this the way you would want to spend them?" I have offered this insight to many of my clients, who have found it quite useful in business situations. So, as we approach the end of this book, I invite you to reflect on the end of other journeys, such as your career and your life.

Near the conclusion of my seminars, I introduce an exercise that explores how being aware of endings can enrich our lives. Endings make things unique and valuable. They highlight the preciousness of experiences. They remind us to stay conscious at every step of the process. Most of us realize that things are impermanent only when the shadow of their ending looms large, when it is too late to change. The best way to benefit from endings is to *project* them into the future while there is still opportunity to correct the present. As the Zen masters say, "Die before you die, so you can truly live."

Imagine your dream retirement. You have accomplished everything you wanted and behaved honorably. You are proud of yourself. Everybody around you deeply appreciates and admires you. You have helped your organization fulfill its mission; you have developed bonds of trust and mutual support with those around you; you feel happy and fulfilled. Now, it is time to hang it up, but first comes the celebratory dinner where people gather to pay their respects to you.

As you imagine this scene, know that this is no time to be humble. On the contrary, the more grandiose you can be, the better. Imagine that one of your managers speaks first, someone who led you and supported you as you supported her. Take a sheet of paper and write a paragraph, referring to yourself in the third person, on what this manager might say as she celebrates your career. For example, "Fred was the team member every manager wishes for. I always felt his unconditional support, not just in pursuit of the task, but as an expression of his care for every person on the team. His commitment to excellence led him to work indefatigably. He was not invested in winning, and not afraid of losing, but he put his heart and soul in the game. He played giving his best all the time. His wisdom, kindness, and compassion were an inspiration for each one of us. In difficult times, we all trusted Fred to stay the course."

Next imagine a colleague, someone who faced challenges with you as a peer. Sometimes you succeeded as a team, sometimes you did not, but you always achieved success beyond success. Write another paragraph on what your colleague might say about you.

Next, imagine a customer, someone who relied on you for service, who trusted you and depended upon you. You always told him the truth; you delivered impeccably, providing excellent service, helping him to succeed and grow. Write another paragraph on what that delighted customer might say at your retirement party.

Now imagine an employee, someone who has looked up to you as a leader and a role model, someone who grew both professionally and personally while working for you. You guided her and helped her become the person she is today. Write another paragraph on what she would say about you, how she would praise you for being the most wonderful leader anybody could have.

Finally, it's time for *you* to reflect on your career. Because you are known to be a humble person who has a hard time appreciating himself, you have been given an ironclad assignment. You can only talk about things that you are proud of. Write a final paragraph appreciating your accomplishments, your relationships, and your personal growth.

(If you are looking for a challenge, I recommend doing this exercise with others. I have seen powerful openings in a variety of teams, and even among strangers participating in open seminars as people share their work. Share the paragraphs you have written with others and listen as they share their writings with you. You can also do this exercise by imagining that you are writing a speech for a retirement party for the team as a whole, speaking about its collective accomplishments and integrity.)

Now consider your current behavior. How does it compare to the actions you would need to undertake in order to receive the accolades you described above? It is often a shock to see how in your day-to-day actions you seem to be targeting goals that are miles away from what you truly want to accomplish in your professional life.

If you feel daring, you can take another step. You can now try a deeper version of the exercise. Instead of focusing on your career, focus on your life. Instead of imagining your retirement party, imagine that you are on your deathbed. Once again, stay positive. Imagine you've had the most wonderful, rewarding life and you are ready to depart. You decide to hold a live-in funeral.[15] At a live-in funeral, people say the same things they would say at a standard funeral; the only difference is that you are there to listen to them—and even to speak.

Imagine the eulogies of a parent, a friend, a spouse or intimate partner, and a child. Finally, imagine that you are asked to prepare your own eulogy appreciating yourself for the things you are most proud of. Write down at least a paragraph for each quality. Remember, this is no time to be shy or to feel constrained by the way you have lived your life so far. Imagine that after reading this book, your life took off, and from this moment until the end of it, it became everything you wanted.

Just as before, you can then share this with your loved ones. And just as before, these eulogies can express the high standards you want to fulfill through your behavior.

Friend, hope for the truth while you are alive.
Jump into experience while you are still alive …
What you call "salvation" belongs to the time before death.
If you don't break your ropes while you are alive,
do you think ghosts will do it after?

The idea that the soul will join with the ecstatic

just because the body is rotten—

that is all fantasy.

What is found now is found then.

If you find nothing now,

you will simply end up with an empty apartment in the City
    of Death.

If you fall in love with the divine now,

in the next life you will have the face of satisfied desire.

KABIR [16]

THE GAME OF BUSINESS

Pursuing your highest aspirations doesn't have to be a serious affair. In fact, it will probably go more smoothly if you view your professional and personal activities as a game. Psychologist Mihaly Csikszentmihalyi found that games provide a setting conducive to what he calls the "optimal experience" of "flow." When you are in flow, you become so absorbed in your activity that you forget yourself. You transcend your self-centeredness and dissolve the boundaries between self and world. You enter into an extraordinary state of consciousness in which there is total awareness without any effort of attention, an experience of no separation in which you feel at one with the game. This not only makes you happy, but it is also very effective. Csikszentmihalyi's studies of top athletes reveal that peak performance occurs while in the state of flow. Players report feeling that "the game plays itself" effortlessly through them, as opposed to them directing their play through will and concentration.

You feel in a state of flow when the experience matters to you more than the outcome. Flow happens when you enjoy the play more than its result. Csikszentmihalyi remarks, "Of course, the ultimate goals … are also important, but true enjoyment comes from the steps one takes toward attaining a goal, not from actually reaching it." [17] We feel relaxed and focused as we face a challenge that taxes our skills without overwhelming us. We feel at our best when we can test our competencies and values without an overwhelming fear of failure. In an optimal experience we feel simultaneously safe and at risk.

The game has clear boundaries. Inside, there are risk, challenge, and drama; outside, security, ease, and calm. When playing a game we can feel the "danger" of losing, while knowing that we are totally "safe." In the game, we face obstacles that test our mettle and push us to perform at our best. We are at the edge. If we slip, we lose. The relaxation comes from knowing that the loss is relatively inconsequential. Inside the game, it's the end. Outside, life goes on.

Two attitudes can ruin the fun: taking the game too seriously and not taking it seriously enough. In the first case, we forget that the risk of the game exists in a larger context of safety. We all know people who take things too seriously, lose their sense of perspective, and play to kill rather than to have a good time while they play to win. In the second case, we never get into the action. I wouldn't want someone on my team who kept saying; "This is just a game, it doesn't really matter, there's no point in playing hard, winning or losing doesn't make any difference."

When the only point of playing the game is to win, it gets too serious. But without an intention to win, the game never gets going. To enjoy the game you need to let it matter and not matter simultaneously. Then you can go all out, knowing that even if you lose you are ultimately okay, that the ultimate point of the game is to succeed beyond success. The synthesis between stress and relaxation, fear and confidence, risk and assurance creates the sense of flow in which we feel and perform at our best.

Business is a risky game. What makes it thrilling rather than frightening is a commitment to consciousness and success beyond success. Only then can we embark on the perilous business journey with total confidence; only then can we experience a security that transcends and includes fear. The main task of a conscious business is to help people succeed (accomplish their mission) while they develop healthy relationships (belong to a community) and experience an unconditional sense of peace, happiness, and growth (actualize and transcend the self).

Consciousness is key. Through a conscious practice of business you anchor yourself in your essential values, choose behaviors in alignment with such values, and act with unconditional responsibility and integrity. Through a conscious practice of business you can succeed beyond success.

A SPIRITUAL HARNESS

During a rock climbing lesson, I found myself paralyzed. I could see an outcrop for my right foot, but no place where I could place my hands or left foot. The situation looked hopeless. I shouted to the instructor that I was stuck. He pointed to the support for my right foot. "I see that, but I can't find anything else to hold on!" I shouted with anxiety.

His advice shocked me, "Take the step. Once you lift yourself up you may find something you can't see from where you stand." "Are you crazy?" I yelled back, "What happens if I don't find anything?" "If you don't find anything," he said calmly, "fall back on the harness and try it again."

When I feel stuck in life, I can't see a way through. I worry about losing my place and making things worse. Perhaps I should follow the climbing instructor's advice, take a step, and trust that my new position will reveal a path that right now is invisible. "What happens if I don't find anything?" "Fall back on the harness and try again."

In life, the harness isn't physical; it is spiritual. I have found that to feel secure I need to rely on a spiritual safety system, a set of values, goals, and behaviors that stills my mind even in the face of the most intense challenges. Whatever I make my business, I need to make it a *conscious* business. Consciousness guarantees success beyond success.

Success beyond success focuses on essential rather than surface values, on unconditional rather than conditional goals, on process integrity rather than outcome achievement. Even though you cannot guarantee that you will win, it is possible to play any game as a full expression of your values. Whatever the outcome, you can demonstrate admirable characteristics such as fairness, courage, respect, determination, and ingenuity in the face of any challenge.

Acting in alignment with your highest values yields a sense of inner peace. Even if you don't succeed, you will feel the pride of having behaved honorably. You will still bear the sorrow of loss, the disappointment of defeat, and the consequences of failure, but you will bear them with poise. When you succeed beyond success, these are small ripples in a vast pool of self-confidence.

A robust confidence cannot depend on outcome success. The result of any endeavor is risky. There are thousands of factors beyond your control that can derail even your best-laid plans. Unshakable confidence relies on success beyond success, on the actualization of your deepest values in the face of the most challenging circumstances. A philosophy of success beyond success allows you to tackle risks that would be daunting without it. It gives you the self-assurance to do your very best, knowing that even if your actions are not enough to achieve the result you want, they will be enough to maintain your dignity and self-esteem. Security in the midst of risk lets you enjoy life to the fullest.

In chapter 3, I introduced *The Bhagavad Gita*, the Indian text that explains how to go to war—or more generally, how to face difficult circumstances with confidence. The teachings of the *Gita*, as it is commonly known, are the basis of Karma Yoga, the yoga of action. The word "yoga" comes from the same root as "yoke" and it means "to bind together"—just as the word "religion" comes from the Latin "religare" and means "to tie back together." Yoga is a discipline for reconnecting the material with the spiritual, and Karma Yoga is a way of doing so through selfless action. He who lets go of the concern for the outcome and acts according to the highest values, says the *Gita*, can rest in his sense of unconditional integrity.

In the *Gita*, Krishna teaches Arjuna to fight his war in the spirit of success beyond success. In the language of modern psychology, Krishna instructs Arjuna on how to be in a state of "flow" and turn any endeavor—even a conflict—into an optimal experience. His first injunction provides the key to success beyond success: Let go of the outcome and act in alignment with your true nature or virtue. "Do your duty to the best of your ability, O Arjuna, with your mind attached to the Truth, abandoning (worry and) attachment to the results, and remaining calm in both success and failure. The equanimity of mind is called Karma-yoga." "Treating pleasure and pain, gain and loss, victory and defeat alike, engage yourself in your duty. By doing your duty this way you will reach salvation." This is the ultimate peace of mind, the spiritual harness that turns any dangerous situation into a noble challenge.

Just as in the Ox-Herding Pictures, Krishna admonishes Arjuna not to eschew action. Advising him to take up his duty as a warrior, a businessman, or a professional, he explains, "One does not attain freedom from the bondage of the world by merely abstaining from work. No one attains liberation by merely giving up work. Perform your duty, because action is indeed better than inaction." Liberation comes from releasing the attachment to results and offering every action to your highest values.

My daily affairs are quite ordinary;
but I'm in total harmony with them.
I don't hold on to anything, don't reject anything;
nowhere an obstacle or conflict.
Who cares about wealth and honor?
Even the poorest thing shines.
My miraculous power and spiritual activity:
drawing water and carrying wood.

LAYMAN P'ANG [18]

SIMPLE, NOT EASY

I started this book inquiring about the sources of exceptional results for organizations and individuals. I defined three dimensions of success: It, We, and I. In the impersonal It dimension, the goal is to accomplish the organization's mission, enhancing its ability to continue doing so in the future, and delivering outstanding long-term returns to shareholders. In the interpersonal We dimension, the goal is to establish cooperative, trusting, and mutually respectful relationships, a community of shared purpose and values in which people feel they belong. In the personal I dimension, the goal is to live in a state of flow, feeling a transcendent happiness that comes from living in full integrity with one's principles and ideals.

I described seven qualities of conscious business, qualities that support an extraordinary business organization and an extraordinary life: unconditional responsibility, essential integrity, ontological humility, authentic communication, constructive negotiation, impeccable coordination, and emotional mastery. Although the concepts are common sense, their application is anything but common practice. This stuff is simple, but not easy. The reason is that all of these practices are based on a shift in consciousness. They cannot work when one sees work as an unavoidable hardship, endured only to acquire the means to satisfy one's basic needs. To develop these skills it is necessary to see work as "love made visible." Then one's professional practice—and one's life—become a work of art, guided by the desire to serve rather than the need to be served.

In this book I invited you to consider work as an arena for the skillful expression of your essential values. I asked you to venture with me through paths that are not traditionally associated with business. Now, at the end of the journey, we close the circle. I invite you to take these skills and enter the market with helping hands. As an old Arab proverb says, although nothing in the external world will have changed, you will have changed, and thus, everything will have changed. And as the Zen masters advise, "Before enlightenment, chop wood and carry water. After enlightenment, chop wood and carry water." I hope that with a higher level of consciousness we will enter the marketplace together to support the liberation of all sentient beings. We might realize then that our business organizations and our work are nothing other than an aspect of Plato's visible sensible God.

We shall not cease from exploration
And the end of all our exploring
Will be to arrive where we started
And know the place for the first time.

T. S. ELIOT, FROM "LITTLE GIDDING" [19]

Epilogue

◆

Security is mostly a superstition.
It does not exist in nature, nor do the children of man as a whole
experience it. Avoiding danger is no safer in the long run than
outright exposure. Life is either a daring adventure, or nothing.

HELEN KELLER

◆

"W hatever happens up there," the expedition cook said, "you'll be changed forever. You won't return the same." Federico observed our departure with a knowing eye. He had seen people like us before, setting out toward the top of the Andes.

Our summit day began in the dark, at thirty below. Rising from a sleepless night, we could taste the peak of Aconcagua three thousand feet above. I left the high camp with trepidation, thinking, "Today is the day." I shivered, and not from the cold. I wondered whether I would make it. I had trained for two years, but I felt more like a weekend hiker than a serious mountaineer. What the hell was I doing at twenty thousand feet? I was in way over my head. Chance of success? Fifty percent, at best.

Summiting was a conditional goal, something I could strive for but not guarantee. I couldn't control the weather; a storm front might envelop the mountain in a blizzard. I couldn't control my body; my muscles could cramp, my brain swell, my lungs fill with fluid. I couldn't even control my mind:

I could decide, "The hell with this! I'm going home." Yet I felt confident. I had an unconditional goal, one that I could achieve regardless of external circumstances: walk till I drop. I was going to climb until I passed out. The trail was not so dangerous; with the help of a guide I could trudge down it even after fainting. I didn't know if I would succeed, but I was certain that I could succeed beyond success.

What would I get from succeeding that was even more important to me than succeeding itself? I wasn't climbing to conquer the mountain, but to learn some deep truth about myself. I undertook this expedition as a transformational learning experience. This was a spiritual journey from which I hoped to return to the marketplace with helping hands. I wanted to come back with a tamed ox, with peace, fullness, and an unshakeable sense of well-being regardless of circumstances. I wanted to find out who I really was, and taste a happiness that embraces sadness. As I approached the crux of my adventure, however, I realized that learning is a double-edged sword. It opens new possibilities while it closes off old ones. Transformation is irreversible. The cook's comments reminded me of Carlos Castaneda's book *Journey to Ixtlán*. In the last chapter, the shaman don Juan tells Castaneda:

> If you survive [the encounter with knowledge] ... you will find yourself alive in an unknown land. Then, as is natural to all of us, the first thing that you will want to do is start on your way back to [your home]. But there is no way to go back ... What you left there is lost forever ... everything we love or hate or wish for has been left behind. Yet the feelings in a man do not die or change, and the [man of knowledge] starts on his way back home knowing that he will not reach it, knowing that no power on earth, not even his death, will deliver him to the place, the things, the people he loved ... [Knowledge] will change your idea of the world ... That idea is everything; and when that changes, the world itself changes.[1]

In order to illustrate this idea, don Juan invites his sorcerer friend, don Genaro, to recount the story of his encounter with knowledge. Walking home from the fields one day, don Genaro encountered his "ally" (a spirit guide), and became entwined in combat with it.

> After I grabbed it we began to spin. The ally made me twirl, but I didn't let go. We spun through the air with such speed and force that I couldn't see any more. Everything was foggy. The spinning went on, and on, and on. Suddenly I felt that I was standing on the ground again. I looked at myself. The ally had not killed me. I was in one piece. I was myself! I knew then that I had succeeded. At long last I had an ally. I jumped up and down with delight. What a feeling! What a feeling it was!
>
> Then I looked around to find out where I was. The surroundings were unknown to me. I thought that the ally must have taken me through the air and dumped me somewhere very far from the place where we started to spin. I oriented myself. I thought that [Ixtlán], my home, must be towards the east, so I began to walk in that direction ...
>
> "What was the final outcome of that experience, don Genaro?" [Castaneda] asked ... [don Juan and don Genaro] both broke into laughter at once.
>
> "Let's put it this way, then. There was no final outcome to Genaro's journey. There will never be any final outcome. Genaro is still on his way to Ixtlán!" ... "I will never reach Ixtlán," [don Genero] said.[2]

Just as your body changes through climbing a mountain, significant learning experiences change your mental model. What you learn changes your world—and who you are as the one who experiences such a world. A spiritual journey has no return because the "home" that you left behind no longer exists—and neither does the "you" who left that home. When you cross the gate of knowledge, reality is not what it used to be. This is why shamans warn that you should meet knowledge with the impeccable spirit of a warrior, ready to face death: death understood not as physical demise, but as the loss of old familiarities and relationships.

Now the sun was high in the sky. We had been hiking for more than six hours. I was tired, but the most challenging terrain lay in front of me. I had heard horror stories about the notorious stretch called "La Canaleta," a pitiless open-faced scree where every step up is followed by a half-step slide. I knew that this short stretch would take at least two hours — if I was able to survive it without breaking a leg or collapsing in exhaustion. When we trained for the climb, my companions and I focused on La Canaleta as the main challenge. My mind likes a single target, an event that determines the outcome. It makes life simple: You overcome it, you succeed; you don't, you fail. But that's not how it is. Significant journeys are processes, not events. They demand sustained energy, not a burst. They require that the traveler develop physical, emotional, mental, and spiritual toughness.

"Train hard, climb easy," became my motto. More significant than my commitment to the climb was my commitment to the practice. Every challenge in my life became a training opportunity. Whether business or personal, every hardship became the "weight" to train my climbing muscles. Enemies became "training partners." This shift was beyond my individual capacity. Just as every climber needs a buddy to hold his rope, I needed friends to support my struggle. And my climbing partners needed me to support theirs. We helped each other embrace all difficulties; we became what Karlfried Graf von Durckheim calls "friends on the Way."

> The man who being really on the Way falls upon hard times, will not turn to that friend who offers him refuge and encourages his old self to survive. Rather, he will seek out someone who will faithfully and inexorably help him to risk himself, so that he may endure the suffering and pass courageously through it, thus making of it a "raft that leads to the far shore." Only to the extent that man exposes himself

over and over again to annihilations, can that which is indestructible arise within him. In this lies the dignity of daring. Thus, the aim of practice is not to develop an attitude which allows a man to acquire a state of harmony and peace wherein nothing can ever trouble him. On the contrary, practice should teach him to let himself be assaulted, perturbed, moved, insulted, broken and battered—that is to say, it should enable him to dare to let go his futile hankering after harmony, surcease from pain and a comfortable life in order that he may discover, in doing battle with the forces that oppose him, that which awaits him beyond the world of opposites.[3]

Even with the training, most of us didn't make it to the peak. Of the twelve who had started out, only four finished the climb two weeks later. There wasn't an obvious distinction between those who turned back and those now struggling for the summit. All of us had trained equally hard, but the altitude sickness and a night with a sixty-mile-per-hour wind convinced eight to return. I looked at my three remaining partners, wondering what distinguished us from the others. We certainly felt as bad and scared as the other eight. One thing came to mind: The four of us had run marathons while none of the others had. Marathon running requires great endurance. Staying the course isn't just a physical challenge, but a spiritual one. We appeared to be the ones willing to bear more afflictions for the sake of a transcendent goal.

It wasn't stoicism; in a perverse sense we seemed to enjoy the pain. The day before, for example, after pitching our tents I told my tent buddy, "Oh God, I feel awful! My head is about to explode, my belly aches, I'm tired to death, even my teeth hurt! This is the worst I've ever felt in my life!" And then, with teary eyes and a huge grin, I added, "I am *sooo* happy!"

In the driest, whitest stretch
Of pain's infinite desert,

I lost my sanity,
And found this rose.

RUMI[4]

No, my buddies and I are not masochists; in fact, we love to enjoy ourselves. As we ran marathons and climbed mountains we found, however, that enjoyment is different from pleasure. In the words of Csikszentmihalyi:

> Enjoyment … is not always pleasant, and it can be very stressful at times. A mountain climber, for example, may be close to freezing, utterly exhausted, and in danger of falling into a bottomless crevasse, yet he wouldn't want to be anywhere else. Sipping a piña colada under a palm tree at the edge of the turquoise ocean is idyllic, but it just doesn't compare to the exhilaration he feels on that windswept ridge … At the moment it is experienced, enjoyment can be both physically painful and mentally taxing; but because it involves a triumph over the forces of entropy and decay, it nourishes the spirit. Enjoyment is the foundation for memories that, in retrospect, enrich lives, and give confidence for facing the future.[5]

After two hours, we made it up La Canaleta. My muscles ached, my lungs burned, and I still had more than a thousand vertical feet to go. I seriously considered giving up. I leaned limply on my poles and sucked the thin air. I was totally exhausted. I couldn't imagine summiting this day and I contemplated heading back down. At that point I remembered my commitment to my unconditional goal—walk till you drop. I decided to keep going until I passed out—which I imagined wouldn't take very long. Then, a thought burst into my mind, hitting me like an avalanche: *There is a finite number of steps from here to the summit, and I am going to walk them one by one.* So I took one step, and then another, and then another. I stopped worrying about the summit, about success, about making it. My world boiled down to *one more step; one more step.*

I felt an unexpected surge of energy. I didn't know where it came from; it originated somewhere beyond the person I thought of as "me." It is hard to put into words. All I know is that something that was both I and not-I kept walking. "It-I" kept moving up the mountain regardless of physical exhaustion. There was still some climbing to do, but I had already received my gift. I had reached the limits of my personal strength and found a way to access something beyond them. That was far more precious than any photograph or bragging rights. I got my peak experience before I got to the peak.

The birds have vanished into the sky,
and now the last cloud drains away.

We sit together, the mountain and me,
until only the mountain remains.

LI PO[6]

❖

Implementing the disciplines presented in this book is less dramatic than climbing Aconcagua, but it is no less demanding. Facing life with unconditional responsibility, enacting your essential values, and humbly accepting that your truth is not *the truth* demands a profound commitment. Communicating authentically, negotiating constructively, and coordinating impeccably require more perseverance than most people can muster. The good news is that these things are no more difficult than running a marathon. The bad news is that they are not easier. The only way to make it is to train hard. To practice, practice, and practice, using everything life gives you. These practices will stretch you beyond yourself. They will challenge you to grow. They will spin you through the air with such speed and force that you may not be able to see any more. They will take you so far that you will never be able to return to Ixtlán.

Challenges will seem insurmountable at times; failure, unavoidable. In those moments, you will need a community to help you expose yourself over and over again to annihilation, so that what is indestructible can arise within you. Taking one step at a time, you may accomplish goals you assumed were impossible. Or you may not. But even if you fall short, your commitment to success beyond success will produce awesome shifts, shifts that you cannot even imagine at this point. As the expedition cook said, no one embarking on this journey remains the same. No matter what happens, you are changed forever.

This Way has no return and it never ends. There is nowhere to arrive, no final summit to conquer. Only higher and higher reaches of the human spirit. Whenever I feel like I've gotten it, that I am finally in control, I am humbled by a challenge that exceeds my ability to respond. However, I have found peace and satisfaction in success beyond success. I am certain that it is always possible to take responsibility, act with integrity, and express my transcendent values through skillful means. There is no doubt, and no place left to hide. Success beyond success is my unconditional accountability. I sometimes wish I could go back: Blame others, feel like a victim, indulge in unconscious patterns. But there is no return. Awareness is irreversible. Once you start seeing, you can't pretend to be blind. You might fool others, but you cannot fool yourself. You can act irresponsibly or unethically, of course, but you cannot avoid knowing that you are doing so.

Someone once asked the climber George Mallory why he wanted to climb Everest. "Because it's there," he answered. When people ask me why they should adopt these practices, I want to give them the same answer. If you feel you can turn your back on these ideas, go ahead. But if you've read this far, I'm afraid you don't have a choice. You may think that you can neglect this material, but if you haven't put the book down yet, you are doomed. You are naturally drawn to this challenge, like a climber to the mountains. Paradoxically, the highest freedom is choiceless discipline. Imagine finding a wallet with a thousand dollars in cash and a driver's license. Do you think you *really* have a choice about what to do with it? You may fantasize about keeping it, but you know you won't. When you reach a certain level of empathy and moral development, you no longer have a choice.

In the process of pursuing the practices in this book, you may encounter great difficulties. You may experience alienation and bewilderment. You may confront cynical or antagonistic coworkers. I don't know any way to avoid these hardships. I suggest taking them as a sign of progress. On the mountain, discomfort is a sign of gaining altitude; in life, a sign of growth. You need to find meaning in the discomfort, a vision of possibilities that gives you a reason to stay the course. Personally, I find sustenance in a comment by the Dalai Lama. "Achieving world peace through the internal transformation of individuals is exceedingly difficult," he once said, and then he added, "and it is the only way." Personal, organizational, and social development are just like world peace.

Although each individual changes internally, it is small groups of committed individuals who change the world. In the words of Margaret Mead, "Never doubt that a small group of thoughtful committed citizens can change the world, indeed it is the only thing that ever has." I had to climb the mountain on my own, but I drew strength from my companions. When I stumbled, they held me. When they stumbled, I held them. It is an intimate connection to share such adventure, to rely on each other so nakedly for survival. When we headed down the mountain, I could feel the new bond that connected us. We had each worked alone and as a group. Now we carried the knowledge that we'd helped each other succeed. We felt a deep respect, almost reverence for each other. It was precious. As we hiked down to base camp, I found a new meaning to the story of the rabbi's gift.

> The story concerns a monastery that had fallen upon hard times. Once a great order, as a result of waves of antimonastic persecution in the seventeenth and eighteenth centuries and the rise of secularism in the nineteenth, all its branch houses were lost, and it had become decimated to the extent that there were only five monks left in the

decaying mother house: the abbot and four others, all over seventy in age. Clearly, it was a dying order.

In the deep woods surrounding the monastery there was a little hut that a rabbi from a nearby town occasionally used for a hermitage. Through their many years of prayer and contemplation the old monks had become a bit psychic, so they could always sense when the rabbi was in his hermitage. "The rabbi is in the woods, the rabbi is in the woods again," they would whisper to each other. As he agonized over the imminent death of his order, it occurred to the abbot at one such time to visit the hermitage and ask the rabbi if by some possible chance he could offer any advice that might save the monastery.

The rabbi welcomed the abbot at his hut. But when the abbot explained the purpose of his visit, the rabbi could only commiserate with him. "I know how it is," he exclaimed. "The spirit has gone out of the people. It is the same in my town. Almost no one comes to the synagogue anymore." So the old abbot and the old rabbi wept together. Then they read parts of the Torah and quietly spoke of deep things. The time came when the abbot had to leave. They embraced each other. "It has been a wonderful thing that we should meet after all these years," the abbot said, "but I have still failed in my purpose for coming here. Is there nothing you can tell me, no piece of advice you can give me that would help me save my dying order?"

"No, I am sorry," the rabbi responded. "I have no advice to give. The only thing I can tell you is that the Messiah is one of you."

When the abbot returned to the monastery his fellow monks gathered around him to ask, "Well, what did the rabbi say?"

"He couldn't help," the abbot answered. "We just wept and read the Torah together. The only thing he did say, just as I was leaving—it was something cryptic—was that the Messiah is one of us. I don't know what he meant."

In the days and weeks and months that followed, the old monks pondered this and wondered whether there was any possible significance to the rabbi's words. The Messiah is one of us? Could he possibly have meant one of us monks here at the monastery? If that's the case, which one? Do you suppose he meant the abbot? Yes, if he meant anyone, he probably meant Father Abbot. He has been our leader for more than a generation. On the other hand, he might have meant Brother Thomas. Certainly Brother Thomas is a holy man. Everyone knows that Thomas is a man of light. Certainly he could not have meant Brother Elred! Elred gets crotchety at times. But come to think of it, even though he is a thorn in people's sides, when you look back on it, Elred is virtually always right. Often very right. Maybe the rabbi did mean Brother Elred. But surely not Brother Phillip. Phillip is so passive, a real nobody. But then, almost mysteriously, he has a gift for somehow always being there when you need him. He just magically appears by your side. Maybe Phillip is the Messiah. Of course the rabbi didn't mean me. He couldn't possibly have meant me. I'm just an ordinary person. Yet supposing he did? Suppose I am the Messiah? O God, not me. I couldn't be that much for You, could I?

As they contemplated in this manner, the old monks began to treat each other with extraordinary respect on the off chance that one among them might be the Messiah. And on the off, off chance that each monk himself might be the Messiah, they began to treat themselves with extraordinary respect.

Because the forest in which it was situated was beautiful, it so happened that people still occasionally came to visit the monastery to picnic on its tiny lawn, to wander along some of its paths, even now and then to go into the dilapidated chapel to meditate. As they did so, without even being conscious of it, they sensed this aura of extraordinary respect that now began to surround the five old monks and seemed to radiate out from them and permeate the atmosphere of the place. There was something strangely attractive, even compelling, about it. Hardly knowing why, they began to come back to the monastery more frequently to picnic, to play, to pray. They began to bring their friends to show them this special place. And their friends brought their friends.

Then it happened that some of the younger men who came to visit the monastery started to talk more and more with the old monks. After a while one asked if he could join them. Then another. And another. So within a few years the monastery had once again become a thriving order and, thanks to the rabbi's gift, a vibrant center of light and spirituality in the realm.[7]

◆

You can't practice these skills without breakdowns. The journey is fraught with mistakes, opposition, embarrassment, and self-doubt. Although the end is worth it, it is easy to get lost at times. When this happens, the traveler needs a simple compass to point to "true north." The best one I've found is the rabbi's advice. Imagine that each person you encounter could be the Messiah, and treat him or her with extraordinary respect. Even if you can't remember a single thing you've read in this book, the power of this noble intention will carry the day.

Let me offer one last tool, one that has helped me incorporate this powerful lesson. I learned it trekking through the Himalayas. As I walked the trails, I passed many people. If I had been in the United States we might have exchanged a smile or a polite "hello." Or we might have simply ignored each other. But in Nepal, we did something different. We each put our hands together in front of our hearts, lowered our heads slightly, and said, "Namaste."

In Sanskrit "Namaste" means "I bow to you"—not to the small "you" but to the vast expression of Consciousness that "You" are. Another way to put it might be, "I honor the Divine Light that shines as you." The more I used this greeting the more I appreciated it. I noticed that it softened my heart. I found it difficult to be harsh with someone after bowing to them and reminding myself that this person may in fact be the Messiah. When I returned home, I adopted "Namaste" as my greeting. I didn't have to use the Sanskrit word. I could say "hi" to anyone and think to myself, "I honor the Divine Light that shines as you." I took to secretly "Namaste-ing" everybody: my family, my friends, my colleagues, my clients—even my dog.

So, as we finish this journey and prepare to go into the market with helping hands, I bow to you. I see the Divine Light that shines as you.

◆

Namaste.

Endnotes

◆

Acknowledgments

1. Quoted in Leo Hartong, *Awakening to The Dream* (Salisbury, Wilts, UK: Non-Duality Press, 2003), 18.

1: Conscious Business

1. Jim Collins, *Good to Great: Why Some Companies Make the Leap and Others Don't* (New York: HarperBusiness, 2001), 11.
2. David Dotlich and Peter Cairo, *Why CEOs Fail: The 11 Behaviors That Can Derail Your Climb to the Top—and How to Manage Them* (San Francisco: Jossey-Bass, 2003), xxiv.
3. Collins, *Good to Great*, 35, 37.
4. Nathaniel Branden, *The Art of Living Consciously: The Power of Awareness to Transform Everyday Life* (New York: Fireside, 1997), 11.
5. Warren Bennis and Burt Nanus, *Leaders: Strategies for Taking Charge* (New York: Harper and Row, 1985), 7.
6. Mihaly Czikszentmihalyi, *Good Business: Leadership, Flow, and the Making of Meaning* (New York: Viking, 2003), 101.
7. Marcus Buckingham and Curt Coffman, *First, Break All the Rules: What the World's Greatest Managers Do Differently* (New York: Simon & Schuster, 1999), 11–12.

8. Gallup research cited in Buckingham et al., *First, Break All the Rules*, 28.

9. Frances Hesselbein, Eric K. Shinseki, and Richard E. Cavanaugh, *Be-Know-Do: Leadership the Army Way* (San Francisco: Jossey-Bass, 2004), 9, 21.

10. Martin Seligman, *Authentic Happiness: Using the New Positive Psychology to Realize Your Potential for Lasting Fulfillment* (New York: Free Press, 2002), 41.

11. Collins, *Good to Great*, 11.

12. Abraham Maslow, *The Maslow Business Reader* (New York: Wiley, 2000), 146.

2: *Unconditional Responsibility*

1. Carlos Castaneda, *Tales of Power* (New York: Simon & Schuster, 1992), 106.

2. Viktor Frankl, *Man's Search for Meaning*, 2nd ed. (New York: Simon & Schuster, 1984), 75.

3. Nelson Mandela, *Long Walk to Freedom* (Boston: Back Bay Books, 1995), 454.

4. Shantideva, The Padmakara Translation Group, tr., *The Way of the Bodhisattva: A Translation of the Bodhicharyavatara* (Boston: Shambhala, 2003), 64.

5. Frankl, *Man's Search for Meaning*, 85.

3: *Essential Integrity*

1. Eknath Easwaran, tr., *The Bhagavad Gita* (Tomales, CA: Nilgiri Press, 1985), 87, 125, 135.

2. Bryan Magee, *The Story of Philosophy* (New York: Dorling Kindersley, 2001), 23.

3. Daniel Goleman, *Emotional Intelligence: Why It Can Matter More Than IQ* (New York: Bantam, 1997), 81.

4. Daniel Goleman, *Working with Emotional Intelligence* (New York: Bantam, 1998), 79.

5. Easwaran, tr., *The Bhagavad Gita*, 66–68.

6. Seligman, *Authentic Happiness*, 133.

7. Csikszentmihalyi, *Good Business*, 86.

8. Easwaran, tr., *The Bhagavad Gita*, 98.

9. Ibid.

10. Maslow, *The Maslow Business Reader*, 141–2.

11. Joseph Campbell, *The Hero With A Thousand Faces* (Princeton, NJ: Princeton University Press, 1972), 30.

12. Rainer Maria Rilke, "The Man Watching" from *Selected Poems of Rainer Maria Rilke*, Robert Bly, tr. (New York: Harper & Row, 1981), 105–07.

13. David Whyte, *The Heart Aroused: Poetry and the Preservation of the Soul in Corporate America* (New York: Doubleday, 1996), 89.

14. Rumi, "Checkmate" from Coleman Barks, tr., *The Essential Rumi* (San Francisco: HarperSanFrancisco, 1997), 176–77.

15. Antonio Machado, "Last night as I slept" from Paul Burns and Salvador Ortiz-Carboneres, tr., *Lands of Castile* (Warminster, England: Aris & Phillips Ltd, 2002), 29.

16. Frankl, *Man's Search for Meaning*, 76.

4: Ontological Humility

1. Branden, *The Art of Living Consciously*, 89.

2. Magee, *The Story of Philosophy*, 135.

3. Douglas Stone et al., *Difficult Conversations: How to Discuss What Matters Most* (New York: Penguin, 2000), 41.

4. Edgar H. Schein, *Organizational Culture and Leadership*, 2nd ed. (San Francisco: Jossey-Bass, 1992), 12.

5. Mark L. Feldman and Michael F. Spratt, *Five Frogs on a Log: A CEO's Field Guide to Accelerating the Transition in Mergers, Acquisitions, and Gut Wrenching Change* (New York: HarperBusiness, 1999), 142.

6. Chris Argyris and Donald Schön, *Organizational Learning: A Theory of Action Perspective* (New York: Addison-Wesley, 1978). Term used throughout.

7. William Glasser, *The Control Theory Manager* (New York: HarperBusiness, 1995), 5–6.

8. Peter F. Drucker, *Management Challenges for the 21st Century* (New York: HarperBusiness, 1999), 20.

9. Chris Argyris and Donald Schön, *Theory in Practice: Increasing Professional Effectiveness* (San Francisco: Jossey-Bass, 1974), 6–7.

10. Chris Argyris, *Overcoming Organizational Defenses* (Boston: Allyn and Bacon, 1990), 29–30.

11. Manfred F.R. Kets de Vries and Danny Miller, *The Neurotic Organization: Diagnosing and Changing Counterproductive Styles of Management* (San Francisco: Jossey-Bass, 1984), 100.

12. Anthony De Mello, *Awareness: The Perils and Opportunities of Reality* (New York: Doubleday, 1990), 5.

5: *Authentic Communication*

1. J.G. Bennett cited in E.F. Schumacher, *A Guide for the Perplexed* (New York: Harper & Row, 1977), 84.

2. Argyris and Schön, *Theory in Practice*, 41.

3. Douglas Stone et al., *Difficult Conversations: How to Discuss What Matters Most* (New York: Penguin, 2000), xv–xvii.

4. The following section owes a great deal to *Difficult Conversations*.

5. David Burns, *Feeling Good: The New Mood Therapy* (New York: Morrow, 1980), 32.

6. Ibid., 79.

7. Stone et al., *Difficult Conversations*, 46.

8. Jack Kornfield, *A Path with Heart: A Guide through the Perils and Promises of Spiritual Life* (New York: Bantam, 1993), 78.

9. Kerry Patterson et al., *Crucial Conversations: Tools for Talking When Stakes Are High* (New York: McGraw-Hill, 2002), 69.

10. Ibid., 145.

11. Ibid., 72.

12. Robert Frost, "The Gift Outright," from Edward Connery Lathem, ed., *The Poetry of Robert Frost*, (New York: Holt 1969), 348.

13. Clifford Notarius and Howard Markman, *We Can Work it Out: How to Solve Conflicts, Save Your Marriage, and Strengten Your Love for Each*

Other (New York: Berkley, 1994), 20–22, 37–38.

14. John W. Jacobs, *All You Need Is Love and Other Lies About Marriage: How to Save Your Marriage Before It's Too Late* (New York: HarperCollins 2004), 53–54.

15. Carl R. Rogers, *On Becoming A Person: A Therapist's View of Psychotherapy* (Boston: Houghton Mifflin, 1961), 18.

16. William Stafford, "A Ritual to Read to Each Other." Reprinted from *The Way It Is: New and Selected Poems* (St. Paul, MN: Graywolf Press, 1999). Copyright © 1960, 1998 by the Estate of William Stafford.

6: Constructive Negotiation

1. Cited in Robert Bolton, *People Skills: How to Assert Yourzself, Listen to Others, and Resolve Conflicts* (New York: Touchstone, 1986), 218.

2. Jacobs, *All You Need Is Love*, xvii–xviii.

3. Drucker, *Management Challenges for the 21st Century*, 11–13.

7: Impeccable Coordination

1. Bennis and Nanus, *Leaders: The Strategies for Taking Charge*, 44.

2. John G. Bruhn, *Trust and the Health of Organizations* (New York: Kluwer Academic/Plenum Publishers, 2002), 5.

3. See Leonard E. Read's classic essay, "I, Pencil" at www.econlib.org/library/Essays/rdPncl1.html.

4. Jacobs, *All You Need Is Love and Other Lies About Marriage*, 57.

5. Personal communication from Art Schneiderman, Total Quality Manager for Analog Devices, 1992.

6. Drucker, *Management Challenges for the 21st Century*, 20–21.

7. Buckingham and Coffman, *First, Break All The Rules*, 11.

8. Ibid.

8: Emotional Mastery

1. Bennis and Nanus, *Leaders*, 56.

2. Cited in Goleman, *Working With Emotional Intelligence*, 19.

3. Ibid., 31.

4. Antonio Damasio, *Descartes' Error: Emotion, Reason, and the Human Brain* (New York: Putnam, 1994), 53.

5. Ibid., 34, 56.

6. Benson, *The Relaxation Response* (New York: Morrow, 1975).

7. Jacobs, *All You Need Is Love and Other Lies About Marriage*, 48.

8. Branden, *The Art of Living Consciously*, 150, 155.

9. Ibid., 157.

10. Goleman, *Emotional Intelligence*, 81.

11. Goleman, *Working With Emotional Intelligence*, 87.

12. David Viscott, *Emotional Resilience: Simple Truths for Dealing with the Unfinished Business of Your Past* (New York: Three Rivers Press, 1996), 1, 6.

13. Jalal al-Din Rumi, "The Guest House," from Coleman Barks, tr., *The Essential Rumi* (New York: HarperCollins, 1995), 109.

14. Robin Casarjian, *Forgiveness: A Bold Choice For a Peaceful Heart* (New York: Bantam, 1992), 16.

15. D. Patrick Miller, *A Little Book of Forgiveness: Challenges and Meditations for Anyone with Something to Forgive* (New York: Viking, 1994), 53.

16. Chuang Tzu, *The Way of Chuang Tzu*, Thomas Merton, tr. (Boston: Shambhala, 2004), 131.

9: *Entering the Market with Helping Hands*

1. Lex Hixon, *Coming Home: The Experience of Enlightenment in Sacred Traditions* (New York: Doubleday, 1978), 79.

2. Ibid.

3. Branden, *The Art of Living Consciously*, 180.

4. Jim Collins and Jerry I. Porras, *Built to Last: Successful Habits of Visionary Companies* (New York: HarperBusiness, 1997), 55.

5. Ken Wilber, *Integral Psychology: Consciousness, Spirit, Psychology, Therapy* (Boston: Shambhala, 2000), 52.

6. Robert Bly, tr., *Kabir: Ecstatic Poems* (Boston: Beacon Press, 2004), 61.

7. Ken Wilber, *Sex, Ecology and Spirituality* (Boston: Shambhala, 1995), 320, 321, 324, 325.

8. Maslow, *The Maslow Business Reader*, 13

9. Quoted in Csikszentmihalyi, *Good Business*, 56.

10. Quoted in Collins and Porras, *Built to Last*, 57.

11. Csikszentmihalyi, *Good Business*, 145, 154.

12. William Barclay, *New Testament Words* (Louisville: Westminster, 1964), 21

13. Nisargadatta Maharaj, *I Am That*, 213.

14. Rumi, "The Worm's Waking," from *The Essential Rumi*, Coleman Barks, tr. (New York: HarperCollins, 1995), 265.

15. See Mitch Bloom, *Tuesdays With Morrie* (New York: Doubleday, 1997).

16. *Kabir: Ecstatic Poems*, Robert Bly, tr. (Boston: Beacon Press, 2004), 8.

17. Csikszentmihalyi, *Good Business*, 42.

18. Stephen Mitchell, *The Enlightened Heart* (New York: Harper Perennial, 1993), 35.

19. T.S. Eliot, "Little Gidding" from *Four Quartets* (New York: Harcourt, 1971), 59.

10: *Epilogue*

1. Carlos Castaneda, *Journey to Ixtlán* (New York: Simon and Schuster, 1991) 265–66.

2. Ibid., 260-64.

3. Quoted in Jordan and Margaret Paul, *Do I Have to Give Up Me to Be Loved by You? Workbook*, 2nd ed. (Center City, MN: Hazelden, 2002), 180.

4. Rumi, in Andrew Harvey, *The Way of Passion: A Celebration of Rumi* (New York: J.P. Tarcher, 2000), 72.

5. Mihaly Csikszentmihalyi, *Good Business*, 29–30

6. Li Po, in Steven Mitchell, ed., *The Enlightened Heart* (New York: HarperCollins Perennial, 1994), 32.

7. Cited in M. Scott Peck, *The Different Drum: Community Making and Peace* (New York: Simon & Schuster, reprint 1998), 13–15.

Further Reading and Viewing List

◆

General

Jim Collins, *Good to Great: Why Some Companies Make the Leap…and Some Don't.* New York: HarperCollins, 2001.

Marcus Buckingham and Curt Coffman, *First, Break All the Rules: What the World's Greatest Managers Do Differently.* New York: Simon & Schuster, 1999.

Elliot Jacques and Stephen Clement, *Executive Leadership.* Arlington, VA: Cason Hall and Co., 1994.

Stephen Covey, *The 7 Habits of Highly Effective People: Powerful Lessons in Personal Change.* New York: Fireside, 1990.

Daniel Goleman, Richard Boyatzis, and Annie McKee, *Primal Leadership: Realizing the Power of Emotional Intelligence.* Cambridge, MA: Harvard Business School Press, 2004.

Schindler's List, Steven Spielgerg, director (film, 1993)

The Matrix I, Andy Wachowski and Larry Wachowski, directors (film, 1999)

Foreword by Peter Senge

Peter Senge, *The Fifth Discipline: The Art & Practice of the Learning Organization.* New York: Doubleday, 1990.

Senge, *The Fifth Discipline Fieldbook: Strategies and Tools for Building a Learning Organization*. New York: Doubleday Currency, 1994.

Senge et al., *The Dance of Change: The Challenges to Sustaining Momentum in Learning Organizations*. New York: Doubleday Currency, 1999.

Senge et al., *Presence: An Exploration of Profound Change in People, Organizations, and Society*. New York: Doubleday Currency, 2004.

Foreword by Ken Wilber

Ken Wilber, A *Theory of Everything: An Integral Vision for Business, Politics, Science, and Spirituality*. Boston: Shambhala, 2000.

Wilber, A *Brief History of Everything*. Boston: Shambhala, 2001.

Wilber, *Integral Psychology: Consciousness, Spirit, Psychology, Therapy*. Boston: Shambhala, 2000.

Wilber, *Kosmic Consciousness* (audio). Louisville, CO: Sounds True, 2003.

Prologue

Leo Hartong, *Awakening To The Dream*. Salisbury, Wiltshire, UK: Non-Duality Press, 2003.

Ramesh Balsekar, *Who Cares?* Redondo Beach, CA: Advaita Press, 1999.

Jed McKenna, *Spiritual Enlightenment: The Damnedest Thing*. Wisefool Press, 2002.

The Official Story, Luis Penzo, director (film, 1985)

Groundhog Day, Harold Ramis, director (film, 1993)

1: Conscious Management

Nathaniel Branden, *The Art of Living Consciously: The Power of Awareness to Transform Everyday Life*. New York: Fireside, 1999.

Mihaly Csikszentmihalyi, *Good Business: Leadership, Flow, and the Making of Meaning*. New York: Viking, 2003.

David Myers, *Pursuit of Happiness*. New York: Morrow, 1992.

Ikiru, Akira Kurosawa, director (film, 1952).

Dead Poets Society, Peter Weir, director (film, 1989).

2: *Unconditional Responsibility*

Viktor Frankl, *Man's Search for Meaning.* New York: Simon & Schuster, 1984.

Peter Koestembaum and Peter Block, *Freedom and Accountability at Work: Applying Philosophical Insight to the Real World.* San Francisco: Jossey-Bass/Pfeiffer, 2001.

William Glasser, *Reality Therapy: A New Approach to Psychology.* New York: Harper & Row, 1965.

The Shawshank Redemption, Frank Darabont, director (film, 1994).

Life is Beautiful, Roberto Benigni, director (film, 1998).

3: *Essential Integrity*

Juan Mascaro, translator, *The Bhagavad Gita.* New York: Penguin Classics, 2003.

Martin Seligman, *Authentic Happiness: Using the New Positive Psychology to Realice Your Potential for Lasting Fulfillment.* New York: Free Press, 2004.

Ayn Rand, *The Fountainhead.* New York: New American Library, 1996.

Braveheart, Mel Gibson, director (film, 1995).

Wall Street, Oliver Stone, director (film, 1987).

4: *Ontological Humility*

Humberto Maturana, *The Tree of Knowledge.* Boston: New Science Library, 1987.

Chris Argyris and Donald Schön, *Theory in Practice: Increasing Professional Effectiveness.* San Francisco: Jossey-Bass, 1974.

Robert Kegan and Lisa Lahey, *How the Way We Talk Can Change the Way We Work: Seven Languages for Transformation.* San Francisco: Jossey-Bass, 2002.

Rashomonn, Akira Kurosawa, director (film, 1950).

Open Your Eyes, Alejandro Amenábar, director (film, 1997).

5: *Authentic Communication*

Douglas Stone et al., *Difficult Conversations: : How to Discuss What Matters Most.* New York: Penguin, 1999.

Kerry Patterson et al., *Crucial Conversations: : Tools for Talking When Stakes Are High.* New York: McGraw-Hill, 2002.

Marshall Rosenberg, *Non-Violent Communication.* Encinitas, CA: PuddleDancer Press, 2003.

Twelve Angry Men, Sidney Lumet, director (film, 1956).

Apollo 13, Ron Howard, director (film, 1995).

6: *Constructive Negotiation*

Thomas Crum, *The Magic of Conflict: Turning a Life of Work into a Work of Art.* New York: Simon & Schuster, 1998.

Roger Fisher and William Ury, *Getting to Yes: Negotiating Agreement Without Giving In.* New York: Penguin, 1991.

William Ury, *Getting Past No: Negotiating Your Way From Confrontation to Cooperation.* New York: Bantam, 1993.

Thirteen Days, Roger Donaldson, director (film, 2000).

Crimson Tide, Tony Scott, director (film, 1995).

7: *Impeccable Coordination*

Kerry Patterson et al., *Crucial Confrontations.* New York: McGraw-Hill, 2005.

Larry Bossidy and Ram Charan, *Execution: The Discipline of Getting Things Done.* New York: Crown Business, 2002.

Carolyn Taylor, *Walking the Talk: The Business Case for Sustainable Development.* New York: Random House, 2005.

Enron: The Smartest Guys in the Room, Alex Gibney, director (film, 2005).

Startup.com, Chris Hegedus and Jehane Noujaim, directors (film, 2001).

8: *Emotional Mastery*

Daniel Goleman, *Emotional Intelligence: Why It Can Matter More Than IQ.* New York: Bantam, 1997.

Richard E. Boyatzis and Annie McKee, *Resonant Leadership: Renewing Yourself and Connecting With Others Through Mindfulness, Hope, and Compassion.* Cambridge, MA: Harvard Business School Press, 2005.

David Burns, *Feeling Good: The New Mood Therapy.* New York: Morrow, 1980.

Ordinary People, Robert Redford, director (film, 1980).

Shadowlands, Richard Attenborough, director (film, 1993).

9: Entering the Market with Helping Hands

Ayn Rand, *Atlas Shrugged.* New York: New American Library, 1996.

Friedrich A. von Hayek, *The Road to Serfdom.* Chicago: University of
    Chicago Press, 1944.

David Whyte, *The Heart Aroused: Poetry and the Preservation of the Soul in
    Corporate America.* New York: Doubleday, 1996.

Other People's Money, Norman Jewison, director (film, 1991).

Erin Brockovich, Steven Soderbergh, director (film, 2000).

Epilogue

Jon Krakauer, *Into Thin Air.* New York: Random House, 1998.

Touching the Void, Kevin Macdonald, director (film, 2003).

My Life, Bruce Joel Rubin, director (film, 1993).